Total E-mail Marketing

Total E-mail Marketing

Maximizing your results from integrated e-marketing

Second edition

Dave Chaffey

AMSTERDAM • BOSTON • HEIDELBERG • LONDON • NEW YORK • OXFORD
PARIS • SAN DIEGO • SAN FRANCISCO • SINGAPORE • SYDNEY • TOKYO
Butterworth-Heinemann is an imprint of Elsevier

Butterworth-Heinemann is an imprint of Elsevier
Linacre House, Jordan Hill, Oxford OX2 8DP, UK
30 Corporate Drive, Suite 400, Burlington, MA 01803, USA

First edition 2003
Second edition 2006
Reprinted 2007

British Library Cataloguing in Publication Data
A catalogue record for this book is available from the British Library

Library of Congress Cataloging-in-Publication Data
A catalog record for this book is available from the Library of Congress

ISBN–13: 978-0-7506-8067-7
ISBN–10: 0-7506-8067-9

For information on all Butterworth-Heinemann publications
visit our website at books.elsevier.com

Printed and bound in *The Netherlands*

07 08 09 10 10 9 8 7 6 5 4 3 2

Contents

Preface

WHY TOTAL E-MAIL MARKETING?

Effective e-mail marketing is not just about creating and running campaigns. E-mail marketing has become an essential, integral part of Internet marketing and, indeed, marketing. So in writing this book I wanted to create a comprehensive guide which not only covers how to create great campaigns and creative, but also describes a strategic approach to integrating e-mail into the communications mix. *Total E-mail Marketing* covers:

- how to use e-mail to support all stages of the customer lifecycle of customer relationship management (CRM) – selection, acquisition, retention and extension

- using e-mail for a range of marketing applications – as a promotional tool, regular communications tool (e-newsletters), conversion tool (multi-stage e-mail), referral tool (viral marketing), research tool and customer support tool

- lists – building and maintaining house-lists and selecting rented lists

- campaign design, from strategy, through conversion modelling, to creative and testing

- managing not only outbound e-mail but also inbound e-mail

- resourcing e-mail, looking at the best options for outsourcing using an e-mail service provider, or in-house management using software packages

- integrated e-mail marketing with the web site, with direct mail, advertising, PR and word-of-mouth.

To illustrate the power of e-mail marketing I also wanted to draw on a range of examples and experiences from different practitioners. Therefore, in each chapter you will find detailed case studies for business-to-consumer, business-to-business and not-for-profit, and viewpoints from a range of e-mail practitioners. To help you improve your e-mail marketing I have also included a series of checklists that can be used to plan future campaigns, and highlighted key insights that are factors for success.

HOW IS THE BOOK STRUCTURED?

Total E-mail Marketing has been developed for fast, efficient learning. It is structured around eight major topics that are of concern to marketers.

Chapter 1 Introduction

Chapter 1 highlights the power of e-mail marketing. We look at the success factors in e-mail marketing and compare it with traditional direct marketing, highlighting its benefits and disadvantages.

Chapter 2 E-mail marketing fundamentals

Permission marketing, customer relationship management, and legal and ethical constraints, the foundations of e-mail marketing, are covered in Chapter 2.

Chapter 3 E-mail campaign planning

Key stages and issues in developing an e-mail marketing strategy and campaign plans are described in this chapter.

Chapter 4 Using e-mail for customer acquisition

Chapter 4 discusses how to use online marketing to acquire new customers and migrate existing offline customers online. This includes building a house list through capture of e-mail addresses and profiling, and using e-mail to support online customer acquisition.

Chapter 5 Using e-mail for customer retention

This chapter covers how to use e-mail to develop customer relationships, and techniques to keep visitors returning to a web site and making repeat purchases.

Chapter 6 Crafting e-mail creative

Chapter 6 is a practical chapter that highlights the different options for developing e-mail creative from the e-mail attributes (message headers), through the structure, style and tone of the message body, to its form (HTML and text).

Chapter 7 E-mail marketing management

This chapter is about making it happen. We look at the best way to implement your plans by discussing how to resource e-mail marketing in terms of partners, purchasing software and managing inbound enquiries.

Chapter 8 E-mail marketing challenges and innovation

This chapter looks at the future of e-mail marketing. Issues covered include combating spam, use of wireless access devices such as PDAs and mobiles, and the opportunities for using rich media such as video streaming.

WHO IS THIS BOOK FOR?

Marketing and business professionals

This book has been developed as a resource to support a range of professionals involved with e-marketing:

- *marketing managers* responsible for defining an e-marketing strategy, implementing strategy or maintaining the company web site alongside traditional marketing activities

- *e-marketing specialists* such as digital marketing managers, e-marketing managers and e-commerce managers responsible for directing, integrating and implementing their organization's e-marketing

- *senior managers and directors* seeking to identify the right e-business and e-marketing approaches to support their organization's strategy

- *information systems managers* also involved in developing and implementing e-marketing and e-commerce strategies

- *technical project managers or web masters* who may understand the technical details of building a site, but want to enhance their knowledge of e-marketing.

Students

This book will also be of relevance to students studying e-marketing, including professionals studying for awards from professional bodies such as the Chartered Institute of Marketing and the Institute of Direct Marketing; to postgraduate students studying specialist masters degrees in electronic commerce, electronic business or e-marketing, and generic programmes in Marketing Management, MBA, Certificate in Management or Diploma in Management Studies which involve modules or electives for e-business and e-marketing; and to undergraduates on business programmes that include marketing modules on the use of digital marketing.

LEARNING FEATURES

A range of features has been incorporated into *Total E-mail Marketing* to help the reader get the most out of it. These have been designed to assist understanding, reinforce learning and help readers find information easily. The features are described in the order in which you will find them.

At the start of each chapter:

- *At a glance*, including an overview, main learning points and the chapter topics.

In each chapter:

- *E-mail marketing excellence boxes* – real-world examples of best practice approaches referred to in the text

- *Campaign checklist boxes* – lists to help you plan e-mail marketing and campaigns
- *E-mail marketing insights boxes* – these highlight factors critical to effective e-mail marketing.

At the end of each chapter:

- *References* – these are references to books, articles or papers referred to within the chapter
- *Web links* – these include resource sites mentioned within the chapter and significant sites that provide further information on the concepts and topics contained in the chapter.

At the end of the book:

- *Index* – all key words and abbreviations referred to in the main text can be found here.

Preface to the second edition

As I have used the book to complement my Chartered Institute of Marketing and e-consultancy training courses, it has been good to see many of my recommendations for improving e-mail marketing being put into practice on attendees' e-mail campaigns. This has inspired me to produce the second edition. Many organizations still have great potential to apply more advanced e-mail marketing techniques, such as event-triggered e-mails, personalized response-based targeting in multi-message campaigns, or simply improved e-mail templates where the creative is more effective in achieving conversion.

A few years on from the first edition, e-mail still works incredibly well as a marketing communications tool. Over the last few years the volume of spam (unsolicited e-mail) has increased dramatically, although it is now plateauing or even declining. However, despite this, the e-mail response benchmarks in Chapter 1 show that e-mail has remained a highly responsive medium. It seems that, fortunately for permission-based e-mailers, consumers can readily distinguish between permission-based e-mail from a trusted brand and spam. The following are some of the highlights of topics that are covered in the second edition:

- *Acquisition*. These improvements in response from e-mail marketing have not been universal. Many marketers have experimented with using e-mail for customer acquisition through using rented lists, but have been disappointed by the results. I think that, today, e-mail is seen primarily as a customer retention medium, and as a result we focus on the use of e-mail for retention. However, renting lists aren't the only option for using e-mail for acquisition, and we will look at other options and many examples of where companies have made acquisition work.

- *Deliverability*. Getting your message through to the recipient's main inbox is a recent challenge for e-mail marketing, which has resulted from efforts by Internet Service Providers (ISPs) and web-based e-mail providers to filter spam. Initially this resulted in 'false positives', where permission-based e-mail was categorized as spam. We will look at the steps to avoid this, and it is widely seen as less of a problem now.

- *Competition*. With publicity regarding the success of early e-mail campaigns, many marketers have been keen to use this still-new medium. The volume of marketing e-mails has therefore increased manyfold over the last five years. The UK Direct Marketing Association E-mail Marketing Benchmarking Council estimated that by 2005, around 4 billion marketing e-mails would be sent by UK e-mail service providers alone! That's a lot of competition, but maybe 100 marketing e-mails per adult per year isn't so high if we think about the e-mail volume in our inboxes every day.

- *Personalization*. This has led to a more crowded inbox and a greater challenge in achieving inbox cut-through. We will look at approaches to achieving this through improved targeting and personalization, and how to craft the creative and subject line to get this cut-through. We will also review the challenges of getting the frequency of e-mail communications right and developing a touch strategy to integrate e-mail with other direct media.

- *Touch strategy*. As companies increase the range and type of e-mail communications, there is a risk of permission-based e-mail marketers becoming spammers. A major challenge of e-mail marketing today is how to balance volume of e-mail sent against the need to hit targets for sales or other marketing outcomes. We will look at how to manage e-mail communications across all channels in keeping with customers' communications preferences.

- *Practical dos and don'ts*. As before, I have designed the book to be very practical, and hopefully you will find ideas and tips on every page you can immediately apply. I have updated the e-mail marketing checklists and added new dos and don'ts for many areas.

- *Technological advances*. Looking to the future, I again use the last chapter to look at emerging approaches such as rich media, mobile marketing and Really Simple Syndication (RSS), which I think will be key messaging approaches for marketers over the next few years.

Acknowledgements

FIRST EDITION

This book has been created using insights and case studies provided by many professionals who are closely involved with e-mail marketing. I would like to thank the following for helping to give the book a range of different viewpoints and opinions.

Jeremiah Budzik, Doubleclick; Pip Chesters, 3M Health Care; William Corke and Rory Teeling, Harvest Digital; Mark Davies, Context Partners; Maddie Davis, Butterworth-Heinemann, Elsevier Science; Philippa Edwards and Robert Perrin, Anderson Baillie Marketing; Stephen Groom, Marketing Law; David Hughes, E-mail Vision; Glenn Jones, glue London; Bill Kaplan, FreshAddress; Matthew Kelleher, Claritas Interactive; Martin Kiersnowski, Interactive Prospect Targeting; David Mill, MediaCo; Caroline Piggins, Corpdata; Derek Mansfield, Bold Endeavours; Duncan Smith, Ashton Court Consultants; Paul Smith, my co-author on *Emarketing Excellence*; Ollie Omotosho, Commontime; Richard Mayer, Befocused; Andrew Petherick, Mailtrack; David Reed, European Centre for Customer Strategies; Stephen Spelman, Altum; Tara Topliff and Naomi Broad, Virgin Atlantic; Sue Ward, Chartered Institute of Marketing, What's New in Marketing; Rhian Whitehead, Elsevier Science; and John Woods, Site Intelligence.

SECOND EDITION

I have again talked to many e-mail service providers and their clients who are at the cutting edge of e-mail marketing, to understand the opportunities and challenges of e-mail marketing. In particular, I would like to thank: Vicky Carne at Email Reaction; Peter Duffy at e-Dialog; David Hughes at E-mail Vision; Sean Duffy at E-mail Center; Ian Scarr at E-RM; and Bertie Stevenson at RedEye.

I am also fortunate that, as a trainer and consultant, I have the opportunity to work in-company with many leading brands. This is very much a two-way learning process, so especial thanks to: Pip Chesters, Lloyd Cole and Peter Boazman at 3M; Bonnie Frankland and Chris Reilly at Euroffice; Piers Dickinson at BP; Matt Dooley and Paul Say at HSBC; Allison Wightman and Lynette Brown at Royal Mail; Sophie Lord at Virgin Wines; Sonia Davidson and Garry Reynolds at Bank of Scotland Corporate; Eileen Pevreall and David Hedges at CIPD; and Martyn Etherington and Mike Rizzo at Tektronix.

The Microsoft product screen shots throughout the book are reprinted with permission from Microsoft Corporation.

Dave Chaffey

Chapter

1

Introduction

INTRODUCTION – TYPICAL E-MAIL MARKETING QUESTIONS

> *What success rate can I expect for an e-mail-shot to 20 000 prospects from a vendor list rented from a vendor, where the e-mail contains a hyperlink to a web site?*

> *We have collected e-mail addresses for 20 per cent of our customer base. We are looking to start using e-mail newsletters and promotions to encourage repeat business. Which factors will govern the success of our e-mail campaigns?*

These are typical questions from marketers keen to run e-mail campaigns, but unsure of the results they are likely to achieve. We have all heard campaign success stories with response rates in double figures, but at the same time we all receive an ever-increasing amount of e-mail in our inbox. As Internet users receive thousands of e-mail messages every year, many of them unsolicited, how can we maximize our response rate?

Think about the factors that will govern the response rate to an e-mail campaign. The starting point is permission – consent is no longer just 'nice to have'; consumer opt-in to receive e-mail communications is required by law in many countries, as we will see in Chapter 2. One factor you may have identified is how well targeted the campaign is to the interests and needs of the recipients – are the e-mails relevant to the audience? The offer made to encourage clickthrough to the site is another key factor. You may also have considered the quality of the creative – is it enticing in drawing the recipient in, how well does the copy explain the offer? These are, of course, very similar to the factors that govern the success of traditional postal mail. You may also have considered some factors that are specific to e-mail marketing – are the copy and e-mail headers compiled such that the message is not intercepted via spam filters and recorded as a 'false positive' which is placed in the inbox? The characteristics of the message are also important – what is the subject line of the e-mail? Which time and day of the week did it arrive? Who is it from – is it a plain text message or is it a HTML page including images? Finally, you may have mentioned the importance of the web page that recipients' click through to – i.e. is the design of this page effective in encouraging further action? So there is a whole host of factors involved – some familiar to direct marketers and some new.

Total E-mail Marketing will give you detailed guidance on all these factors to enable you to devise powerful e-mail campaigns that maximize response. To start this process, consider my mnemonic of the 'CRITICAL' factors for e-mail marketing success. CRITICAL is a useful checklist of questions to ask about your e-mail campaigns. CRITICAL represents:

- *Creative*. This assesses the design of the e-mail, including its layout, use of colour and image, and the copy. The form and location of the calls-to-action are also critical.

- *Relevance*. This is arguably the most important factor. Ask yourself, does the offer and creative of the e-mail meet the needs of recipients?

- *Incentive* (or offer). This is the WIFM (what's in it for me?) factor for the recipient. What benefit does the recipient gain from clicking on the hyperlink(s) in the e-mail?

- *Targeting and timing*. Targeting is related to the relevance – is a single message sent to all prospects or customers on the list, or are e-mails with tailored creative, incentive and copy sent to the different segments on the list? Timing refers to when the e-mail is received – the time of day, the day of the week, the point in the month and even the year, does it relate to any particular event? There is also the relative timing – when is the e-mail received compared to other marketing communications? This depends on the integration.

- *Integration*. Are the e-mail campaigns part of your integrated marketing communications? Questions to ask include the following: are the creative and copy consistent with my brand? Does the message reinforce other communications? Does the timing of the e-mail campaign fit with offline communications?

- *Copy*. This is part of the creative, and refers to the structure, style and explanation of the offer together with the location of hyperlinks in the e-mail.

- *Attributes* (header attributes of the e-mail). Assess the message characteristics, such as the subject line, From address, To address, date/time of receipt, and format (HTML or text).

These can also influence deliverability of the message if they contain the wrong structure, or keywords identified as spam.

- *Landing page* or microsite. These are terms given for the page(s) reached after the recipient clicks on a link in the e-mail. Typically, on clickthrough recipients will be presented with an online form to profile or learn more about them. Designing the page so the form is easy to complete can affect the overall success of the campaign.

E-MAIL MARKETING INSIGHT

Don't focus solely on the e-mail when trying to maximize response – remember that the quality of the landing page(s) or microsite also affects the success of your e-mail campaign.

Figure 1.1   Virgin Wines deliver relevance

Which of the CRITICAL factors do you think are more important? While the mnemonic starts with 'Creative', other aspects, such as Targeting, Integration and Incentive, are arguably more important. This is in keeping with the old direct marketing adage that success is based 40 per cent on offer quality, 40 per cent on list quality and 20 per cent on creative quality. The content and structure of *Total E-mail Marketing* is in keeping with this, with much of the material we will cover looking at how we can achieve *Relevance*. Figure 1.1 gives an example of an e-mail that delivers Relevance and combines all of the CRITICAL factors well. It is a brief, timely e-mail, sent just after Christmas in the sales period to entice bargain hunters.

MODELLING AND MEASURING E-MAIL MARKETING EFFECTIVENESS

Further common questions from marketers starting out with e-mail marketing include:

How do I build my e-mail list to meet my objectives?

How do I assess the success of my campaign?

Looking at the second question, one of the great benefits of e-mail, in common with other forms of direct marketing, is its accountability. In *Total E-mail Marketing* I present a simple Excel spreadsheet-based model that you can use for setting objectives and comparing the effectiveness of different tests or campaigns. Figure 1.2 shows the framework used for this model, and some points to bear in mind.

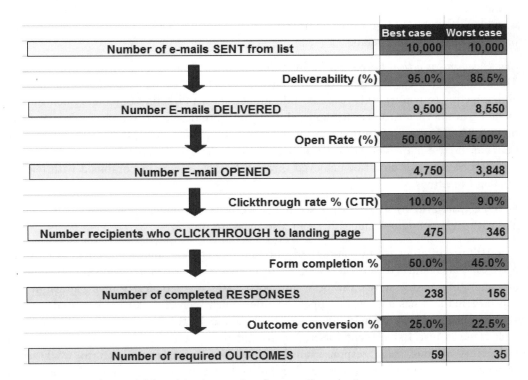

	Best case	Worst case
Number of e-mails SENT from list	10,000	10,000
Deliverability (%)	95.0%	85.5%
Number E-mails DELIVERED	9,500	8,550
Open Rate (%)	50.00%	45.00%
Number E-mail OPENED	4,750	3,848
Clickthrough rate % (CTR)	10.0%	9.0%
Number recipients who CLICKTHROUGH to landing page	475	346
Form completion %	50.0%	45.0%
Number of completed RESPONSES	238	156
Outcome conversion %	25.0%	22.5%
Number of required OUTCOMES	59	35

Figure 1.2 A simple model for objective setting for e-mail marketing

To evaluate the success of a direct response e-mail campaign, we can best understand what worked and what didn't if we break down response into different stages. The effectiveness of each stage can be assessed by two measures – the absolute number of people who interact with the message, and the relative percentage effectiveness compared to the previous stage. The key measures for e-mail marketing are as follows.

- *Number of e-mails sent.* How many e-mails are broadcast to list members?

- *Number of e-mails delivered* (deliverability,%). How many e-mails get through to the inbox? This is dependent on the accuracy of the addresses, i.e. how up-to-date and clean your list is, and the proportion of e-mails that are blocked by spam filters. Improving deliverability is a key issue for e-mail marketers, and we will look at this in detail in Chapter 8.

- *Number of e-mails opened* (open rate,%). How many e-mails are viewed by recipients? As we explain later, this figure is approximate, since it is calculated by images in an e-mail downloaded from a server. This is dependent on the combination of the proportion of people who click on the e-mail to open it, have the preview pane enabled and have images blocked.

- *Number of clickthroughs* (clickthrough rate,%). This is the percentage of recipients who respond to the e-mail by clicking on a link. It is best to measure this as *unique clicks* from unique individuals, since some recipients may click on an e-mail more than once.

- *Number of completed responses* (form completion,%). This is the percentage of the recipients who click through and go on to complete a form or a combination of forms of a shopping basket process for an e-retailer.

- *Conversion rate to action.* Direct marketing campaigns are always aimed at achieving a response. Those that complete the landing page have responded, but we often have an additional aim, which is to convert this response into an action or marketing outcome. Such outcomes include gaining a customer through achieving an initial sale or a repeat sale. To achieve these outcomes there will often need to be a follow-up. For example, a sales representative that has used e-mail marketing to gain a qualified lead will aim to convert the lead into a customer, and this could be achieved through follow-up e-mails combined with telephone calls and meetings.

- *Referrals* (forward,%). If recipients see relevance in their e-mails, they will share what they like with friends and colleagues; we can also measure this.

By modelling different combinations of the number of e-mails sent, clickthrough rates, completion rates and conversion rates, it is possible to set more realistic objectives for a campaign. Figure 1.2 shows the best and worst cases for a typical e-mail campaign which is well targeted and has a relevant, appealing offer. Such scenarios can be discussed with your e-mail marketing agency to help agree a realistic target. In the worst case here the efficiency at each stage is just 10 per cent lower, but overall this results in 40 per cent less outcomes because it is a multi-stage response mechanism. E-mail marketers need to work hard at isolating the reasons for response at each stage and improving accordingly; this book shows you how.

Obtaining the spreadsheet

This spreadsheet is available free at www.davechaffey.com/Spreadsheets. While you're on my site, don't forget to opt-in to my *E-marketing Essentials* – a monthly briefing on the latest trends in e-marketing. The spreadsheet has been devised to enable 'what-if' objective setting. For example, it is possible to work back to the number of e-mails that need to be sent to achieve the desired number of outcomes with a given clickthrough, completion rate and conversion rate, as shown in Figure 1.2.

E-MAIL MARKETING INSIGHT

Use conversion-based modelling to set realistic objectives and to help learn for future campaigns.

WHY E-MAIL MARKETING MATTERS

The marketing potential of e-mail can be clearly seen by the way it is rivalling other media as a form of direct communications. Worldwide, the compilations of research published at ZDNET (http://blogs.zdnet.com/ITFacts/?cat=8) estimated that the number of e-mails sent increased from 5.1 million per day in 2000 to 135 million per day in 2005. A lower volume had been indicated by IDC, which predicted that nearly 84 billion e-mails would be sent daily in 2006. Of these, more than 33 billion would be spam messages.

In the UK, we saw, in 2005, the first fall in overall direct mail volumes for six years, as assessed by the Direct Mail Information Service (www.dmis.co.uk). Contrast this with commercial, permission-based e-mail, which has increased in volume for the last few years. Table 1.1 suggests the importance of e-mail as a communications medium for business-to-consumer and business-to-business companies. This compilation is taken from the national benchmarking hub of the E-mail Council of the Direct Marketing Association. The volumes are based on around 75 per cent of e-mails sent by E-mail Service Providers (ESPs), rather than clients, so they underestimate the total, since some clients (such as Dell and Lastminute.com) may send e-mails direct. While figures such as these quickly date, I recommend visiting the research section of the DMA site for the latest figures, which are also broken down by sector.

Table 1.1 Volume of e-mail marketing from e-mail service providers, Q3 2005

Measure	Acquisition campaigns	Retention campaigns
Average hard bounce	9.0%	8.0%
Average unique open	25.0%	33.9%
Average unique click	6.1%	9.2%
Opt-out rate	1.0%	0.7%

Source: UK DMA E-mail Marketing Council (www.dma.org.uk), reprinted with permission.

For US and European figures on e-mail deliverability and responsiveness, the best place to check the latest trends is the Doubleclick resource centre (http://www.doubleclick.com/us/ knowledge_central). An example is shown in Figure 2.1. Other ESPs, such as Email Labs and Bronto, also do their own compilations.

WHY E-MAIL MARKETING BEATS DIRECT MAIL

E-mail offers many practical benefits over traditional direct mail. Its lower cost means it is possible to send more and better-targeted messages to each recipient as part of the campaign, which can be used to convert more of the audience to respond. E-mail can be used to send reminders about a sales promotion or event, and different follow-up messages according to response – i.e. those who open but don't click, or those who click but don't respond overall. Figure 1.3 gives an example of a multi-message campaign which achieved double-digit response. It shows that following an initial e-mail (1) with different creative for four segments offering entry into a prize draw, a reminder (2) was sent to those who had not entered. Those entering the prize draw had the opportunity to provide the e-mail addresses and names of friends or colleagues, who were sent an e-mail offering them the opportunity to take part in the campaign (3). This is a 'viral referral' (see Chapter 4 for more on viral marketing). Finally, an e-mail was sent to losers (4), offering participation in a further draw. Clearly such a campaign structure can achieve a better response than traditional direct marketing, where sending this many communications is usually impractical because of cost.

It can be seen that e-mail gives more options for converting the audience to action. It is even possible to follow up losing contestants with the option of further competition. Finally, the e-mail is not a one-way communication – feedback from customers via the landing page about their

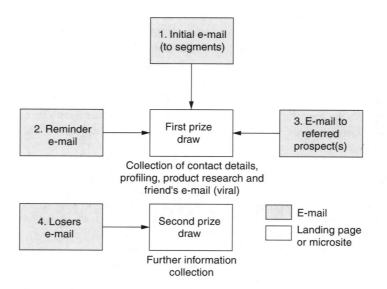

Figure 1.3 Example e-mail campaign structure (supplied by and published with permission of UK-based digital marketing specialists Harvest Digital, www.harvestdigital.com)

buying behaviour and positioning of products can also be incorporated into the campaign to inform market research.

The many well-known benefits of e-mail marketing in comparison with traditional direct marketing have been summarized by Gartner G2 (2002). According to these analysts, e-mail marketing offers the following:

- *Higher response rates*. On average, response rates are between 6 and 8 per cent for permission-based e-mail – a significantly higher figure than in the majority of direct marketing campaigns.

- *A shorter duration for campaign creation*. Gartner G2 estimates that e-mail campaigns are completed in seven to ten business days on average, compared to four to six weeks for direct mail.

- *A more rapid response*. Gartner G2 reports that responses to e-mail accumulate in an average of three days, while direct mail requires an average response time of three to six weeks.

- *A faster overall cycle–cycle time*. Gartner G2 suggests that the overall cycle time of an e-mail campaign from creation to delivery and response is one-tenth the time of traditional direct mail.

- *Lower costs*. It is estimated that, currently, e-mail costs range from \$5 to \$7 per thousand compared to \$500 to \$700 per thousand for direct mail.

We can also add that we can use viral campaigns to effectively increase response rates further, that we can use e-mail for market research and that the medium is more accountable – we can find out how many respond to the medium (open rates).

Claritas estimated the differences between e-mail and direct mail costs for 60 000 prospects, as shown in Table 1.2, for a customer acquisition campaign. It is evident that while the list cost may be higher, this is offset by the reduced print, postage and fulfilment costs. For a campaign to an in-house list which does not have the cost of list rental, the benefits of e-mail are clearer still. A more detailed budget model for campaign planning is presented in Chapter 3.

One opportunity provided by the lower costs is that of communicating more frequently with customers. Take the example of a business-to-business company that can supplement events and

Table 1.2 Cost estimate comparing a direct mail campaign to an e-mail campaign for 60 000 prospects

Cost item (£)	Direct mail campaign (£)	E-mail campaign (£)
List cost	5000	15 000
Design	5000	5000
Print	6000	0
Postage	13 000	0
Fulfilment	7500	2500
Total	35 500	22 500

Source: Claritas Interactive (www.claritasinteractive.co.uk).

visits by account managers with more frequent technical e-newsletters for its users and other decision-makers, as shown in Figure 1.4. The content of this e-newsletter delivers relevance by using a combination of appropriate content and product offers to get the balance right between selling and informing – as discussed further in Chapter 5, where we look at best practice for e-mail newsletters.

Figure 1.4 Business-to-business e-newsletter from Tektronix targeting the needs of a technical audience (reproduced courtesy of Tektronix, Inc.)

Table 1.3   Comparative costs and responses for different forms of direct communications

Media type	Cost per thousand (£)	Response rate (%)	Cost per response (£)
Acquisition e-mail – rented list	100	0.1	100
Acquisition e-mail – co-branded	50	0.2	25
Paid search advertising	8	0.2	4
Affiliate marketing	N/A	NA	8
Online ad.	20	0.02	100
Direct mail	500	2	25
National press	10	0.05	20
Direct response TV	8	0.04	20
Magazines	40	0.2	20
Radio	2	0.01	20

I have to give a further word of caution on costs, though. As experienced with banner adverts, there has been a decline in the average clickthrough rate for e-mail, particularly from those from rented lists. Combining a high cost per thousand with the low clickthrough rate can lead to a high cost per sale. Table 1.3 shows a compilation of cost-effectiveness for different media based on the example of acquiring a customer for a new credit card which might have an allowable cost per acquisition of £40–£50. The compilation of offline media is from Tapp (2005), and I have added estimates based on my experience of digital media. Although you may be asking what the value of tabulating such high-level cross-media averages is, this does show that e-mail is not necessarily the right acquisition tool. Although it can be made to work with the right list, targeting and creative, it may well be that there are more cost-effective forms of online media – such as paid search or affiliate marketing. I have met some marketers who say that, for their sector, using rented or cold e-mail lists for acquisition is impossible at the right cost of acquisition, but they have found that co-branded e-mails that are warmer for the audience can work.

You can also see from the table that the cost per sale for e-mail to a rented list is higher than that for direct mail to a rented list, since the response rate is higher in the latter case. The data in Table 1.3 suggest that it is never worthwhile e-mailing to a rented list. The Virgin Atlantic case study later in this chapter and many other successful campaigns show it can still definitely be worthwhile to undertake campaigns to an opt-in list. Looking at it the other way, it is still possible to produce a campaign to a house list that isn't cost-effective if the campaign planning is wrong.

To summarize, e-mail offers many advantages as a communications tool – immediacy, targeting and accountability, and it is relatively cheap. Additionally, it can be more cost-effective to target niche groups. For example, a bank could e-mail female customers aged eighteen to twenty-five, who read a particular newspaper, have a credit card and have responded to an e-mail campaign within the last six months. Such precision targeting is known as using multiple selects. For rented lists, the cost per thousand is increased for multiple selects.

WHY E-MAIL MARKETING BEATS WEB-SITE BASED MARKETING

E-mail marketing is a vital part of the e-marketing communications mix. It is arguably as important, or more important, than the web site itself. How can I justify this statement? Well, a web site's greatest strength is also its greatest weakness. A major benefit of the web site is that its audience is self-selecting. The audience is mainly attracted (or 'pulled') to the web site by the content that is on offer, which is indicated by search-engine listings or links from other sites (or 'pushed' using offline media). The problem is that once visitors leave the site, they may never return. This is where e-mail wins: it is a 'push' medium. If visitors' e-mail can be captured on their visit to the site, the e-mail can be used to remind them about the company and its products, together with relevant incentives to visit the web site. Of course, this is the key elements of permission marketing, which is described in more detail in Chapter 2.

Since e-mail is a push medium, this makes it a great medium for time-critical information. E-mail alerts and offers about promotions are the obvious application. A less obvious (but very powerful) application is the use of e-mail which is automatically triggered based on the marketer's understanding of the customers' lifecycle and the content they are interested in, and the marketer's objectives in converting the customer from one stage to the next. My US contacts call this approach 'sense and respond'.

Less frequent e-mail alerts can also be of value – weekly and monthly alerts can be used for less critical knowledge. Such alert information can be added-value information in e-mail newsletters – you act as a source of knowledge for your customers.

E-mail is also potentially better than a web site for targeted communications. It is superior since you, not the visitor, choose who sees what information. Web-site designers have to cater for a range of audiences, and this can make it difficult for customers in any segment to find the communications that have been developed for them. Similarly with special offers; these often have to be highlighted by a space on a panel little more than a postage stamp, and it's often better to use the space provided by an e-newsletter. With e-mail you choose the customers who will receive the communications, using standard database marketing selects. For example, Boots the Chemist has used e-mail to target customers within a 30-minute drive of a new range of opticians – try doing that via a web site!

Customers can also choose the information they need and when they need it. Advanced e-mail services give customer choice regarding which information is delivered and when it is delivered. This and other forms of personalization are discussed in more detail in Chapter 2.

Of course, there are areas where the web site does work better; providing a depth of information is only possible through multiple web pages. Here, the e-mail is best used in combination with the web, to direct customers to the more detailed information. The web can help in delivering targeted messages that fit buyer behaviour if combined with search marketing, since the visitors are delivered to the relevant page on the site.

So, e-mail marketing does not beat web site marketing in all respects – the two are perfect partners.

WHY 'TOTAL E-MAIL MARKETING'?

Much that has been written about e-mail marketing is limited to best practice about e-mail copy or creative, or creating e-mail campaigns based on rented lists. This misses the value of e-mail in supporting all aspects of the buying process and the entire customer lifecycle. Total e-mail marketing:

- includes building and maintaining house lists as well as renting lists

- reviews changes to customer relationship management (CRM) and web analytics systems needed to integrate data from different sources, to enable companies to sense when customers click on their web sites and e-mail and respond with targeted, personalized messages

- covers using e-mail for the entire customer lifecycle, from customer selection, through acquisition and retention to extension

- is integrated with the web site and other direct communications

- uses a range of different e-mail types, from e-mail offers and regular e-newsletters to multi-stage and viral e-mails

- includes management of inbound communications to improve customer satisfaction

- incorporates best practice on the practical details of how to improve results of e-mail templates and landing pages.

E-mail marketing – it's not just e-newsletters

Many marketers immediately think of e-newsletters and sales promotions as the main opportunities for deploying e-mail, but the opportunities are much greater. Think about how many of the following techniques you could deploy.

- *Acquisition tool*. Here, e-mails are sent to members of a bought-in list to acquire new customers. Alternatively, you could advertise in an established e-newsletter to drive traffic to your web site.

- *Conversion tool*. Many sites use offers to capture leads in the form of e-mail addresses. E-mails can then be sent to these leads, aimed at converting leads to customers. Multi-stage e-mails can be automated to help encourage conversion to a sale.

- *Retention tool*. This is the classical e-newsletter or promotional e-mail sent to your house list of customers. It is aimed at keeping your company at 'front-of-mind', and achieving repeat purchases through offers delivered by e-mail. Automated multi-stage e-mails can also be used to retain customers at renewal – for example, for insurance or utility services.

- *Awareness raising tool*. E-mail, particularly the viral variety, can be used to let customers know about new entrants into a sector and new product launches, for example.

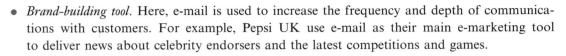

- *Brand-building tool*. Here, e-mail is used to increase the frequency and depth of communications with customers. For example, Pepsi UK use e-mail as their main e-marketing tool to deliver news about celebrity endorsers and the latest competitions and games.

- *Research tool*. Many marketers do not immediately think of e-mail as a way of learning more about prospects and customers, but research is straightforward to build into e-newsletters and e-promotions. Questionnaires within the e-mail itself do not work well, so are not widely used, but using e-mail to encourage customers to participate in a web site survey or focus group does work, and this is more widespread.

- *Viral tool*. Viral e-mail does not only mean shock videos for the eighteen to thirties. It is more widely applicable in using e-mail to encourage acquisition of new customers by referrals from existing customers – the classic 'member-get-member' approach.

- *Service delivery tool*. Many customers prefer queries answered via e-mail as a way of avoiding the 'our call is important to you' holding systems of phone support. Many organizations are now receiving tens of thousands of e-mail enquiries. Managing these in a cost-effective manner that improves rather than damages the brand is a major challenge for e-marketers.

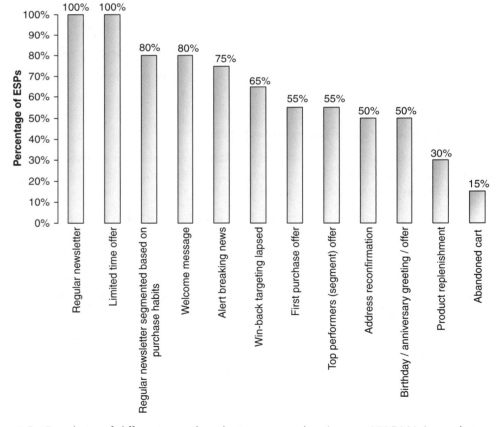

Figure 1.5 Popularity of different e-mail marketing approaches (source: UK DMA (www.dma.org.uk))

Figure 1.5 summarizes the popularity of some of these different e-mail marketing approaches. You can see that while the e-newsletter is ubiquitous, more sophisticated triggered approaches to target customers with more relevant messages are less common.

MEETING THE CHALLENGES OF TOTAL E-MAIL MARKETING

Although the potential for e-mail marketing is clear, it presents a steep learning curve for marketers. The following are some of the solutions that will be proposed in this book.

Permission challenges

Spam, unsolicited commercial e-mail, is the main barrier to the acceptance of e-mail marketing, and is well-known and reviled. Likewise, the need for a permission-based approach is well-recognized. Rather than taking up too much space repeating these well-known problems, we will concentrate on giving detailed guidance regarding how to achieve permission marketing. What exactly does this mean when you are designing an online form for collecting customer needs? What are the options – which are legal, which are ethical, and which result will result in the highest response rates?

Permission marketing is covered in Chapter 2. In Chapter 8 we look at the future of e-mail given the ever-increasing wave of spam, and the measures taken by governments, the industry and consumer organizations to combat it.

E-mail marketing strategy

Rather than concentrating on individual campaigns, which encourages an approach of moving from one campaign to another without focus, we describe an integrated approach to e-mail strategy that links marketing objectives and e-marketing objectives to different forms of e-mail marketing.

Campaign design strategies

E-mail marketing gives the potential for more complex e-mail campaigns. How can we develop the best form of campaign to achieve our objectives?

Campaign design strategies for customer acquisition are described in Chapter 4, and for customer retention in Chapter 5.

Buying lists

If you are familiar with buying lists for direct marketing, what are the similarities and differences in buying e-mail lists? How can you tell whether a list meets your needs? What are the questions to ask list-brokers or list-owners when purchasing lists?

Of course e-mail marketing also provides new challenges for marketers. Managing lists, producing a new form of creative, response rates, and privacy issues all need to be considered, as they do for conventional direct marketing.

Buying lists is covered in more detail in Chapter 4.

Developing creative

We have seen that the response rates for e-mail campaigns can be impressive, but what is the best design practice to achieve these? What are your alternatives for the subject line? Why is the 'From' address important? How should a promotional e-mail be structured? How do you write compelling copy? Where and how should the call-to-action link to the web site?

Developing creative is covered in Chapter 6.

Testing and measurement

E-mail marketing gives marketers much greater visibility regarding how their campaigns are performing, but the detail may obscure the critical points. We describe approaches to testing and ask: which are the measures that matter? What options should reporting systems contain?

Testing and measurement is covered in Chapters 2 and 7.

List fulfilment/e-mail management

For your initial forays into e-mail marketing, you may decide to use a specialist e-mail fulfilment house. However, there are big cost savings for those companies that dispatch e-mails from in-house. There are many pitfalls for the unwary when dispatching e-mails. List fulfilment and e-mail management is measured in Chapter 6. Improving deliverability is summarized in Chapter 8.

So, *Total E-mail Marketing* aims to equip you with the background knowledge to make a flying start in exploiting these opportunities for e-mail. We finish this chapter with a case study that shows how a powerful offer and high impact creative can achieve a successful acquisition campaign. A successful viral element is also included. Finally, it illustrates how e-mail marketing can integrate different forms of offline and online media.

**CASE STUDY 1.1: E-MAIL MARKETING EXCELLENCE –
VIRGIN ATLANTIC FLY FREE FOR LIFE**

The campaign

To celebrate the launch of Virgin Atlantic's new web site, a viral campaign was launched offering one customer the chance to Fly Free For Life (paying applicable passenger taxes). A competition and game were used to encourage people to visit a microsite and provide their e-mail address. This campaign was promoted via cold e-mails to bought-in lists (Figure 1.6 shows the e-mail creative), banners on various sites, the flying-club newsletter, a radio campaign, and a poster site driving traffic to a specially built microsite. To maximize exposure, it was expected that the campaign would take off virally (i.e. the game would be forwarded by e-mail to friends to play, and they would forward it to others, etc.). The main objective of the campaign was to sign up customers to Virgin's site registered base, to receive e-mail alerts on Virgin Atlantic offers and news.

Figure 1.6 E-mail creative for the Virgin Atlantic Fly Free For Life campaign

The microsite

Once at the microsite (Figure 1.7), customers had to answer a simple question in order to gain entry to the competition. The microsite offered customers the choice of three types of entry:

- enter for the competition only (for people who may already have joined up to the flying club, site-registered, or who were just competition 'junkies')

- enter for the competition and site register (to receive e-mail alerts on special offers and news)

- enter for the competition and enrol in the flying club.

To gain a further entry into the competition, entrants also had the opportunity to play the interactive game on the microsite. This game was called *Globetrotter*, and was based on visitors navigating their way around the world (depicted by icons

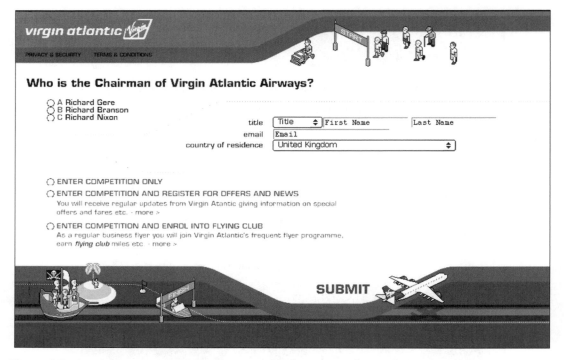

Figure 1.7 Landing page competition creative for the Virgin Atlantic Fly Free For Life campaign

of Virgin's network, such as the Statue of Liberty, palm trees, etc.) within a time limit while being chased by a pack of 'wannabe mates' (who have come out of the woodwork to go on holiday with you now you have won this fantastic prize!). If the players bumped into anything they slowed down and their mates had a chance of catching them up, thereby sending them back to the beginning.

The ability to send the game to a friend was present throughout. If the game was forwarded to a friend, it contained a score to beat (time taken to complete/fail game), to provide a challenge aspect. Once the game was completed, users were given the option of playing again and prompted to refer friends. Users were also prompted to visit the new web site.

For each friend who went on to enter the competition, the original entrant (who forwarded the game in the first place) received another entry into the competition, thereby increasing his or her chances of winning.

As well as launching in the UK, the campaign also launched in the USA, Hong Kong, India and South Africa, offering free flights for life to London. The 'Lovin' London' game was specific to the UK, with icons and landscapes of the UK to navigate through.

E-mail lists

The e-mail lists and the relevant selects used for this campaign were:

TheMutual.net	HTML and text	10 000	30+, £40k+, have clicked on travel offers
Doubleclick	HTML and text	15 000	Economy, professional
Claritas	HTML and text	15 000	Economy travellers, non-European destinations
Guardian newsletter	Text	5 × 35 000	Long-haul travellers
Virgin Wines database	HTML and text	90 000	

These lists were selected primarily on the audience being long-haul, leisure economy travellers who had expressed an interest in travel.

Results

The total traffic from all online advertising and all e-mail activity was 241 460 visits, and the following statistics emerged:

Delivered	190 523	
HTML open rate	82 686	43%
Clickthrough	53 939	31%
Clickthrough from opened e-mails		65%
Pass along (e-mail referrals)	2932	1.53%

Banner advertising delivered 10 296 clickthroughs, with an average clickthrough rate of 0.63 per cent.

In addition to e-mail pass alongs, the viral contribution of the campaign was successful with, on average, just under one e-mail per visitor being sent from the site to friends to spread the word about the site. It resulted in 200 000 additional e-mails being delivered from the site – the main source of visitors. Clickthrough for opened e-mails was extremely high, averaging around 80%, suggesting that the offer and creative were compelling.

Over 100 000 registrants with e-mail addresses available for future campaigns were achieved, breaking down as follows:

Registration online	Globetrotter	Lovin' London	Total
Competition only	67 138	29 906	97 044
Site registered	70 508	27 661	98 169
Flying Club	8891	4763	13 654
			208 867

(Case study courtesy of Tara Topliff and Naomi Broad at Virgin Atlantic, and Glenn Jones at glue London.)

REFERENCES

Gartner G2 (2002). Gartner G2 says E-mail Marketing campaigns threaten traditional direct mail promotions. Gartner G2 Press release, 19 March.

Tapp, A. (2005). Clearing up media neutral planning. *Interactive Marketing*, **6(3)**, 216–221.

WEB LINKS

Clickz (www.clickz.com/experts) has great columns on e-mail marketing, e-mail marketing optimization and e-mail marketing case studies.

DaveChaffey.com (www.davechaffey.com) is the author's site, which has a blog on e-mail marketing to update you with the latest developments.

Doubleclick (www.doubleclick.com) Knowledge Centre has a compilation of the response rates to e-mail marketing.

Digital Marketing Association (www.dma.org.uk) gives best practice guidelines, including UK legal interpretations and response rates.

DM News (www.dmnews.com) provides updates on e-mail campaigns and new practices from the US.

E-consultancy.com (www.e-consultancy.com) is a portal on all aspects of improving digital marketing, with a channel on e-mail marketing.

Chapter

2

E-mail marketing
fundamentals

CHAPTER AT A GLANCE

Overview

This chapter looks at best practice for the concepts of permission marketing and customer relationship management. We ask and answer questions such as: what does permission marketing mean beyond 'opt-in'? What legal constraints do e-mail marketers operate under?

Chapter objectives

By the end of this chapter you will be able to:

- identify all the characteristics of permission marketing
- assess the legal constraints on e-mail and know sources to keep updated
- evaluate how e-mail marketing can be used to support customer relationship management.

Chapter structure

- Introduction
- Permission marketing
- E-permission marketing principles
- Legal constraints
- Customer relationship management (CRM)
- Online CRM
- Personalization and mass customization
- An integrated e-mail marketing approach to CRM
- References
- Web links

INTRODUCTION

In this chapter we lay the foundations for detailed guidelines in later chapters which describe approaches for developing and implementing e-mail strategies. The well-established concepts underpinning e-mail marketing described in this chapter are permission marketing and customer relationship management.

Permission marketing, or gaining consent for marketing communications to be received, is fundamental to successful e-mail marketing. We will explore the development of the permission marketing concept and ask what it means in practice – for example, how do opt-in and opt-out relate to permission marketing, and what are the legal constraints on e-mail marketing? Meanwhile, the concept of customer relationship management (CRM) has proved popular as an approach to improving customer focus and customer loyalty. Companies have found the customer lifecycle of customer acquisition, retention and extension provides an essential framework for bringing focus to creating different marketing strategies and tools. If you are already familiar with the permission marketing and CRM concepts you may want to fast-forward to Chapter 3, where we look at the specifics of developing an e-mail marketing strategy. However, in this chapter we do challenge some of the conventional wisdom about permission marketing and CRM, and also explain how e-mail can be used in conjunction with the web site and traditional communications.

PERMISSION MARKETING

Permission marketing is an integral part of e-mail marketing. 'Permission marketing' is a term coined by Seth Godin, formerly a VP of marketing at Yahoo! It is best characterized with just three (or four) words:

> *Permission marketing is ... anticipated, relevant and personal [and timely].*

Godin (1999) argues that there is a need for permission marketing, since there are ever-increasing numbers of marketing communications bombarding consumers. He notes that while research shows that we used to receive 500 marketing messages a day, with the advent of the web and digital TV this has now increased to over 3000 a day! From the marketing organization's viewpoint, this leads to a dilution in the effectiveness of the messages – how can the communications of any one company stand out? From the customer's viewpoint, time is seemingly in ever-shorter supply; customers are losing patience and expect reward for their attention, time and information. Godin refers to the traditional approach as 'interruption marketing'.

However, some direct marketers have criticized the permission marketing approach in that it is not an entirely new, radical approach. Ross (2001) says:

> *the large number of direct marketers who start the selling process with an ad offering information and take it from there with a graduated programme of data collection and follow-ups will wonder how it is that they have been practising permission marketing for all this time without knowing.*

Ross also notes that in order to achieve permission it is necessary to gain the attention of prospects, and this, of course, is only possible using ... interruption marketing.

A further implication of permission marketing is that by providing choice you will, in all likelihood, be reaching fewer people with your communications. Research by Evans *et al.* (2000) found a continuum between consumers who recognized that in order to receive targeted communications they had to provide their details, and those who felt that there was an invasion of privacy. Typical comments from the former group about collection of personal data include:

> *I'm not particularly bothered about that. I've nothing terrible to hide! It doesn't really bother me, I'm just mildly interested to know how they get hold of your name sometimes. (Female, 45–54)*

> *It's more targeted. (Female, 45–54)*

> *Don't mind if a company wants to know more about me. (Male, 18–24)*

Comments from those more concerned about their personal details include:

> *I think it's quite unnerving really what people might know. How much detail they do actually have on you regarding income and credit limits. I don't know what details are stored. (Female, 25–34)*

> *Junk mail, God. I give to one charity and the next thing I know I've got 10 charities coming in daily. They've obviously sold it on for profit. (Female, 45–54)*

Clearly, those consumers in the second group are less likely to enter into a permission-based relationship unless their privacy concerns and worries about data-sharing between organizations are overcome. Advocates of permission marketing argue, however, that if consumers opt out of communications, it is not a bad thing. The cost of communications with such consumers is avoided, and they may have a low propensity to buy.

Incentivization

Incentives are not only used at the outset of a relationship; they can also be used throughout the customer lifecycle. This process is often likened to dating someone. Godin (1999) suggests that dating the customer involves:

1. Offering the prospect an incentive to volunteer

2. Using the attention offered by the prospect, offering a curriculum over time, teaching the consumer about your product or service

3. Reinforcing the incentive to guarantee that the prospect maintains the permission

4. Offering additional incentives to get even more permission from the consumer

5. Over time, leveraging the permission to change consumer behaviour towards profits.

Notice the importance of incentives at each stage. Which incentives have you or your partner offered during your relationship? In the context of e-mail marketing, the incentive is used initially to gain a prospect's or customer's e-mail address and to profile them. E-mail is then vital in permission marketing to maintain the dialogue between company and customer, and offer further incentives and learn about the customer through stages 1 through 5.

Of course, likening customer relationship building to social behaviour is not new; as O'Malley and Tynan (2001) point out; the analogy of marriage has been used since the 1980s at least – particularly for business-to-business marketing. They also note that this concept also rests uneasily with the customer. Many do not want a continuous relationship with their supplier; they may prefer a discontinuous relationship based more on exchanges. They perceive the business-to-consumer relationship quite differently from that with friends or family. O'Malley and Tynan debunk much of the relationship marketing mythology by stating that:

> *They [consumers] continue to trade with organisations that use information about them to get the offer right, but they do not consider this false intimacy an interpersonal relationship. It is not driven primarily by trust, commitment, communication and shared values, but by convenience and self-interest.*

E-PERMISSION MARKETING PRINCIPLES

It is now over five years since Seth Godin launched his permission marketing mantra, so we need to ask, how can the original principles of permission marketing be applied by today's digital marketer? Writing in *What's New in Marketing* (www.wnim.com) in 2004, I defined these 'e-permission marketing principles' to prompt you to think about how you can e-mail smarter:

1. *Offer selective opt-in to communications.* Offer choice in communications preferences to the customer to ensure more relevant communications. Some customers may not want a weekly e-newsletter; rather, they may only want to hear about new product releases. Remember, opt-in is a legal requirement in many countries. Four key opt-in options, selected by tick-box are:

    - content – news, products, offers, events

    - frequency – weekly, monthly, quarterly or alerts

    - channel – e-mail, direct mail, phone or SMS

    - format – text vs HTML.

    Of course using a range of communications preferences needs to be managed carefully since it sets expectations, and resources must be available to deliver on these expectations. Care must be taken *not* to restrict opportunities for e-mail marketing. In many ways, e-mail marketing is about opportunities or reasons to communicate; if the customer opts-out of some communications, then the opportunity to market and sell to them is reduced – so you can give too much choice. I know of one company that had a tick box for a product catalogue. Many customers ticked this and this only, meaning that the company could only communicate once per year!

2. *Create a 'common customer profile'.* A structured approach to customer data capture is needed, otherwise key data needed for delivering targeted e-mails will be missed. It sounds obvious, but … consider the utility company that collected 80 000 e-mail addresses, but forgot to ask for the postcode for geo-targeting! This can be achieved through a common customer profile – a definition of all the database fields that are relevant to the marketer in order to understand and target the customer with a relevant offering. These forms belie their importance – I think they are the second most important pages on a site after the home pages. B2B company Tektronix (www.tektronix.com) uses three levels of profile; level 1 (basic contact information), level 2 (position, market sector and application) and level 3 (detailed information about standards and preferences). Through having goals to grow level-2 and -3 detail, improved targeting is possible. Chapter 4 provides some practical recommendations on how to obtain opt-in from web-site enquirers, and explains why using an opt-out approach may be better in some circumstances. We also look at some refinements of the technique, such as double opt-in and notified opt-in.

3. *Offer a range of opt-in incentives.* Many web sites now have 'free-win-save' incentives to encourage opt-in, but often it is a case of one incentive fits all visitors. Different incentives for different audiences will generate a higher volume of permission, particularly for business-to-business web sites. We can also gauge the characteristics of the respondents by the type of

incentives or communications they have requested, without the need to ask them. If you're a business-to-business marketer take a look at Siebel (www.siebel.com) or Oracle (www.oracle.com), which offer a range of information resources for different members of the buying unit, such as IT managers, marketing director and CxO.

4. *Don't make opt-out too easy.* My view is that we often make it too easy to unsubscribe. Yes, providing a straightforward opt-out is part of permission marketing and, in many countries, a legal requirement due to privacy laws, but a single click to unsubscribe is arguably making it too easy. Instead, wise e-permission marketers use the concept of 'My Profile'. Instead of 'unsubscribe', they offer a link to a web form to update a profile, which includes the option to unsubscribe to some or potentially all communications. Amazon's communications preferences page is a good example of this approach. The use of 'My Profile' can be tied to the principle of 'selective opt-in' – you could call it selective opt-out. Put the 'My Profile' option in the e-mail to prompt the user to keep their contact details up-to-date.

5. *'Watch don't ask'* or *'sense and respond'.* The need to ask interruptive questions to profile customers better can be reduced through the use of monitoring of clicks to understand customer needs better, and to trigger follow-up communications or 'sense and respond'. Examples include:

   - Monitoring clickthrough to different types of content or offer. The interests of individual list members can be assessed through monitoring what they click through to. Lastminute.com reputedly tailors its newsletters to many different template types according to content clickthrough. For example, if you click through to theatres or city-breaks, then you will receive more of this type of content in future.

   - Monitoring the engagement of individual customers with e-mail communications. This is achieved by monitoring trends of opening and clickthrough by individual customers. These metrics indicate the level of interest of individuals, and we can monitor how these vary through time and use follow-up communications. For example, a buying signal may be suggested by a customer who has not previously responded to e-mails but starts clicking through to the web site more frequently. This could be followed up by a tailored e-mail communication or a phone call.

   - Follow-up of response to a specific e-mail. If a B2B vendor offers information about a new product launch which encourages clickthrough to a landing page, then they have two main choices of follow-up. First, the form could contain a question asking about the future buying intentions of the customer, or whether contact from a sales rep is required. Alternatively, if there is the capability to monitor an individual who has clicked through to a page, then it may be best to use this to prompt a call from an account manager or sales person. The second approach may result in more sales, but of course there is the danger that the customer may react negatively to monitoring or 'stalking' of this type, and it is arguably not permission marketing.

6. *Create an outbound contact or touch strategy.* A good starting point is to ask, what will annoy the customer? Clearly, if e-mail communications are too frequent, then the customer is less likely to have the time or inclination to open an e-mail. Therefore, one approach is to monitor the response for e-mail communications. According to a posting on this topic at E-consultancy,

Alex Chudnovsky, an e-commerce analyst (at Phones4U at the time), recommends that the following criteria need to be monitored by e-tailers to assess whether the frequency is right:

● drop off (unsubscribe)

● opens

● clicks

● sales (or profits for cases with high variation in margins)

● costs.

The alternative, particularly for non-retail brands, is to research customer preferences or, as we have said before, to offer a choice of frequencies at the point of initial opt-in.

The contact strategy should indicate the following aspects of communications, which are explained in more detail in later chapters:

1. Communications targeting

2. Communications frequency

3. Communications interval

4. Content and offers scheduling

5. Links between e-newsletters and campaign e-mails

6. Links between online communications and offline communications

7. A control strategy

8. Flexibility in communications rules.

CAMPAIGN CHECKLIST: PERMISSION MARKETING – IT'S MORE THAN OPT-IN

To summarize this section, here is a checklist of what permission marketing means in practice. Check it to see to what extent you practise permission marketing:

1. Permission marketing is an alternative approach to interruption marketing ☐

2. Prospects or customers agree to receive information according to their communications preferences; this is selective opt-in (i.e. it is not spam) ☐

3. Incentives are usually used to achieve opt-in ☐

4. Customers are usually profiled when they opt-in, or order to place them in a segment and understand their future needs from the relationship ☐

5. Subsequent communications are tailored in-line with customer needs, based on the initial profiling ☐

6. Incentives are used for continued dialogue – customer needs are researched as further data are collected throughout the customer lifecycle. The aim is to increase the level of permission by collecting more detailed information and responding accordingly ☐

7. Customers can also decline receipt of information, effectively ending the relationship; this is opt-out ☐

The battle against spam

For some consumers, all e-mail marketing is spam. They do not know about the concept of 'permission marketing' – only the annoyance of unwanted e-mail. Understanding spam can help the e-mail marketer to avoid the risk of being classified as such. It is often said that 'spam is in the eye of the beholder'. This conjures up an intriguing image, but it helps with understanding spam and the laws to protect against it to think about consumer expectations, which start from the point of opt-in.

Customers need to be reassured that what you are offering is not spam. Potential customers can be reassured that they will not be spammed, and that they will have control through communications preferences. Spam is formally referred to within the e-mail industry as unsolicited commercial e-mail (UCE). For example, the Coalition against Unsolicited Commercial E-mail pressure group CAUCE (www.cauce.org) has been active in encouraging the enactment of new laws to reduce spam. The term originally referred to 'spiced ham', which US GIs contracted to 'spam' during the Second World War. It has been said that, today, spam stands for 'Sending Persistent Annoying e-Mail'. You will know it as the instantly identifiable 'Get rich quick' offers that flood into e-mail inboxes. Later, we will review how to make your e-mail easily distinguishable from spam. Fortunately, and perhaps incredibly, despite the problem of spam, permission-based e-mail marketing still works incredibly well, as indicated by Figure 2.1. This shows that, on average, 90 per cent of e-mails are delivered, around one-third of those that are delivered register as opens, and around 10 per cent are clicked on (this is based on total clicks, not unique clicks). Although Figure 2.1 suggests that e-mail marketing works well, we still need to work hard to ensure that our e-mails are not classified as 'false positives' – permission-based commercial mail that is incorrectly identified as spam. We cover this topic in detail in Chapter 7.

LEGAL CONSTRAINTS

Nowhere is the maxim 'consult a lawyer' more relevant than for e-mail marketing, since new legislation and case law means that it is frankly impossible for a marketer to keep up to date with the details of legislation. In fact, the maxim should read 'consult a specialist lawyer'. Legal constraints on e-mail marketing naturally vary by country. Here, we concentrate on European legislation. E-mail marketers operating in European countries are subject to several existing laws, and there are also emerging laws. Of the established laws, the most pertinent are the EU Data Protection Directive, and local advertising standards and telecommunications laws. Of the new laws, the EU Privacy and Electronic Communications Directive is the most important.

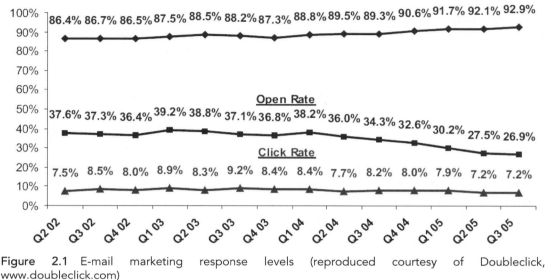

Figure 2.1 E-mail marketing response levels (reproduced courtesy of Doubleclick, www.doubleclick.com)

LEGAL NOTICE

This information provides a summary interpretation of current and emerging law. It is not intended as legal advice or counsel, and is not represented as such by the author or publisher. The author or publisher makes no warranties regarding the legal acceptability of the information provided. It is advised that legal counsel is sought to ensure compliance with legislation.

Within many companies, there is tension between achieving legal compliance in e-mail marketing, which is enforced by legal representatives, and maximizing the commercial success of e-mail marketing, which is the aim of the marketers. This tension is often evident when agreeing the details of consent through opt-in. For example, a legal advisor may state that a check box is essential for opt-in of customers, yet this is arguably not essential and is likely to restrict sign-up. In many countries (such as the UK) the implementation isn't specific and only refers to clear consent, which may be achieved through a pre-ticked box, if a purchaser is opting in, or even by just pressing a button to indicate agreement.

This tension is often difficult to resolve since although compliance with the laws may sound straightforward, in practice different interpretations of the law are possible, and because these are new laws they have not been tested in court. As a result, companies have to make their own business decision based on weighing the business benefits of applying particular marketing practices against the financial and reputational risks of less strict compliance. Marketers often need to negotiate with the legal team, and negotiation is difficult if your level of knowledge is a lot lower than that of the legal experts. At the end of this chapter, we give several references with detailed interpretations and guidelines on the emerging laws.

Data protection legislation

Data protection legislation is there to protect the individual – to protect their privacy and prevent misuse of their personal data. Indeed, the first article of the European Union Directive 95/46/EC, on which legislation in individual European countries is based, specifically refers to personal data. It says:

> *Member states shall protect the fundamental rights and freedoms of natural persons, and in particular their right to privacy with respect to the processing of personal data.*

In the UK, the enactment of the European legislation is the Data Protection Act 1998 (DPA), managed by the 'Information Commissioner' and summarized at www.informationcommissioner. gov.uk. This law is typical of what has evolved in many countries to help protect personal information. Any company that holds personal data on computers or on file about customers or employees must be registered with the data protection registrar (although there are some exceptions, which may exclude small businesses). This process is known as *notification*.

So what do personal data consist of, from a marketing point of view? Well, the data can simply be the name, address or e-mail address of an individual, or the sales history of the customer and the record of all communications with a person (outbound marketing or inbound e-mails where they ask a question or express an opinion). Data can also refer to an individual's use of the web site, as found in web-site logs; if a server places a cookie on an individual's PC, then this also provides personal data.

Note that this clause refers to personal data regardless of whether it is a consumer (B2C) or an individual working for an organization (B2B). 'Natural person' refers to the individual rather than the organization he or she works for. The implication of this is that e-mailing to generic addresses such as info@company.com or support@company.com is not subject to data protection legislation, but the moment you contact a named individual, then data protection legislation does apply. So an e-mail address such as dave.chaffey@marketing-online.co.uk is personal data, as are all facts, opinions or behaviour you record about the customer.

An organization's data protection or information management policy must cover all aspects of processing personal data that are shown in Figure 2.2. It indicates that we must start by considering the perception of the individual before he or she has even entered any data. Individuals must be clear about the future uses their data will be put to, such as whether the data will be used for marketing purposes or shared with any third parties. Sharing data with third parties is a key concern of the e-mail receiving public, so you can increase the number of registrants if you explicitly declare that 'we will not sell your data to third parties under any circumstances'. This may be good, in the short-term, but, have you considered all the circumstances? What if an opportunity arises to sell your list to a third party? What if your company is taken over by another company that does have the opportunity to pass it on to a third party? In these cases, a 're-consenting' operation may be required. For example, if prospects opt-in to an e-newsletter, this does not mean they have agreed to receive other communications which are aimed at converting them from prospects to customers. In this case, there should be an opt-in to the type of information that will be received and the channel it will be used through.

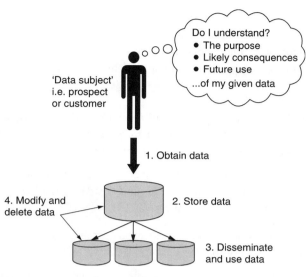

Figure 2.2 Stages in the processing of personal data

Your future use of a data statement should therefore cover:

- recipients' options – opt-in

- the form of communication – e.g. newsletter or other promotional e-mail

- the channel of communication – e.g. e-mail, phone, fax or direct mail

- whether you will share data with third parties.

It follows that the form of words, the position or the size of text for an opt-in is vital, since this will govern whether data subjects understand the use to which their data will be put. A broad opt-in for consent to receive e-mail communications gives more scope than narrow agreement to receive 'an e-newsletter'. You will want to avoid an expensive re-consenting exercise, where it is necessary to contact customers because you are unsure what use of data they have consented to in the past.

The following principles are important to understanding e-mail marketing laws:

- *Personal data* – the Data Protection Directive and the UK Data Protection Act 1998 were essentially created to protect personal data. The Act defines 'personal data' as '*data which relate to a living individual who can be identified: from those data; or from those data and other information which is in the possession of, or is likely to come into the possession of, the data controller.*' This begs the question, are e-mail addresses personal data? Since personal data are deemed to uniquely identify an individual, the answer is yes, even if it is a generic address such as dave@yahoo.co.uk.

- *Sensitive personal data* – additional protection is given for these data, which include personal details such as religious beliefs, political affiliations, gender, health information and racial origins. Such data cannot be processed or used in any way on anything other than an 'opt-in' basis.

The guidelines on the eight data protection principles are produced by the Information Commissioner (www. informationcommissioner.gov.uk), on which this overview is based. We will review the main principles, since clear understanding of these is important to e-mail marketing. The DPA states that personal data should be:

1. Fairly and lawfully processed. In full:

    Personal data shall be processed fairly and lawfully and, in particular, shall not be processed unless – at least one of the conditions in Schedule 2 is met; and in the case of sensitive personal data, at least one of the conditions in Schedule 3 is also met.

    The Information Commissioner has produced a 'fair processing code' which suggests how an organization needs to achieve 'fair and lawful processing' under the details of Schedules 2 and 3 of the Act. This requires:

    - appointment of a data controller, who is a person with defined responsibility for data protection within a company

    - clear details in communications, such as on a web site or direct mail, of how a 'data subject' can contact the data controller or a representative

    - before data processing, 'the data subject has given his consent' or the processing must be *necessary* either for a 'contract to which the data subject is a party' (for example, as part of a sale of a product) or because it is required by other laws (consent is defined in the published guidelines as 'any freely given specific and informed indication of his wishes by which the data subject signifies his agreement to personal data relating to him being processed')

    - sensitive personal data require particular care; these include

        - the racial or ethnic origin of the data subject

        - political opinions

        - religious beliefs or other beliefs of a similar nature

        - membership of a trade union

        - physical or mental health conditions

        - sexual life

        - the commission or alleged commission or proceedings of any offence

    - no other laws must be broken in processing the data.

2. Processed for limited purposes. In full:

    Personal data shall be obtained only for one or more specified and lawful purposes, and shall not be further processed in any manner incompatible with that purpose or those purposes.

    This implies that the organization must make it clear why and how the data will be processed at the point of collection. For example, an organization has to explain how your data will be used if you provide your details on a web site when entering a prize draw. You would also have to agree (give consent) to further communications from the company. Figure 2.2 suggests some of the issues that should be considered when a data subject is informed of how the data will be used. Important issues are:

- whether future communications will be sent to the individual (explicit consent is required for this in online channels, this is clarified by the related Privacy and Electronic Communications Regulation Act which is referred to below)

- whether the data will be passed onto third parties (again explicit consent is required)

- how long the data will be kept for.

3. Adequate, relevant and not excessive. In full:

    Personal data shall be adequate, relevant and not excessive in relation to the purpose or purposes for which they are processed.

    This specifies that the minimum necessary amount of data is requested for processing. For example, it would not be applicable in the Virgin Atlantic case study (see Case study 1.1) for the company to ask about your credit history. There is difficulty in reconciling this provision between the needs of the individual and the needs of the company. The more details that an organization has about a customer, the better it can understand that customer and so develop products and marketing communications specific to that customer, who will then be more likely to respond to them.

4. Accurate. In full:

    Personal data shall be accurate and, where necessary, kept up to date.

    It is clearly also in the interest of an organization in an ongoing relationship with a customer that the data are kept accurate and up to date. The guidelines on the Act suggest that additional steps should be taken to check data are accurate, in case they are in error – for example, due to mis-keying by the data subject or organization, or some other reason. Inaccurate data are defined in the guidelines as: 'incorrect or misleading as to any matter of fact'. The guidelines go on to discuss the importance of keeping information up to date. This is only necessary where there is an ongoing relationship and the rights of the individual may be affected if information is not up to date. This implies, for example, that a credit-checking agency should keep credit scores updated.

5. Not kept longer than necessary. In full:

    Personal data processed for any purpose or purposes shall not be kept for longer than is necessary for that purpose or those purposes.

    The guidelines state: 'To comply with this Principle, data controllers will need to review their personal data regularly and to delete the information which is no longer required for their purposes.' It might be in a company's interests to 'clean data', so that records that are not relevant are archived or deleted – for example, if a customer has not purchased for ten years. However, there is the possibility that the customer may still buy again, in which case the information would be useful. If a relationship between the organization and the data subject ends, then data should be deleted. This will be clear in some instances – for example, when an employee leaves a company, his or her personal data should be deleted. With a consumer who has purchased products from a company this is less clear, since frequency of purchase will vary – for example, a car manufacturer could justifiably hold data for several years.

6. Processed in accordance with the data subject's rights. In full:

   Personal data shall be processed in accordance with the rights of data subjects under this Act.

   One aspect of the data subject's rights is the option to request a copy of their personal data from an organization; this is known as a 'subject access request'. For payment of a small fee, such as £10 or £30, an individual can request information which must be supplied by the organization within 40 days. This includes all information on paper files and on computer. If such information is requested from a bank, the individual may find there are several boxes of all transactions! Other aspects of a data subject's rights which the law upholds are designed to prevent or control processing that:

   - causes damage or distress (for example, repeatedly sending mailshots to someone who has died)

   - is used for automatic decision-taking (for example, automated credit checks may result in unjust decisions on taking a loan; these can be investigated if you feel the decision is unfair)

   - is used for direct marketing (for example, in the UK consumers can subscribe to the mail, e-mail or telephone preference services to avoid unsolicited mailings, e-mails or phone calls). This invaluable service is provided by the Direct Marketing Association (www.dmaconsumers.org). If you subscribe to these services, organizations must check against these 'exclusion lists' before contacting you. If they don't – and some don't – they are breaking the law.

7. Secure. In full:

   Appropriate technical and organisational measures shall be taken against unauthorised or unlawful processing of personal data and against accidental loss or destruction of, or damage to, personal data.

   This guideline places a legal imperative on organizations to prevent unauthorized internal or external access to information and also its modification or destruction. Of course, most organizations would want to do this anyway, since the information has value to their organization.

8. Not transferred to countries without adequate protection. In full:

   Personal data shall not be transferred to a country or territory outside the European Economic Area, unless that country or territory ensures an adequate level of protection of the rights and freedoms of data subjects in relation to the processing of personal data.

Transfer of data beyond Europe is likely for multi-national companies. This principle prevents export of data to countries that do not have sound data processing laws. If the transfer is required in concluding a sale or contract, or if the data subject agrees to it, then transfer is legal.

E-mail-specific legislation

Since writing the first edition of this book, new privacy laws similar to the principles of permission marketing, and specifically designed to protect the consumer from spam, have been enacted in many countries. These usually build on data protection legislation and give additional details regarding which e-mail marketing activities are acceptable.

In 2002, the European Union passed an Act, the 2002/58/EC Directive on Privacy and Electronic Communications, to complement previous data protection law. This Act is significant from an information technology perspective, since it applies specifically to electronic communications such as e-mail and the monitoring of web sites.

As with other European laws, this law has been implemented differently in different countries. Some countries consider infringements more seriously. A company that is in breach of the Directive in Italy is threatened by fines of up to €66 000, while in the UK the maximum fine is £5000. It is clearly important for managers to have access to legal advice that applies not only to their country but also other European countries.

In January 2004, a new federal law known as the CAN-SPAM Act was introduced in America to assist in the control of unsolicited e-mail. CAN-SPAM stands for 'Controlling the Assault of Non-Solicited Pornography And Marketing (an ironic juxtaposition between pornography and marketing). This harmonized separate laws in different US states, but is less strict than the former laws in some states, such as California. The Act requires unsolicited commercial e-mail messages to be labelled (though not by a standard method) and to include opt-out instructions and the sender's physical address. It prohibits the use of deceptive subject lines and false headers in such messages. Anti-spam legislation in other countries can be accessed at www.spamlaws.com.

As an example of European privacy law, we will now review in some detail the implications for managers of the UK enactment of 2002/58/EC Directive on Privacy and Electronic Communications. This came into force in the UK on 11 December 2003 as the Privacy and Electronic Communications Regulations (PECR) Act, and is published at: http://www. hmso.gov.uk/si/si2003/20032426.htm. Consumer marketers in the UK also need to heed the Code of Advertising Practice from the Advertising Standards Agency (ASA CAP code, www.asa.org.uk/the_codes). This has broadly similar aims, and places similar restrictions on marketers as does the PECR Act.

The PECR Act is a surprisingly accessible and commonsense document – many marketers were practising similar permission marketing principles already. Clauses 22 to 24 are the main clauses relevant to e-mail communications. We will summarize the main implications of the law by picking out key phrases. The new PECR Act:

1. *Applies to consumer marketing using e-mail or SMS text messages.* Clause 22(1) applies to 'individual subscribers'. Individual subscribers means consumers, although the information commissioner has stated that this may be reviewed in future to include business subscribers, as is the case in some other countries (for example, Italy and Germany). Although this sounds like great news for business-to-business (B2B) marketers, and some take the view that 'great, the new law doesn't apply to us', this could be dangerous. There has been adjudication by the Advertising Standards Agency which found against a B2B organization that had unwittingly e-mailed consumers from what it believed was an in-house list of B2B customers. Sole traders and limited liability partnerships are also classified by the commissioner as individual subscribers, so in practice, for many B2B organizations such as a business bank, it will not be possible to distinguish between the types of subscriber; therefore many will follow the law as it applies to consumers.

2. *Is an 'opt-in' regime.* The new law applies to 'unsolicited communications' (Clause 22(1)). It was introduced with a view to reducing spam, although its impact will be limited on spammers beyond Europe. The relevant phrase is part of Clause 22(2), where the recipient must have 'previously notified the sender that he consents' or has proactively agreed to receiving commercial e-mail. This is opt-in.

3. *Requires an opt-out option in all communications.* An opt-out or method of 'unsubscribing' is required so that the recipient does not receive future communications. In a database, this means that a 'do not e-mail' field must be created to avoid e-mailing these customers. The law states that a 'simple means of refusing' future communications is required both when the details are first collected and in each subsequent communication.

4. *Does not apply to existing customers when marketing similar products.* This commonsense clause (Clause 22(3)(a)), known to lawyers as the 'soft opt-in exemption', states that previous opt-in is not required if the contact details were obtained during the course of the sale or negotiations for the sale of a product or service. While this is great news for retailers, it is less clear where this leaves not-for-profit organizations such as charities and public sector organizations where the concept of a sale does not apply. Clause 22(3)(b) adds to the definition of soft opt-in, in that when marketing to existing customers the marketer may market 'similar products and services only'. Case law will help in clarifying this. For example, for a bank, it is not clear whether a customer with an insurance policy could be targeted for a loan.

5. *Requires that contact details must be provided.* It is not sufficient to send an e-mail with a simple sign-off from the 'Marketing team' or 'Web team', with no further contact details. The law requires a name, address or phone number so that the recipient can contact the organization about their privacy if required.

6. *Requires that the 'From' identification of the sender must be clear.* Spammers aim to disguise the e-mail originator. The law says that the identity of the person who sends the communication must not be 'disguised or concealed', and that a valid address to 'send a request that such communications cease' should be provided.

7. *Applies to direct marketing communications.* The communications that the legislation refers to are for 'direct marketing'. This suggests that other communications involved with customer service, such as an e-mail about a monthly phone statement, are not covered, so the opt-out choice may not be required here. It may also be possible to use these messages for promotional purposes.

8. *Restricts the use of cookies.* Some consumers and privacy campaigners consider that the user's privacy is invaded by planting 'cookies' or electronic tags on the end-user's computer. The law states that companies must clearly describe how cookies are employed, particularly if they are used for tracking rather than in delivery of a service. This may be an issue with tracking viral marketing, for instance.

For traceability to answer future privacy queries, organizations should not record permission but also different acceptable form of communications to the customer (phone, fax, direct mail, e-mail), the date and time the data were collected, and the form of consent given – was it opt-in or opt-out? This should even reference the form of privacy statement in force at the time of registration.

Questions for list owners

This is what happens when you get permission-based marketing wrong. The extract below is from an e-mail received by a marketer after renting a list.

> *No request was made to me nor permission given to use my personal data and it is therefore an offence under UK and European Data protection legislation ... I am copying this correspondence to the Information Commissioner with a request to initiate action against you.*

Scary stuff, but it can generally be avoided if you follow these guidelines:

- ask for the form of opt-in used for the list, and require proof of double opt-in from the list owner
- check the list owner is a member of the DMA and is on the list warranty register
- use a 'statement of origination' or a message 'why am I receiving this e-mail?', explaining that the customer has agreed to receive communications
- have traceability of contact – ideally, the date and physical location of opt-in and when the profile was last updated
- ensure the opt-out mechanic works satisfactorily.

Here is some more detail on these points. It is often in the interests of list brokers to state that their lists are opt-in, when in fact they may not be. If you use such a list, you may be breaking data protection laws, have an unsatisfactory response rate and receive complaints that tarnish your brand. Therefore, with all list brokers or vendors you should initially ask whether the list is opt-in or not, and find out the exact form of the opt-in – what text was used, and what was the source? One list vendor in the UK has a privacy statement that states that the recipient's address was collected at a conference, via a magazine subscription or direct mail. This is not sufficiently specific. Some individuals will want to know exactly where their data were collected. When renting a list, it can be safer to ensure that the list is 'double opt-in'. This means that consumers have confirmed that they want to receive e-mails by replying to an initial message actively agreeing to receiving e-mail. For building in-house lists this approach is not recommended, since it does tend to reduce subscription rates.

If the form and source of opt-in is not known, then there can be no reassurance that you are not spamming, and damage to your brand will result. You should ask that it is written into the contract that the list is warranted for use in direct marketing under current data protection legislation. This will be useful if you later receive a complaint from a recipient.

You can also check whether the list owner is on the List Warranty Register (which was originally developed for direct mail). The List Warranty Register is a central database of list-owner and list-user warranties. There are four types of warranties: consumer list owner, consumer list user, business list owner and business list user. Warranties are renewed every year. By signing a warranty, the signee agrees to comply with the Direct Marketing Association's Code of Practice and, in case of a complaint, to be bound by the decisions of the Direct Marketing Authority.

CAMPAIGN CHECKLIST: STAYING WITHIN THE LAW

What are the implications for e-mail marketers arising from these emerging laws? We can use these guidelines:

1. Consent to e-mail communications is required unless there is 'soft opt-in' during the course of a sale or negotiations for sale, in which case the marketer may communicate about related products.

2. When buying e-mail lists, care should be taken to ask exactly how those on the list were asked whether they wished to opt in or opt out. This may even require assessing the form of the question (see Chapter 4).

3. Be aware of and counter the possibility of a spammer using your server for spamming. It can be hijacked if you do not have adequate security measures in place. If this does happen, your server could be suspended by the ISP.

4. When devising campaigns, ensure that:.

   - the e-mail is clearly a marketing communication – this should be the case if the offer and sender are clear

   - the originator of the e-mail is clear – provide a statement of origination for clarity

   - you respect opt-in lists

   - there is a clear privacy statement

   - online promotional competitions or discounts are clearly identifiable as such, and conditions are easily accessible and presented clearly and unambiguously

- all price indications online are clear/unambiguous and indicate whether inclusive of packaging/delivery costs.

CUSTOMER RELATIONSHIP MANAGEMENT (CRM)

Building long-term relationships with customers has always been essential for any sustainable business. However, for many years marketing theory and practice suggested an emphasis on a short-term approach, concentrating on achieving transactions rather than building customer lifetime value. A shift from transactional marketing thinking to relationship marketing thinking was highlighted by Regis McKenna (1991), who suggested a change:

from manipulation of the customer to genuine customer involvement; from telling and selling to communicating and sharing knowledge.

This change has been facilitated by advances in technology, enabling customers to be profiled in more detail and their needs assessed through market research. The Deutsche Bank case study below shows that even an international company with a large customer base can achieve this approach.

CASE STUDY 2.1: E-MAIL MARKETING EXCELLENCE – CUSTOMER PROFILING AND ANALYSIS AT DEUTSCHE BANK

Technology enables Deutsche Bank to manage its customers on an amazing scale. Deutsche Bank has 73 million customers, of whom 800 000 are online and 190 000 use its online brokerage service; it has 1250 branches, 250 financial centres, 3 call centres and nearly 20 000 employees.

To manage customer data, the DataSmart infrastructure was created on four levels – to provide a technical infrastructure across the company, to consolidate data, to enable data analyses and segmentation, and to manage multi-channel marketing campaigns.

According to Jens Fruehling, head of the marketing database automation project, for each customer over 1000 fields of data are now held. These allow the bank to understand customers' product needs, profile, risk, loyalty, revenue and lifetime value. For each customer there is also a range of statistical models, such as affinity for a product and channel, profitability overall and by type of product. External data, such as Mosaic from Experian, are also used where there is less information, such as for new prospects in every household – the type of house, the number of householders, status, risk, lifestyle data, financial status and age.

Models are run monthly in order for time-series analysis to be performed to see whether the profitability of an existing customer is falling or at risk, so a mailing can be targeted to that customer.

> For customer acquisition, the bank's customer acquisition programme, called AKM, uses up to 30 mailings per year with as many as 12 different target groups and very complex selection criteria. The bank is looking to move to a higher communications frequency so every customer gets a relevant offer.
>
> Customer opinion polls are also run frequently, aiming to assess customer satisfaction twice a year.
>
> (Source: ECCS (2001), available at the European Centre for Customer Strategies (www.uk.eccs.com))

Customer relationship management (CRM) is an approach to marketing that seeks to increase customer loyalty, resulting in greater customer lifetime value. O'Malley and Tynan (2001) refer to the need for this to be a win–win approach, where the relationship is characterized by trust, commitment, communication and sharing, resulting in the mutual achievement of goals. Some have gone further and questioned the concept of CRM, saying that customers do not want a relationship and show little loyalty to companies. For those, perhaps a more appropriate term is 'customer management'. However, I believe that e-mail marketing assists in forming both emotional and behavioural loyalty between a company and its customers as part of forming a relationship. The concepts of e-permission marketing, such as selective opt-in and opt-out and ownership of communications preferences described earlier in this chapter, can help in this. These give the customer more control of the relationship, and change CRM towards CMR or Customer Managed Relationships.

To introduce CRM, many organizations use a simple framework to develop various CRM initiatives. This is the customer lifecycle, which is divided into stages of customer selection, acquisition, retention and extension (see Figure 2.3).

This shows common themes within customer selection, acquisition and extension. As the customer moves through the different stages from acquisition and retention to extension, the loyalty of the customer and their value to the organization increases. Customer selection is key at each stage to identify potential high-value customers who will have the right connection with a brand. Other common themes include the need to deliver a great experience and customer service at each stage, and integrate communications across different channels.

Benefits of relationship marketing

Relationship marketing is aimed at increasing customer loyalty, which has clear benefits. As Reicheld (1996) has explained, loyalty or retention within a current customer base is a highly desirable phenomenon since it not only results in more transactions from each customer, but these transactions are more profitable. This occurs for these reasons:

- no acquisition costs (which are usually far higher than 'maintenance' costs)
- less need to offer incentives such as discounts, or to give vouchers to maintain their custom (although these may be desirable)

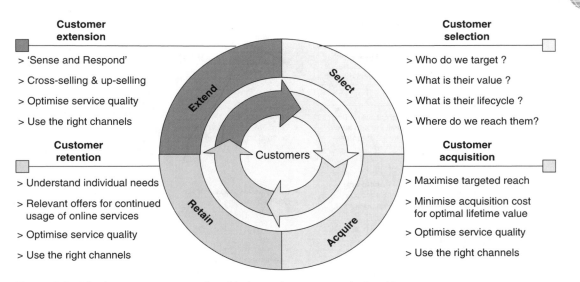

Figure 2.3   The key components of multi-channel customer relationship management

- loyal customers are less price sensitive enabling premium pricing to be used (loyal customers are happy with the value they are getting)
- loyal customers will recommend the company to others ('referrals')
- individual revenue growth occurs as trust increases.

Failure to build long-term relationships in this way largely caused the failures of many dotcoms following huge expenditure on customer acquisition. Research summarized by Reicheld and Schefter (2000) shows that acquiring online customers is so expensive (20–30 per cent higher than traditional methods) that start-up companies may remain unprofitable for at least two to three years. The research also shows that by retaining just 5 per cent more customers, online companies can boost their profitability by 25–95 per cent. According to Reicheld and Schefter (2000), 'if you can keep customers loyal, their profitability accelerates much faster than in traditional businesses. It costs you less and less to service them.'

Discussion of the factors that drive loyalty is covered at the start of Chapter 5.

Customer selection

Customer selection needs to occur at each stage of customer relationship management. This relates CRM with segmentation and target marketing. Figure 2.4 shows that customer selection starts with identifying customer characteristics through profiling and understanding their product needs. In e-mail marketing, we may want to identify those customer groupings that have the best propensity for forming an online relationship. Once these have been identified, a suitable proposition and campaign plan will be developed for each.

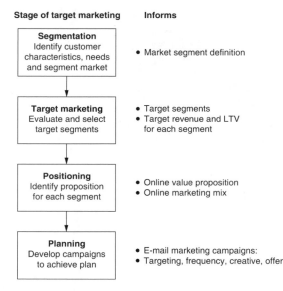

Figure 2.4 A segmentation and target marketing approach for e-marketing planning

The implication of Figure 2.4 is that achieving relevance in communication starts with how well we know the prospects and customers on our list. To deliver relevance, we need to capture the full range of data from these five areas:

1. Demographic (characteristics of an individual customer, such as age and sex)

2. Transactional (customer interactions, including purchase history and contacts via phone or e-mail)

3. Behavioural (the response history, showing how customers interact with a site and respond to e-mail campaigns)

4. Relationships (between family or decision unit members)

5. Derived data (such as customer profitability or lifetime value, customer growth potential and propensity to purchase).

However, the online marketer's capability to deliver relevance may be limited if there is insufficient focus on customer knowledge within an organization, and the following problems can arise:

- limited capacity to target, leading to lower response and higher cost for direct marketing campaigns

- no clear responsibilities for managing data quality

- no targets for data quality, strategies to achieve them or measures for data quality

- no coordination of improving customer knowledge quality at different touchpoints and for capturing e-mail details

- data stored in separate databases with duplication and lack of integrated information accessed from a single source.

To avoid these types of problems, having specific targets and responsibilities for list quality is a big help. Often marketers will only look at list volume, using measures such as subscriber number, including unsubscribes and percentage change through time, and coverage (percentage of database with e-mail addresses). However, additional list quality measures can help improve the capability to target. Such measures include:

- permission (opt-in percentage to different communications types within the list preferences)

- profile depth (from levels 1 to 3, as described in the section 'E-permission marketing principles')

- audience composition (are the demographics or roles of list members consistent with your target audience – for example, what proportion of gatekeepers?)

- deliverability (percentage bounces and messages that are delivered)

- response activity (percentage opens/clicks across the year) – you may want to break this down by segments to see how well your communications are received by different audiences; you can setup an 'activity score' which shows the number of opens, clicks or outcomes per year

- value delivered – you can calculate the revenue/cost and profitability per list member; again it may help to break this down by segment and compare to other media.

In Chapter 5, we look in more detail at five alternative customer-centric approaches for effective targeting. These approaches are based on customer selection and targeting according to:

1. Customer lifecycle groups

2. Customer profile characteristics (demographics)

3. Customer behaviour in response and purchase

4. Customer multi-channel behaviour (channel preference)

5. Customer tone and style preferences.

Customer acquisition

Customer acquisition involves techniques used to form relationships with new customers leading to a sale. It involves using marketing communications to convert potential customers into actual customers. Figure 2.5 shows the well-known funnel model applied to web marketing. This model, which applies particularly well to business-to-business permission marketing, shows how e-marketing is used to gain new customers. The web site is at the heart of this model as a lead generation tool. Lead generation happens as prospects become registered site visitors in response to offers on site, such as a free newsletter or web seminars in return for providing their contact details and profile information. For this lead generation tool to work to maximum effect, it first needs as many targeted visitors as possible. This is where a range of e-marketing techniques described in Chapter 4 are used to drive suspects to the site. Once on site, the site design and offers should be constructed to maximize capture of customer details. To convert leads into sales, a combination of traditional sales and e-mail follow-up is used.

Figure 2.5 The funnel model applied to e-marketing

Customer acquisition can have two meanings in an e-mail marketing context. The obvious meaning is the use of the web site to acquire new customers for a company as qualified leads that can be converted into sales. However, organizations should also actively encourage *existing* customers to engage in online dialogue. Many organizations concentrate on the former, but where acquisition is well managed, campaigns will be used to achieve conversion or migration of offline customers to online customers. The online dialogue referred to here means, in practice, encouraging customers to use web-site services and also encouraging communications by e-mail.

E-MAIL MARKETING INSIGHT

Online customer acquisition involves both acquiring new customers and converting existing customers to online customers.

Customer retention and extension

Customer retention refers to the strategies and actions an organization takes to keep existing customers or to reduce churn. These strategies are typically based on value. The most effort should be put into keeping the most profitable customers with the highest growth potential. For e-marketers, an important aspect of retention is continuing the customer dialogue, using e-mail to encourage repeat visits to a web site and to keep the company or brand 'front of mind'. Retention also involves learning more about the customers through their behaviour or through marketing research.

We will review in detail in Chapter 5 how e-mail techniques such as solus or standalone e-mail and e-newsletters can be used to assist customer retention.

The phase of customer extension refers to increasing the depth or range of products that a customer purchases from a company. This is targeted at customers who have the most potential for growth. For example, an online bank may initially acquire a customer through use of a credit card. The relationship will be extended if the customer can be persuaded to purchase other financial services, such as loans or insurance.

We summarize this section on the customer lifecycle by reviewing the guidance provided by Peppers and Rogers (1993) in *The One-to-One Future* on how to prioritize activity on different phases of the customer lifecycle. They say:

- Focus on share of the customer as well as market share – this means increasing the revenue from each customer as far as possible

- Focus on customer retention, which is more cost-effective than acquisition

- Concentrate on repeat purchases by cross- and up-selling; these also help margins increase

- To achieve the above use dialogue at all stages to listen to customer needs and then *respond to them* in order to build trusting and loyal relationships.

ONLINE CRM

Peppers and colleagues (Peppers and Rogers, 1998; Peppers *et al.*, 1999) have suggested the IDIC (Identification, Differentiation, Interaction, Customization) framework as an approach for using customer relationship management and the web effectively to form and build relationships. IDIC refers to these stages of relationship building:

1. *Customer identification*. This stresses the need to identify each customer on his or her first visit and subsequent visits. Common methods for identification are use of cookies, or asking a customer to log on to a site. In subsequent customer contacts, additional customer information should be obtained using a process known as drip irrigation. Since information will become out-of-date through time, it is important to verify, update and delete customer information.

2. *Customer differentiation*. This refers to building a profile to help segment customers. Appropriate services are then developed for each customer. Examples of such segments include the top customers, non-profitable customers, large customers who have ordered less in recent years, and customers who buy more products from competitors.

3. *Customer interaction*. This refers to interactions provided on the web site, such as customer service or creating a tailored product. More generally, customers should listen to the needs and experiences of major customers. Interactions should be in the customer preferred channel – for example, by e-mail, by phone or by post.

4. *Customer customization*. This refers to dynamic personalization or mass customization of content or e-mails according to the segmentation achieved at the acquisition stage. Approaches for personalization are explained in the section on retention. This stage also

involves further market research to find out whether products can be further tailored to meet customers' needs.

Personalization and mass customization can be used to tailor information content on a web site, and opt-in e-mail can be used to deliver it to add value and at the same time remind the customer about a product. Personalization and mass customization are terms that are often used interchangeably. In the strict sense, personalization refers to customization of information requested by a site customer at an *individual* level. Mass customization involves providing tailored content to a *group or individuals* with similar interests. It uses technology to achieve this at an economic basis. An example of mass customization is when Amazon recommends similar books according to those that others in a segment have ordered, or when it sends a similar e-mail to customers who have an interest in a particular topic such as e-commerce.

Mass customization can range from minor cosmetic choices made by the customer (for example, the choice of colour, trim and specification available to the customer via the multimedia kiosks in Daewoo's car showrooms) to a collaborative process facilitated by ongoing dialogue. Peppers and Rogers (1993) give the example of Motorola, which can manufacture pagers to any of over 11 million different specifications.

For e-mail marketing, there is a range of options for personalization; these include variation according to the following:

1. *The salutation*. This is the most basic level of personalization, and should be offered in all customer communications although it is not generally used for newsletters.

2. *The content*. For newsletters and alerts, this can be varied according to user selection. For example, Silicon.com, a news service for IT professionals, enables a range of items to be offered. These can be selected by checking boxes for the type of content. A further method of content personalization is keyword-based. This is offered by analysts such as Gartner, where particular keywords such as 'metrics' can be selected. Forbes.com offers a keyword-based e-mail service which alerts recipients when a particular company name is covered. For e-mail promotions the content can be personalized for different segments, although it will rarely be personalized on an individual level.

3. *The offer*. The offer can be varied according to past behaviour, such as amount spent.

4. *The landing page*. It is sometimes worth tailoring the landing page, which can be personalized if e-mails have been targeted for different segments. Content can also be personalized for individuals if they are already registered on a site. The landing page can use cookies to tailor information for an individual.

When planning e-mail campaigns, always consider how they can best be combined with offline promotions such as direct mail or advertising. The same landing pages or microsite can be used for both e-mail and direct mail components of a campaign. Hughes (1999) has called this approach the web response model. The web site is used as the direct response mechanism where the customers expresses their interest in the offer, hence 'web response'. Web response can be taken further by developing different offers for different segments. For example, a Netherlands-based bank devised a campaign targeting six different segments based on age and income. The e-mail or initial letter contained a PIN (personal identification number) which had to be typed in when the customer visited the site. The PIN had the dual benefit that it could be used to track responses to the campaign, while at the same time personalizing the message to the consumer. When the PIN was typed in, a 'personal page' was delivered for the customer with an offer that was appropriate to his or her particular circumstances.

CAMPAIGN CHECKLIST: SETTING YOUR LEVEL OF MASS CUSTOMIZATION

Figure 2.6 summarizes the options available to organizations wishing to use the Internet for mass customization or personalization. You should start by considering the vertical axis. What level of profiling information do you collect about each prospect or customer? Increasing levels of information collection are indicated by how many of these boxes you can tick:

☐ E-mail address

☐ Name

☐ Postal address

☐ Company details (B2B)

☐ Personal characteristics – demographics (B2C), position in decision-making unit (B2B)

☐ Buying intentions

☐ Buying behaviour and sales histories

☐ E-mail campaign response characteristics

☐ Loyalty

☐ Advocacy

Turning now to the horizontal axis, this refers to the extent to which the information you collect can be applied. To what extent do you personalize e-mails or web-site content, according to information collected?

If there is little information available about the customer and it is not integrated with the web site, then no mass customization is possible (A). To achieve mass customization or personalization, the organization must have sufficient information about the customer. For limited tailoring to groups of customers (B), it is necessary to have basic profiling information such as age, gender, social group and product

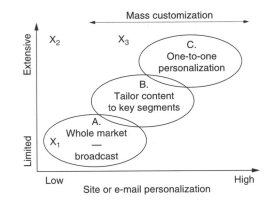

Figure 2.6 Options for mass customization using the web site and e-mail

category interest, or for B2B the role in the buying unit. This information must be contained in a database system that is directly linked to the content management system used to produce web-site content. For personalization on a one-to-one level (C), more detailed information about specific interests, perhaps available from a purchase history, should be available.

You can use Figure 2.6 to plan and explain your e-marketing relationship marketing strategy. The symbols X_1 to X_3 show a typical path for an organization. At X_1, information collected about customers is limited. At X_2, detailed information is available about customers, but it is in discrete databases that are not integrated with the web site. At X_3, the strategy is to provide mass customization of information and offers to major segments, since it is felt that the expense of full personalization is not warranted.

Of course, how far you want to progress to the top right quadrant of this diagram will depend on the balance between costs and reward. To move in this direction will require expenditure on personalization systems which may be difficult to recoup. Many companies identify major customer segments rather than operating on a true one-to-one basis. In Case study 2.1, Deutsche Bank used twelve segments. Dell uses these segments on its web site, e-mail and offline marketing communications:

- Home or small office (<5 employees)

- Small and medium enterprise (5–500 employees)

- Preferred accounts division (500–5000 employees)

- Large corporate accounts (>5000 employees)

- Public sector.

Remember that profiling is not a one-off operation. As we have said, one of the aims of permission marketing is to continue learning about the customer. Ideally, this should be made as unobtrusive as possible. The watchword could be summarized as 'Watch, don't ask'. We will see in Chapter 3 that it is possible to learn about recipient behaviour with regard to e-mail campaigns by recording their propensity to open, clickthrough and respond to e-mails. Campaigns can then be devised in line with these behaviours.

E-MAIL MARKETING INSIGHT

Take a staged view of data gathering: 'Watch, don't ask.'

REFERENCES

ECCS (2001). Deutsche Bank Finds Value In Its Customer Data (ed. David Reed). Case study on European Centre for Customer Strategies. Available online at www.uk.eccs.com

Evans, M., Patterson, M. and O'Malley, L. (2000). Bridging the direct marketing–direct consumer gap: some solutions from qualitative research. In: *Proceedings of the Academy of Marketing Conference*, University of Derby, UK.

Godin, S. (1999). *Permission Marketing*. Simon and Schuster, New York.

Hughes, A. (1999). Web Response – Modern 1:1 Marketing. Database Marketing Institute article, available at www.dbmarketing.com/articles/Art196.htm

McKenna, R. (1991). *Relationship Marketing: Successful Strategies for the Age of the Customer*. Addison Wesley.

O'Malley, L. and Tynan, C. (2001). Reframing relationship marketing for consumer markets, *Interactive Marketing*, **2(3)**, 240–246.

Peppers, D. and Rogers, M. (1993). *Building Business Relationships One Customer at a Time. The One-to-One Future*. Piatkus.

Peppers, D. and Rogers, M. (1998). *One-to-one Fieldbook*. Doubleday.

Peppers, D., Rogers, M. and Dorf, B. (1999). Is your company ready for one-to-one marketing? *Harvard Business Review*, **Jan/Feb**, 3–12.

Reicheld, F. (1996). *The Loyalty Effect*. Harvard Business Press.

Reicheld, F. and Schefter, P. (2000). E-loyalty, your secret weapon. *Harvard Business Review*, **Jul/Aug**, 105–113.

Ross, V. (2001). Review of permission marketing. *Interactive Marketing*, **Jan/Mar**, 292–294.

WEB LINKS

The following sites offer good guidelines on law for e-mail marketing:

DMA Guidelines (www.dma.org.uk) is produced by the Direct Marketing Association, which has introduced guidelines for e-mail marketing by its members which are available from this site.

Information Commissioner (www.informationcommissioner.gov.uk) has the latest developments and guidelines on data protection and personal information-related law in the UK.

Marketing Law (www.marketinglaw.co.uk) is an up-to-date source on all forms of law related to marketing activities.

iCompli (www.icompli.co.uk) is a portal and e-newsletter concentrating on privacy law.

Chapter **3**

E-mail campaign planning

CHAPTER AT A GLANCE

Overview

This chapter sets out a structured approach to planning e-mail campaigns. It also describes how an overall e-mail strategy can be developed.

Chapter objectives

By the end of this chapter you will be able to:

- develop a plan for how e-mail marketing integrates with other marketing
- identify the cost components of an e-mail campaign
- assess the main success factors in designing an e-mail campaign
- devise measurement and testing approaches to improve campaign performance.

Chapter structure

- Introduction
- Objective setting
- E-mail campaign budgeting
- Campaign design: targeting – offer – timing – creative
- Campaign integration
- The creative brief
- Measurement
- Continuous improvement of campaigns
- Testing
- Campaign management and resourcing
- References
- Web links

INTRODUCTION

In Chapter 1, we explored the CRITICAL factors that influence the success of an e-mail marketing campaign. In this chapter, we look in more detail at how we can select the best options for these factors at the start of a campaign. This involves answering these types of questions:

- What are we trying to achieve through our campaign(s)?
- What are long–medium term e-marketing objectives and our campaign-specific objectives?
- What are our options for the type of incentives or offers in a campaign?

- How do we segment the list to target recipients with a relevant offer and creative?

- How can we integrate the e-mail campaign with other marketing campaigns through time?

- How do we measure the success of the campaign, and how can the metrics collected be used to improve future campaigns?

OBJECTIVE SETTING

To develop objectives for an e-mail campaign, a good starting point is to look at how the campaign fits into your overall e-marketing plans across the next year. A key question when setting e-marketing objectives is the balance between e-marketing activities for customer acquisition, retention and brand-building. Figure 3.1 shows how an acquisition-focused strategy will be aimed at increasing turnover through adding new customers. However, since the cost of acquisition is higher for new customers, this will typically result in a relatively low profitability in comparison with a retention strategy. A retention-focused strategy, achieving incremental sales, will have a lower cost of acquisition, so will typically be more profitable. Of course both of these strategies will usually be conducted simultaneously, since acquisition is necessary to offset churn and grow a customer base, but the balance of resources into each will need to be set by setting objectives for each. Examples of typical overall e-marketing objectives are as follows.

Customer acquisition:

- For an e-tailer – gain 10 000 new customers with an average spend of £80 per year

- For a B2B service – gain 1000 new leads via the web site and convert to at least 50 new customers

- For a B2C financial service – migrate 5 per cent of offline customers to online customers.

Customer retention:

- For an e-tailer – gain an average repeat purchases spend of £100 per year within customer base

- For a B2B service – reduce customer churn to less than 15 per cent

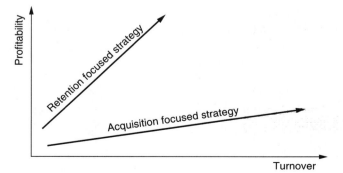

Figure 3.1 Focus for acquisition and retention strategies

- For a B2C financial service – achieve purchase of additional products in 10 per cent of customer base.

Brand building:

- Achieve brand interactions with 500 000 consumers through the web site and e-mail.

There may also be other aims that are not directly related to sales, such as gaining more insight into online customer behaviour – a research objective. Complete the campaign checklist: range of e-mail marketing applications, to think about your typical aims.

CAMPAIGN CHECKLIST: RANGE OF E-MAIL MARKETING APPLICATIONS

The list below gives potential future e-mail marketing applications. Tick those that are relevant to you and assess their suitability on a scale of 1–3, where 1 is immediate (this year), 2 is next year and 3 is possibly in the future. For the priority 1 applications, write SMART (Specific, Measurable, Achievable, Relevant, Time-related) objectives.

Six high-level aims of e-mail marketing:

1. Generate leads from prospects ☐
   (Example goals: number/percentage of leads from bought in e-mail campaigns, number of leads generated by web site, potential reach of web site, web site visitors)

   - Generate leads from prospects (using a rented list) ☐

2. Convert leads to customers ☐
   (Example goals: conversion rate)

   - Convert leads to customers (follow-up e-mails) ☐

3. Sell more/additional products to existing customers ☐
   (Example goals: number of e-mails/percentage e-mail coverage of customer base (including distributors), percentage of valid e-mail addresses, reduced churn/attrition rate, increase renewals)

   - Sell more/additional products to existing customers (using a house list) ☐
   - Reduce churn – remind of renewals, e.g. subscription, contract expiry ☐
   - Deliver loyalty programmes ☐
   - Sales promotions ☐
   - Announce new products, services, pricing and policies ☐

4. Reduce marketing costs ☐
    (Example goals: reduce target cost of acquisition, e.g. £40 for a new credit card, reduce cost of customer service contact)

5. Improve brand awareness/perception ☐
    (Example goals: reach of web site, frequency of communications, brand awareness and perception)

    - Increase brand awareness and interactions with brand ☐
    - Deliver regular information to keep brand at front of mind (e-newsletters) ☐
    - Deliver customer service ☐
    - Deliver value, e.g. alert customers to events in marketplace ☐

6. Conduct market research by recruiting to surveys and focus groups ☐
    (Example goals: Increase knowledge of customers, percentage of customers surveyed)

    - Conduct market research by delivering surveys and focus groups ☐
    - Conduct market research by pre-testing response to different offer and creative for TV or print ad campaigns ☐
    - Invite customers to take part in online discussion, webinar or offline event ☐

Note that many of these applications are achieved in conjunction with the web site and, of course, offline marketing.

To achieve the overall e-marketing goals referred to above, Chaffey *et al.* (2006) say that three main types of targets are needed:

1. *Traffic-building targets.* Use online and offline communications to drive or attract visitors' traffic to a web site. Examples of SMART traffic-building objectives are:

    - to generate awareness of web offering in 80 per cent of existing customer base in one year
    - to achieve 10 000 new site visitors within one year
    - to convert 30 per cent of existing customer base to regular site visitors.

    Although traffic-building objectives and measures of effectiveness are often referred to in terms of traffic *quantity*, such as the number of visitors or page impressions, it is the traffic *quality* that really indicates the success of interactive marketing communications (see, for example, van Doren *et al.*, 2000; Smith and Chaffey, 2005). The traffic quality is indicated by how many of the visitors are within your target market, and how many convert to action (see the section on conversion objectives below).

2. *Web-site communications targets.* Use on-site communications to deliver an effective message to the visitor which helps shape customer behaviour or achieve a required marketing outcome. The message delivered on site will be based on traditional marketing communications objectives for a company's products or services – for example, to create

awareness of a product or brand, to inform potential customers about a product, to encourage trial, to persuade customer to purchase, to encourage further purchases. Examples of SMART 'on site' communications objectives are:

- to generate 1000 new potential customers in Europe by converting new visitors to the web site to qualified leads

- to capture e-mail addresses and profile information for 100 leads in the first 6 months

- to convert 3 per cent of visitors to a particular part of site to become buyers, across the year

- to achieve relationship-building and deepen brand interaction by encouraging 10 per cent participation of customer base in online competitions and forums

- to acquire 100 new contacts through viral referrals.

3. *Mixed-mode buying targets.* This refers to sales achieved offline through follow-up of leads gained on the web site or via e-mail, and is dependent on successful integrated marketing communications. Examples of mixed-mode buying objectives are:

- to achieve 20 per cent of sales achieved in the call centre as a result of web-site visits

- to achieve 20 per cent of online sales in response to offline adverts.

- to reduce contact-centre phone enquiries by 15 per cent by providing online customer services.

The three different types of objectives described above can be integrated by using conversion marketing objective setting as described in the next section.

Conversion-based e-marketing objectives

Web marketing and e-mail marketing objectives can also be usefully stated in terms of conversion marketing. It is helpful to create separate objectives for the overall e-marketing plan and then identify specific conversion objectives for each e-mail marketing campaign. The objectives for the overall e-marketing plan will typically be over a year period, with the e-mail marketing campaign supporting the overall e-marketing plan. So, we can develop two types of objectives:

1. *Annual marketing communications objectives.* For example, objectives for achieving new site visitors or gaining qualified leads should be measured across an entire year since this will be a continuous activity based on visitor-building through search engines and other campaigns. Annual budgets are set to help achieve these objectives.

2. *Campaign-specific communications objectives.* Internet marketing campaigns such as a direct e-mail campaign will help to fulfil the annual objectives. Specific objectives can be stated for each campaign in terms of gaining new visitors, converting visitors to customers and encouraging repeat purchases. Campaign objectives should build on traditional marketing objectives, have a specific target audience and have measurable outcomes which can be attributed to the specific campaign.

Overall e-marketing objective setting

Objective setting for gaining new customers using conversion marketing takes a bottom-up approach – i.e. you start with the number of new customers you require to meet financial targets, and then work backwards to see the different conversion rates needed to achieve this number of new customers.

Take, for example, the objectives of a campaign for a large, international B2B services company, such as a consultancy company selling search engine optimization. Here the ultimate objective, across different geographical markets, is to achieve 5000 new clients using the web site in combination with telesales and sales representatives to convert leads to action. To achieve this level of new business, the marketer will need to make assumptions about the level of conversion that is needed at each stage of converting prospects to customers. Such a model can be built bottom-up for key segments and major markets. Let's assume that a 10 per cent conversion rate occurs at each of the three stages shown in Figure 3.2.

There are three stages of converting a suspect to a client using an online approach:

- *Stage 1: Conversion of web browsers to visitors.* This is referred to as 'attraction efficiency'. The main source of visitors will be from search engines and related sites. As we will explain in a later section, this highlights the importance of search engine registration, optimization and advertising using banner advertising and pay-per-click sponsorship. Of course, offline promotion techniques such as direct mail and advertising can also be used to gain site visitors. In fact, we should divide site visitor objectives into those gained through online communications and those gained through offline communications.

- *Stage 2: Conversion of site visitors to registered site visitors.* This is referred to as the 'site conversion efficiency'. This is dependent on a combination of the design of a site and the lead generation offers. This is effectively how good you are at gaining the customers permission to start a dialogue.

- *Stage 3: Conversion of leads generated from the site to customers.* This is referred to as the 'lead conversion efficiency'. You have gained leads from the web site, what do you now do with

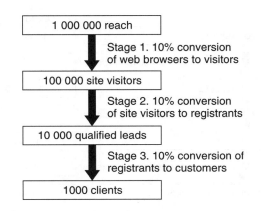

Figure 3.2 Conversion marketing approach to objective setting

these leads? One option will be to use e-mail promotion follow-ups to encourage prospects to sign up to the service. However, for high-value products with a complex decision process, e-mail alone may not be sufficient to gain the customer. In this example of a B2B company, the customer will be phoned in order to clinch the sale or to arrange further meetings.

How does this conversion-based approach relate to business-to-consumer sites? For a B2C business where the product is high value, high involvement and typically purchased offline, as with a car, the conversion process is similar to the B2B example above. Here, Stage 2 is a site visitor signing up for a brochure or arranging a test drive. Stage 3 conversion will often occur in the car dealership.

For a lower-value product that is commonly purchased online, such as books, CDs, software or travel services, the first two stages are similar. Building traffic or visitors is important in all cases. From here on, the exact conversion process will depend on the type of business model for a site. For a retail site (say, selling software) where the purchase is online, Stages 2 and 3 may overlap. Stage 2 registration will be part of Stage 3, where purchase occurs. In this case, Stage 2 conversion is typically where the customer becomes engaged with the site, perhaps by performing a product search and then clicking on a particular product and adding it to the shopping basket. E-tailers are concerned about the attrition rate, which is defined as how many customers visit the site and then add products to their shopping baskets but do not complete the sale.

Figure 3.3 shows how best case and worst case scenarios can be developed for objective setting. This spreadsheet model is available free at www.davechaffey.com/Spreadsheets. The best case scenario here uses 10 per cent conversion for simplicity. It can be seen that because conversion involves a three-stage process, reducing each of the three stages from 10 per cent to 2 per cent causes a large fall in the number of leads. This highlights the necessity of setting objectives for different conversion rates and then having good visibility of the status of conversion rates through the year. Knowing the drivers that affect the conversion rates and being able to control them is equally important.

	Scenario 1	Scenario 2
REACH of web site	1 000 000	200 000
S1. Attraction efficiency	10.00%	2.00%
Web site VISITORS	100 000	4000
S2. Site conversion efficiency	10.00%	2.00%
LEADS generated	10 000	80
S3. Lead conversion efficiency	10.00%	2.00%
Number of required OUTCOMES	1000	2

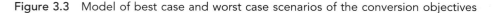

Figure 3.3   Model of best case and worst case scenarios of the conversion objectives

Cost objectives

A further aspect of objective setting to be considered is the constraints on objectives placed by the cost of traffic-building activities. A campaign will not be successful if it meets its objectives of acquiring site visitors and customers if the cost of acquisition is too high. This constraint is usually imposed simply by having an annual or campaign-specific budget – a necessary component of all campaigns. However, in addition it is also useful to have specific objectives for the cost of getting the visitor to the site, and the cost of achieving the outcomes during their visit. Typical cost measures include:

- cost per response – a basic measure to compare the cost-effectiveness of a campaign based on total campaign costs divided by unique clicks

- cost of acquisition per visitor – the cost of gaining a new site visitor regardless of whether he or she registers or purchases; this is dependent solely on the promotional method used

- cost of acquisition per lead or enquiry – this measure is of greater relevance, since it measures a marketing outcome; however, it is dependent on both the promotional method and the effectiveness of the web-site design and communications in achieving an action.

- cost of acquisition per sale (customer acquisition cost) – the cost of gaining a sale or new customer; this is the most cost important measure, which is usually constrained by defining an allowable cost per sale.

These cost measures for e-mail marketing will be compared against other traffic-building techniques, such as banner advertising or pay-per-click search engine advertising.

In the next section, on budgeting, we will look at how overall cost estimates are made. These are then divided by the relevant number of visitors, leads or sales to derive the measures given above.

A summary of this section on objective setting is given in the campaign objective checklist.

CAMPAIGN CHECKLIST: OBJECTIVE SETTING

General purpose of campaign

- Acquisition or retention balance?
  - new customer acquisition targets
  - migrating existing customers online target
  - customer retention targets
- Researching customers?

Target audience

- Segments targeted by geodemographics, lifestyle, customer value, psychographics, etc.

> *Success measures (conversion e-marketing)*
>
> ● Campaign reach
> ● Influence on awareness or perception of target audience
> ● Campaign conversion rate (response to action)
> ● Cost of acquisition (per visitor, lead or customer).

E-MAIL CAMPAIGN BUDGETING

In this section we look at the main elements of an e-mail campaign budget, starting with the revenue estimate and then moving on to the variable and fixed costs. The budgeting process is determined by calculating the return on investment (ROI) to ensure the campaign is profitable and that it has a satisfactory ROI. The budgeting process is also useful for determining an *allowable cost per outcome*. The outcome will depend on the campaign, but typically this is an allowable cost per lead or sale. For example, a credit card company may have an allowable cost per sale of £50 for a credit card. By modelling e-mail response rates and conversion rate to sale, as shown in this section, they can then assess whether e-mail marketing is viable as an acquisition medium or whether they have to look at other approaches or media, such as direct mail or paid search marketing such as Google Adwords.

For some campaigns, where the main aim is list building, it is useful to have an *allowable cost of e-mail address acquisition*. This is a notional figure for addresses from new prospects, since it is difficult to put a precise value on an address when it depends on its quality – i.e. how well it is likely to convert to sale. However, it is useful to help control spend on media such as paid search. Examples include a B2B software company which places an allowable cost of e-mail acquisition of $0.40 per e-mail, and a recruitment company which places an allowable cost of an e-mail address (as part of a job application) at $0.70.

Return on investment (ROI) is a vital concept in assessing all types of outlay, ranging from a simple pay-per-click campaign through to a major investment in a CRM system. Return on investment simply presents profitability in a different form. Profit is shown as relative to the original investment, typically expressed as a percentage. The general form of a ROI equation for any form of investment is:

$ROI \% = 100 \times Return\ from\ investment/cost\ of\ investment$

For a marketing communications investment, the formula is:

$ROI \% = 100 \times (Revenue - (cost\ of\ goods\ sold + communications\ cost))/ communications\ cost$

Using ROI has the benefit that it gives a simple way of comparing the returns of different marketing activities relative to each other. This is not possibly simply using profitability, which is an absolute amount.

For example, a net profit of £10 on a product sale appears superior to a net profit of £5 on a different product, but if the £10 profit is based on an investment of £8 then this is a 25% ROI (100 × 2/8) whereas if the £5 profit is based on an investment of £2.50 then this is a 100% ROI (100 × 2.5/2.5).

Figure 3.4 provides a typical example that you may want to refer to as we look at the individual components of budget. This budget model is based on immediate sales. Sometimes, for acquisition campaigns in particular, marketers use a more realistic lifetime value (LTV) model, which takes into account repeat sales over time and referrals. The LTV concept is explained in Chapter 5.

Revenue estimate

The revenue estimate is calculated as follows:

$$\textit{Total revenue} = \textit{Number of e-mails sent} \times \textit{Average value of response}$$

Starting with revenue, the simplest form of revenue calculation is on a revenue-per-response basis for a single campaign. The budget component is simply an average value per response. This form of estimate is most suitable for a retailer where there is product sales directly tied into the e-mail campaign. Say, for simplicity, there is a single product available to a value of £10 for each response, then £10 will be the average value per response. If there is a range of

		Best case	Worst case
E-mail campaign characteristics	Number of e-mails SENT from list	10 000	10 000
	CTR	10.00%	5.00%
	Number of recipients who CLICKTHROUGH to landing page	1000	500
	Completion	80.00%	60.00%
	Number of completed RESPONSES	800	300
	Average value per response	£10.00	£10.00
Variable costs	List rental (per thousand)	£150	£150
	Cost per e-mail sent	£0.050	£0.050
	Fulfilment cost per response, e.g. offers and response management	£0.800	£0.800
	Total list cost	£1500	£1500
	Total sending cost	£500	£500
	Total fulfilment cost	£640	£240
Fixed costs	E-mail creative	£500	£500
	Landing page/microsite creative	£800	£800
	Set-up cost for sending list and/or fixed fulfilment costs	£250	£250
	Total cost	£4190	£3790
Campaign success measures	**Total revenue**	£8000	£3000
	Profitability	£3810	−£790
	Return on investment	90.9%	−20.8%

Figure 3.4   An example of an e-mail campaign budget

products available from the e-mail we will have to make assumptions about the relative popularity of the different products to give an average price. There is also the likelihood that respondents to the campaign will purchase other products from the site which are not part of the e-mail offer.

Where products are not offered directly from the e-mail, it is more difficult to estimate the value per response. An idea of incremental revenue can be assessed on the probability that future purchases will be made. For a B2B company marketing a high-value product, it could be assumed that if 1 in 20 respondents were directly influenced to buy a product within the next 3 months due to the e-mail, the average value per response would be the value of the product divided by 20.

Variable costs estimate

Costs are divided into the variable costs, which are dependent on the number of e-mails sent or responses received, and fixed costs, which are independent of the number of e-mails sent. Typical variable costs are:

Total list cost = (Number of e-mails sent × List rental price)/1000 (0 for house list)

Total sending cost = Number of e-mails sent × Cost per e-mail sent (0 if sent inhouse)

Total fulfilment cost = Number of responses received × Fulfilment cost per response.

The total list cost is a media cost that is only incurred if you are renting an opt-in list of prospects. This will typically be charged per thousand. The amount may range from £100 to £300, depending on the quality of the list and the degree with which it is possible to target prospects by how many variables are used to select the members of the list. Buying lists is described in more detail in Chapter 4. If you are e-mailing to a house list, set this cost to zero.

The total sending cost arises if you outsource the sending of messages to an E-mail Services Provider (ESP), such as E-mail Vision or Email Reaction, which fulfils the broadcasting of your messages. The cost of broadcast per message varies widely according to the number sent (the larger the volume, the smaller the cost), the size of the message, the volume of graphics to be served, and security arrangements. Typical costs are between 1p and 5p per message, but may be over 10p for small-volume, large-size messages. If you are mailing a house list from inside an organization and this is part of your overall IT costs, you can also assign zero to this cost.

The total fulfilment cost is dependent on what your offer is. For example, Parker Pens offered a free pen to businesses looking to subscribe to their service for customized business gifts. The fulfilment cost here was that of the pen plus processing plus postage, which would usually be handled by a single fulfilment house. We are still reminded of the danger of providing an offer that costs too much to fulfil by the domestic appliance manufacturer which offered international flights costing in excess of the average value of the products it was selling.

Fixed costs estimate

Variable costs include:

- E-mail creative costs
- Landing page creative and database integration costs
- Set-up costs for sending
- Fixed fulfilment costs (e.g. prize draw).

E-mail creative is the cost of designing and producing the e-mail layout, text and graphic content. These costs will clearly be higher for an HTML e-mail.

Landing page or microsite creative costs are for the design of the page(s) that will be reached following clickthrough. We have already emphasized the importance of these in the overall success of the campaign, since you need to maximize the number of clickthroughs who go through to complete the offer. A significant additional cost here is the programming and database integration used to capture the customer profile details. This will often be higher than the costs of designing and producing the page in HTML.

Some e-mail marketing bureaux charge a set-up cost for the first time their service is used. For others, this is included within the per-message broadcast fee.

There may also be fixed fulfilment costs, depending upon the offer. If, for example, you are offering a free computer or 'fun in the sun' prize, these will be included here.

Other costs

These other costs are not shown in the budget model of Figure 3.4, for simplicity. You may want to identify these costs:

- list-building costs for house list, i.e. revising the web site in order to capture new e-mail lists
- database management, i.e. upgrades to the database to store additional fields required for profiling
- testing; a separate spreadsheet model similar to Figure 3.4 could also be produced for each series of tests
- software purchase, e.g. for web page or HTML e-mail design, e-mail broadcasting or tracking
- list-cleaning and de-duplication (these are often outsourced); it is best if the costs are assigned to a particular campaign or series of campaigns
- measurement and reporting; some e-mail bureaux will charge separately for e-mail tracking or reports, although increasingly these are included as part of the service.

Costs within the campaign can be compared for different sources of traffic, such as referrals from banner adverts on different sites. To be able to measure cost per action, we need to be able to track individual customers from when they first arrive on the web site through to when the action is taken.

CAMPAIGN DESIGN: TARGETING – OFFER – TIMING – CREATIVE

In Chapter 1, we looked at all the CRITICAL variables under the control of the e-mail marketer which will govern the success of a campaign. Here we will look at a simpler framework from Smith and Taylor (2002), which will help you design an effective campaign. The four main variables are:

1. *Creative* – the design and layout of the mail shot

2. *Offer* – the proposition or the benefits of responding

3. *Timing* – the season, month or day when the offer or mailshot lands on a desk or in a house

4. *Targeting* – the segments we are targeting (the mailing list or section of a database).

Since no one has unlimited time and resources for designing the campaign, it is useful to think about the relative importance of these variables. Which would you say is most important? Rating these out of 4, where 1 is least important and 4 most important, the UK Institute of Direct Marketing suggests these scores for a mailshot:

Creative	1
Offer	2
Timing	2
Targeting	4

We suggest that the results for e-mail campaigns are likely to be similar to those for a mailshot, so don't neglect targeting in favour of creative!

We will now look at each of these four aspects of campaign design in rough order of importance. Since these variables are well known from direct marketing, explanations will be brief and we will focus instead on specific issues in e-mail marketing.

Targeting

Targeting e-mails for a house list as part of a contact strategy is a major strategic decision, which we introduced in Chapter 2. We identified five major approaches to targeting:

1. Customer lifecycle groups

2. Customer profile characteristics (demographics)

3. Customer behaviour in response and purchase

4. Customer multi-channel behaviour (channel preference)

5. Customer tone and style preferences.

Targeting for e-mail marketing involves selecting a subset of the list for mailing, whether it is a bought-in or a house list. There is a whole host of methods of breaking down a list. Imagine your list as a cube representing all the list members – what are all the different ways to slice and dice this cube to identify the special characteristics of the list members? Figure 3.5 gives an indication of the many different ways of targeting an e-mail list.

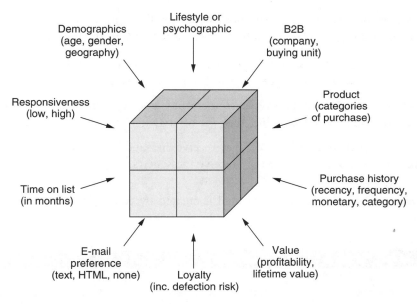

Figure 3.5 Options for targeting an e-mail list

Let's run through 10 of the common options for targeting, highlighting their relevance to e-mail marketing.

1. *Demographics (age, gender, geography)*. These are generally the preserve of B2C markets. With the relatively low cost of creating and dispatching e-mail creative, a different style and tone of creative can be developed according to age and sex. For example, a whisky brand developed different creative styles for younger and older drinkers and also developed creative for female partners to encourage gift purchases. The Boots Dentalcare example used postcodes to target potential customers within a 20-minute drive of the branches.

2. *Lifestyle or psychographic*. The providers of lifestyle classifications, such as MOSAIC or ACORN, supply services to integrate these data with e-mail lists in order to target according to lifestyle.

3. *B2B (company or individuals)*. For business-to-business organizations, the primary segmentation is usually according to company characteristics such as sector or size, proxied by number of employees or turnover. Dell Computers uses a classification based on companies' employee numbers as its primary segmentation, and different web-site and e-mail content is targeted at each of these segments. The individuals that make up the decision-making unit can also be targeted separately.

4. *Product (categories of purchase)*. This refers not to particular products, but general categories. For example, an IT supplier might distinguish between customers who focus most on hardware and those who focus most on software categories.

5. *Purchase history*. This evaluates the characteristics of purchase through time using evaluation schemes such as recency, frequency and monetary-value analysis. E-mail offers great potential for targeting according to history of purchase and category of interest.

E-mail Vision has developed a rules-based personalization approach for retailers which allows them to target by product and other characteristics in the following manner:

- by spend (over last n months) – customers who have spent £300+ get message A, while customers who have spent up to £300 get message B

- by product – if the profile says customers buy books online, they get offer C; if the profile says they buy CDs online, they get offer D

- by interest – if customers like golf they receive message E, if they like tennis they receive message F, if they like neither they receive message G.

The rules are devised such that the e-mail is created by combining these messages to form a unified e-mail.

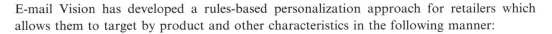

E-MAIL MARKETING INSIGHT

Use automated rules-based personalization for targeting groups of consumers with similar characteristics such as product interest or responsiveness.

6. *Customer value*. The simplest form of customer value calculation looks at the value to customer over a fixed period. For example, we could assess total spend across the last 3, 6 or 12 months, and customers could be placed in categories of spend (see (5) above) and given different offers. The future value of customers can also be calculated using lifetime value calculations. These include assumptions about the rate of churn, average spend per category and referrals to other members. Some companies, such as Deutsche Bank, use complex modelling of profitability for targeting purposes (see Nitsche, 2002, for a summary). Their approach is iterative, enabling the targeting capability to be refined through time.

7. *Customer loyalty*. Loyalty has been defined by Sargeant and West (2001) as 'the desire of the customer to continue to do business with a give supplier over time'. Customer loyalty is linked in with purchase history and customer value. Customer loyalty can be measured simply by the length of time a customer has been with the company, but more meaningfully by the frequency and value of purchase, using RFM analysis. Understanding different levels of loyalty and developing campaigns to appeal to these different levels is part of retention planning, so we return to this topic in Chapter 5.

8. *E-mail preference*. This can simply refer to the format required for e-mails – whether text or graphical (HTML). Many companies are now also establishing a communication channel preference (phone, e-mail or post). E-mail preferences may also state the type of content or the offers a list member has expressed an interest in receiving.

9. *Time on list (in months)*. This is arguably a more critical tool for targeting in e-mail than it is in traditional direct marketing. With opt-in for e-mail communications, we would expect that the susceptibility to response is highest immediately following opt-in. Response rates tend to be highest when the most recent list members are targeted.

10. *Responsiveness to e-mail campaigns.* This measure combines a number of targeting methods we have talked about, such as purchase history, loyalty and time on list as part of the customer lifecycle. Jeremiah Budzik of Doubleclick (www.doubleclick.com), building on established models, suggests that customers should be segmented into different 'buckets' dependent on their time on list, susceptibility and buying characteristics. Figure 3.6 shows how the new members on the list, referred to as 'Nellie New', have the greatest susceptibility or responsiveness to offers. Through time, however, responsiveness will fall, and the aim is to target customers with good potential ('Peter Potential') to become high-value, loyal customers ('Betty Best'). Effectively, we are looking to minimize the number of unresponsive customers who are ignoring their e-mail but remain on the

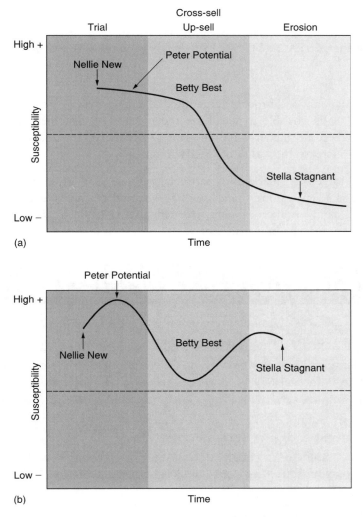

Figure 3.6 Customer lifecycle model of customer responsiveness to e-mail campaigns: (a) without incentivization, (b) with incentivization (source: Jeremiah Budzik, Business and Technical Manager, EMEA Doubleclick, DARTmail, www.doubleclick.com)

		0 units	1–2 units	>3 units
	% of list	10%	4%	2%
	% of gross sales	0%	1.50%	1.50%
	Average £/list member	0	£25	£50
	Average units/list member	0	1.3	3.9
		0 units	**1–2 units**	**>3 units**
Mailings				
6–12	# of members	1500	650	300
	% of list	15%	6%	4%
	% of gross sales	0%	1.30%	2.20%
	Average £/list member	0	£33	£65
	Average units/list member	0	1.5	4.2

Nellie New
Betty Best

Stella Stagnant
Peter Potential
Betty Best

Example of customer buckets based on buying behaviour mapped to lifestyle curve

Figure 3.7 Enhancing customer value through e-mail targeting (source: Jeremiah Budzik, Business and Technical Manager, EMEA Doubleclick, DARTmail, www.doubleclick.com)

list ('Stella Stagnant'). Through targeting the high-potential new customer as shown in Figure 3.7, it is possible to maximize the revenue of customers by converting more customers to become higher-value customers. Special offers and creative can also be developed to increase the value of 'Stella Stagnant'.

In databases used for e-mail marketing, particularly those that are currently separated from the main transactional or customer database, 'flags' should be included that indicate the type of customer – e.g. main product segment, frequent user. Decide on 5–10 key characteristics which will determine the type of e-mail sent.

E-MAIL MARKETING EXCELLENCE: ENHANCING CUSTOMER VALUE THROUGH E-MAIL CAMPAIGNS

A summary is given of guidance from Jeremiah Budzik for maximizing customer value through e-mail campaigns:

- A small percentage of Nellies become Bettys; however, a majority need incentives to move to Peter status.
- Treat your Bettys well and they will treat you well; they are your core customer base!
- Some Peters will need an extra push to move to Betty status, or there is the fear that they might end up in Stella's bucket.
- When the population of Stellas increases, Bettys dwindle and Peter makes no traction, it's time to refresh your house list and attract some Nellies.

(Source: Jeremiah Budzik, Business and Technical Manager, EMEA Doubleclick, DARTmail, www.doubleclick.com)

David Hughes of E-mail Vision suggests that targeting can be refined during campaigns or in follow-up campaigns according to their response to the initial e-mail. This is a response-behaviour based segmentation. We can again leverage the technology to automate this response process. E2Communications refers to this as 'response-based segmentation'. The categories of response to the e-mail we can identify are:

- A. *Don't open*. If recipients do not open the message, this suggests the list members are not responding to the subject line. This can be revised to have greater impact or refer to a different offer. Recipients may not be responding because of a lack of time, so another option is to send it out on a different day of the week, or at a different time. It is only possible to tell whether an e-mail is opened for an HTML e-mail. One approach for using this information is shown in Figure 3.8.

- B. *Open, don't click*. If recipients do open the e-mail but don't click on it, this shows they are not responding to the creative or the offer. They have indicated a good level of susceptibility, however, so there could be a follow-up with different creative and/or offer.

- C. *Click, but don't act*. In this case recipients have clicked through on one of the hyperlinks in the e-mail to the microsite or landing page. They have a very high propensity to act, but something has stopped them acting. A specific e-mail, perhaps acknowledging their interest but offering an improved incentive as an additional carrot to persuade them to act, might be effective here.

- D. *Do act*. If recipients do click through and follow the instructions on the landing page, then they should be flagged in the database as having a high susceptibility. A follow-up with a complementary offer should be planned.

E-MAIL MARKETING INSIGHT

Use response-based segmentation to plan follow-up offers according to how recipients responded to e-mails.

A summary of the alternative responses and the related follow-up options is presented in Figure 3.9. Further details on how we test for these actions are provided in the 'Measurement' section later in this chapter.

We have considered a range of targeting options. Later in the chapter we will look at testing that can be applied to targeting. Remember that the more of these different alternative ways of targeting are combined, the greater the targeting and the higher the response.

E-MAIL MARKETING INSIGHT

Combine different types of targeting, such as response behaviour, purchase behaviour and demographic data, for tighter targeting.

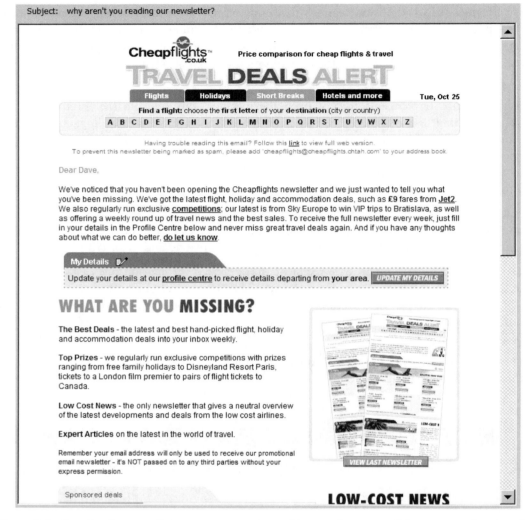

Figure 3.8 Reactivation e-mails to encourage renewed interest in an e-mail (source: opt-in subscriber newsletter, a marketing add-on to the Cheapflights Ltd main site (www.cheapflights.co.uk), as is the travel news (http://news.cheapflights.co.uk) blog site

Offer

The offer is the next of our direct marketing variables which is critical to the response to the campaign. The offer is the incentive that we use to encourage action. In e-mail marketing, we use incentives to encourage two distinct types of action. The first type of action is encouraging prospects and customers to provide their e-mail address, profile information and permission to contact as part of an acquisition campaign through MyOffers. This action can occur on the web site or offline media. This requires a lead generation offer. Figure 3.10 is an example of such a campaign where the aim is to encourage e-mail recipients to enter the prize draw on a microsite in return for providing profile details and opting in to future communications.

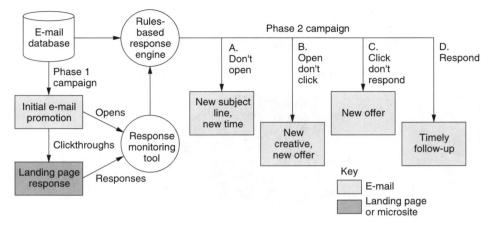

Figure 3.9 Automated response-based segmentation options

The second action is encouraging clickthrough from e-newsletters or e-mail promotions. This requires a sales generation or conversion offer.

As part of campaign planning, suitable offers should be identified for each situation. However, we can make some general comments about offers that apply to both situations. First, the offer must always be relevant to the target audience – consistent with their needs, interests or aspirations. Clearly we need the offer to appeal to the target audience, but there is also a problem if the appeal is too broad. Imagine an offer for a B2B company which involves winning tickets to a Rugby World Cup. This will appeal to consumers who may respond even though they have no interest in the company's products.

A decision should be taken as to whether these offers are available on the web only as a 'web exclusive'. In some cases it may be more cost-effective or practical to deliver offers using the web. It may also encourage an online dialogue. If, however, you want to give the customer the choice of which channels to use to deal with you, then the offer may also be made using traditional media. If a 'web exclusive' approach is taken, then this gives a great reason to visit the web site for offline communications rather than the bland 'visit our web site'.

Your options for types of offers can usefully be divided according to the type of value they represent to their audience. Farris and Langendorf (2001) identify five different types of information value:

1. *Information value*. This can take a variety of forms. Most common for B2B is access to a report or white paper that can be downloaded as an Adobe Acrobat (.pdf) or Microsoft Word document. It may be that you already have this type of information available, so this can be a low-cost, effective option for B2B. What we are trying to do is to achieve one of the key success factors for Internet marketing identified by Patricia Seybold (1999), which is 'Help the customer do their job'. Such incentives are very effective, so it may be worthwhile creating some information specifically to achieve this for different audiences. Examples include white papers about improving the efficiency of workflow in a particular job, or information about the marketplace. Such information may not necessarily be in

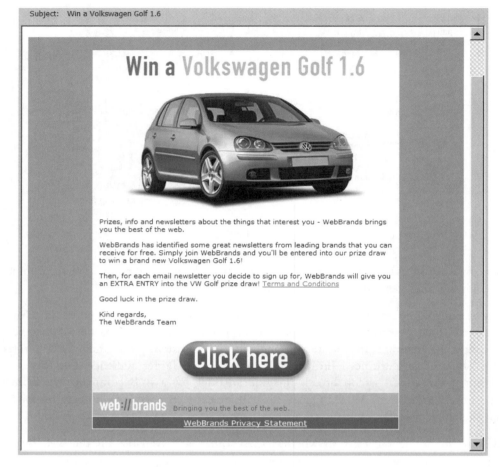

Figure 3.10 Data capture E-mail with Prize Draw from MyOffers (www.myoffers.co.uk) (WebBrands is a co-registration product from IPT, a leading UK e-mail data and delivery solutions provider)

report form or delivered online. Registration that leads to further dialogue with the prospect at an online or real-world seminar is often most effective. The JD Edwards case study later in this chapter (Case study 3.1) is an example of this. A research survey where the results are sent to a respondent is another form of dialogue. E-newsletters or industry alerts are yet another common form of information value, as are software tools or spreadsheet calculators. However, care must be taken that the offer does not act as a barrier to acquiring the customer. With the case of prospective loan customers, for example, customers might go elsewhere rather than entering their details.

E-MAIL MARKETING INSIGHT

Assess carefully the balance between the strength of the incentive and the barrier of the customer having to provide information.

A final example of information value, and a favourite of mine, is to use the e-mail itself to deliver the value. Some companies offer a sequence of several e-mails over a period of several days or weeks to add to the customers' knowledge about a particular topic. The *Dummies Books* offer a tip of the day delivered by e-mail, which is perhaps too frequent.

2. *Monetary value.* This is a straightforward discount or a buy-one-get-one free offer. E-tail e-commerce sites often offer an online discount on the first order. Loyalty programmes that can be administered online are another way of offering monetary value. Finally, monetary value is also offered through prize draws or other contests.

3. *Privilege value.* This is most likely to be privileged access to information. For example, media sites and information providers such as the industry analysts Forrester (www.forrester.com) and E-consultancy (www.e-consultancy.com) have tiered levels of information access. This approach works particularly well if the information is of high quality and isn't readily available from other sources. A limited amount of information showcasing the content and service is available to all site visitors, further information is available to those who register, and all information is available to paying subscribers. Here, the offer is fulfilled as providing a username and password to access an extranet. This approach can also be used in consumer applications – for example, giving fans access to exclusive footage or clips of a band.

4. *Service value.* Farris and Langendorf refer to offering a service that does something worthwhile for the customer, whether it is making their lives more convenient, keeping them informed or automating mundane tasks. Examples given include online surveys or polls that offer learning and possibly entertainment; reminder services; and personalized content, such as that available at Silicon.com for IS managers and gift registries.

5. *Transactional value.* For e-commerce sites, the purchase process is clearly an opportunity to profile customers; however, we don't want to increase attrition by asking too many questions in what may already be a lengthy process.

A sixth value, *entertainment value*, was not in Farris and Langendorf's original list but is worth identifying separately. This is typically (but not exclusively) a B2C offer. It may take the form of a game or quiz, screensaver or movie clip. Such offers are often tied in with viral campaigns. Here, the offer should be devised according to how well it can be passed onto a friend or colleague. Ways of communicating the offer to others applies to each of the different offer types.

Multiple offers are more effective than single offers, so it is useful to identify at least a primary offer and a secondary offer. The power of the two offers together will increase the pulling power of the campaign. The primary offer is used as the main appeal to the target audience to respond; the secondary offer is an additional tool to help convert those who are inclined to respond but need a further stimulus. The prospect's perception of the company and its web site services can also be part of the secondary offer. The offer won't work if the company or web site does not have the credibility to deliver.

Another way of thinking about these offers is as 'free–win–save', and of course these keywords are often used to communicate the offer. Remember that 'save' can refer to saving time as well as to saving money.

Finally, as we have mentioned before, the cost of the offer and fulfilling it must fit within the budget of the campaign. This must be modelled to ensure there is a satisfactory return on investment for the campaign.

Timing

Starting with the absolute timing, a frequently asked question is: when is the best time to broadcast an e-mail promotion? The flippant answer is that it will vary according to audience, so you should always test to find the best timing for your audience. Results of tests suggest that the e-mail will have the greatest impact if it arrives in the recipients' inbox while they are using the computer. This would suggest that, for consumer audiences, evenings or weekends might be the best time to dispatch. For business customers we want the e-mail to arrive when they will give it the most attention, so we are looking for times in the week when business people are likely to be less busy. Industry wisdom dictates that the best days of the week for e-mail broadcasting are Tuesdays and Thursdays. Presumably, on Monday we are all recovering from the weekend and have Monday planning meetings, on Friday, we are winding down for the weekend or frantically trying to finish work scheduled for the week. However, there are dangers with general rules – each company needs to test for its own markets. A good starting point is your web analytics results – look at your web-site stats to see which are naturally the most popular days of the week. For financial services providers, Sunday and Monday at work can be important, after consumers have reviewed financial products in the Sunday papers. For an FMCG brand seeding a viral campaign, Friday may work well, as people's attention at work falls. Similarly, B2B audiences may have more time to look at e-mails when they arrive on Friday, when businesses are winding down, and many marketers find this a good time to send them. To summarize, currently Friday is the new Tuesday, but it may not be next year!

Note that many e-mails are dispatched overnight, when costs may be cheaper or the IT department argues that workload on the servers is lower. This is a serious mistake, since maximum impact will always be higher during the day for the business user or during the evening for a consumer with an 'always on' broadband connection, since many will open e-mails as they arrive. If permission e-mails are sent overnight they are caught amongst the spam, and recipients are in 'delete mode' as they go through their inbox.

Relative time considers the timing of the e-mail campaign in comparison to other media. For example, does it precede or follow the offline launch of a cross-media campaign?

Another aspect of relative timing is frequency compared to the last e-mail. Is weekly, bi-weekly or monthly best? How important is it that these messages are sent out on the same day of the week? Selecting the best frequency is covered in Chapter 5.

Creative

The creative of an e-mail campaign includes the message header (subject line, From, To) and the design of body of the message, including the text structure and copy and graphics (if used). Creative also refers to the creative used for the web-site landing page. We cover options for designing the creative in depth in Chapter 6, so will not discuss it further at this stage.

CAMPAIGN INTEGRATION

Many books and articles on e-mail marketing tend to describe it in isolation from other media. However, an integrated campaign can increase the impact and response rate to the e-mail. Kotler *et al.* (2001) describe integrated marketing communications as:

> ***the concept under which a company carefully integrates and co-ordinates its many communications channels to deliver a clear, consistent message about the organisation and its products.***

Integrated marketing communications will use a range of media, such as TV, print advertising, direct mail and web site, in addition to e-mail. A range of promotional tools may also be used from advertising, direct or interactive marketing and PR. The different media and promotional tools that are used also need to be integrated through time such that the sequence of communications is most effective.

Clearly there is a danger if e-mail marketing is managed by a different agency to the traditional DM agency and the two are not briefed on consistency of message. A useful mnemonic referred to by Pickton and Broderick (2000), which highlights the characteristics of integrated communications, are the 4 Cs of:

- *Coherence* – different communications are logically connected
- *Consistency* – multiple messages support and reinforce, and are not contradictory
- *Continuity* – communications are connected and consistent through time
- *Complementary* – synergistic, or the sum of the parts is greater than the whole!

Case study 3.1 illustrates these points well and uses a range of media, with promotional tools carefully integrated through time. In this case the different communications had a theme of retaining customers, but different metaphors were used in each to highlight the approach, from the restrictive 'rope and straitjacket' to blandishments such as chocolates and cheesecake. In this way, the sequence of messages supported and reinforced. Different media, including telemarketing, a DM mailer and e-mail, were also used in a synergistic way such that the sum of the parts was greater than the whole. Through the use of telemarketing and direct marketing JD Edwards was at front of mind, so the e-mail was not unexpected – and this contributed to the large number of responses.

CASE STUDY 3.1: E-MAIL MARKETING EXCELLENCE – JD EDWARDS LAUNCHES CRM SYSTEM USING AN INTEGRATED CAMPAIGN

Campaign objectives

Software supplier JD Edwards wanted to launch its CRM programme in the UK. A 'Window into the World of CRM' event was organized for 21 March 2002, with a minimum of 30 attendees required from the direct marketing campaign.

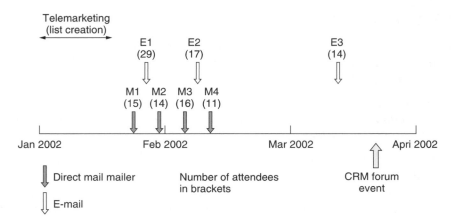

Figure 3.11 Campaign timing for JD Edwards CRM launch

Campaign tactics

An integrated campaign, using four direct mail and three e-mail campaigns, was produced (see Figure 3.11). All messages were each received by each list member. These were supported by a microsite to gather customer details. Telemarketing was used throughout the campaign to gain prospects. Those contacted were offered the choice of hearing about a new product or hearing from independent experts on CRM. Those contacted included both JD Edwards' customers and prospects obtained from a bought-in list.

Creative

A series of high-impact direct mail pieces using key statements and imagery related to a Valentine's Day theme were used (Figure 3.12). The background of the e-mail was red, to fit in with the theme and to achieve high impact. The following images and strap lines were used:

- Mailer 1/e-mail 1 – man wrapped in rope: 'There Are Other Ways Of Keeping Your Customers'

- Mailer 2 – cheesecake: 'Keep Them Coming Back For More'

- Mailer 3/e-mail 2 – man in straitjacket: 'Once You've Got Them You'll Want To Keep Them'

- Mailer 4/e-mail 3 – heart shaped chocolate box: 'Keep Them Sweet'.

Results

The target of 30 attendees was exceeded, with 80 registrations achieved via the microsite (see Figure 3.11). Over 200 prospects showing an active interest in the product were also gained. The e-mail was more effective at generating visits to

Figure 3.12 JD Edwards creative – e-mail 3

> the microsite than was direct mail, but not significantly so – for example, Mailer 1 generated 100 visits to the site while e-mail 1 generated 120 visits.
>
> (Source: Philippa Edwards and Robert Perrin, Anderson Baillie Marketing (www.andersonbaillie.com))

The exact form of integration will vary in each case. However, we can draw out some general principles. Taking the example of the campaign to support relaunch of a web site (Figure 3.13), we can make the following observations:

1. *A combination of online and offline communications techniques is used.* The techniques to promote the launch include a range of communications media and promotion tools.

2. *Search engine registration must be planned well in advance.* This is important for all e-mail related marketing where a web site is part of the offer. For example, when the UK's Chartered Institute of Marketing launched its 'Whats New in Marketing?' Newsletter, registering the site was not seen as a priority. Consequently, word-of-mouth recommendation of the newsletter which led to someone searching for a site they could not find was wasted. Also there is a delay in each search engine indexing a site and then publishing it, even with paid-for express-inclusion services.

3. *Online and offline PR can be useful in driving traffic to a newsletter site.* Online PR takes the form of online articles on related web sites, with links referring to the site. Offline PR can play a similar role. For example, briefing newspapers or magazines about the launch of a high-impact viral campaign in advance will assist in the success of the campaign.

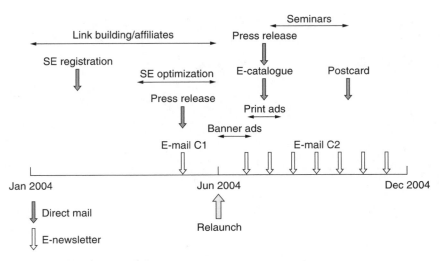

Figure 3.13 An integrated campaign for a web-site relaunch

4. *Developing an e-newsletter takes time.* While a one-off e-mail campaign can be produced in days, the same is not usually true for a newsletter. Newsletters stand or fail according to their content. Commissioning, editing and assembling content, even when sourced from within a company, takes weeks rather than days. To produce the first newsletter following the relaunch shown in Figure 3.13, work will typically need to start two months before the first issue. The first issue will also require a design template to be produced as well as sourcing content.

THE CREATIVE BRIEF

The creative brief is a summary of the purpose of the campaign. It is used to communicate the aims of the campaign to the alternative agencies who may be conducting the work, or as a summary of intent if undertaken internally. The detail in the brief will depend on the experience of and control required by the marketer directing the campaign. If relatively new to e-mail marketing, the marketer may leave the details more open and look to the agencies who have been asked to submit a tender to provide their creative input.

The brief covers many of the topics we have referred to already in this chapter, so this section acts as a summary of this chapter to this point.

CAMPAIGN CHECKLIST: THE CREATIVE BRIEF

- *Aims*: lead generation, customer acquisition, retention – number required, level of sales anticipated. Changing awareness or perceptions about brand. Different response mechanisms (e.g. e-mail only, or e-mail and phone) and method of tracking response.

- *Target audience*: the demographics of consumers or characteristics of businesses or those in the decision-making unit. Pyschographic profile of the type of person you are trying to reach.

- *Offer*: the nature of the offer – a general indication of information value, monetary value, saving, or a more specific offer consistent with brand. Generally there should be a primary offer, and a secondary offer to engage people who don't buy.

- *Timing*: target date for completion of campaign. Relation to campaign in other media.

- *Integration*: how does the e-mail campaign integrate with offline media campaigns such as advertising, direct mail or PR?

- *Creative*: the details will usually be left to the agency to devise, but a theme or tone may be suggested.

- *Brand*: the communications in the campaign must support the brand in terms of the brand values and its rational and emotional elements. Brand identities such as logos must also be prominent to achieve a connection with customers who are familiar with the brand.

- *Style and tone of voice*: related to the brand values, the e-mail style and tone of voice should support the brand; however, for large lists this should be tailored to different segments – for example, older or younger consumers, or male or female.

- *Microsite*: location of microsite – part of the sponsoring company's site, or separate site. Notification pages required, e.g. successful completion, notification of error in form completion.

- *Information collection needs*: what fields should be used to profile the customer or research their views (including mandatory fields)? Specific form of wording required for opt-in. What validation will be used to check the data (e.g. valid postcode, e-mail address format)? In what format is the data required in (e.g. comma delimited ASCII text file, Access database)?

- *Mandatory inclusions*: logo, link to privacy statement, terms and conditions, unsubscribe, is contact number required?

- *Budget*: an indication of maximum budget may be included.

MEASUREMENT

A valuable characteristic of e-mail marketing is that it enables detailed analysis of direct marketing campaigns. To date, we have simplified the measurement of campaigns to refer to four variables (number sent, number of clickthroughs, number who complete the form, and the number of recipients who become customers). For detailed analysis of a campaign more metrics are available, and it is important to dissect these to identify the weaknesses in the campaign. Figure 3.14 summarizes the metrics in diagrammatic form. Figure 3.15 illustrates a typical solution for presenting results from an ESP.

			Campaign 1	Campaign 2
Number of e-mails SENT from list			10 000	10 000
	Receipt rate		98%	90%
Number of e-mails RECEIVED from list			9800	9000
	Reader rate (open rate)		60%	40%
Number of e-mails READ or opened			5880	3600
	Response rate 1 (CTR of readers)		30%	10%
	Response rate 2 (CTR of recipients)		18.0%	4.0%
	Response rate 3 (CTR of number sent)		17.6%	3.6%
Number of CLICKTHROUGHS to landing page			1764	360
	Completion rate		80%	60%
	Response rate 4 (responses of number sent)		14.1%	2.2%
Number of FORMS COMPLETED (RESPONSES)			1411	216
	Referral rate		10%	2%
Number of REFERRALS			141	4

Figure 3.14 Detailed e-mail campaign diagnostics

One way to remember the different type of measures for e-mail marketing is the 7 Rs. We will relate this back to Figure 3.14 and also to a traditional door-drop campaign. The 7 Rs are:

1. *Receipt rate* (based on number of recipients), calculated as

   Receipt rate = (nSent − nBounced)/nSent

   'Bounces' are returned e-mails that are not received by the intended recipient. There are two types of bounces:

   - soft bounce – an e-mail returned because the e-mail server is not working (will resend later)

   - hard bounce – an e-mail returned with address unknown.

   The level of 'bounces' compares to level of 'gone-aways' of a conventional direct mail campaign – i.e. people who no longer live or work at a particular address. With e-mail

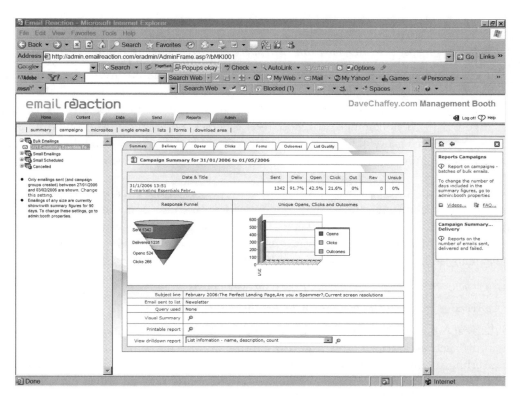

Figure 3.15 Typical e-mail marketing reports from an E-mail Service Provider (reproduced courtesy of Email Reaction Ltd, www.emailreaction.com)

we have the benefit that it is easier to see when someone has moved on, and we don't have to waste funds by continuing to contact them.

Hard bounces are of the greatest concern to e-mail marketers. A high bounce rate indicates an e-mail list with a high proportion of e-mail addresses with errors or that have become out-of-date. In the next section we look at what can be done to reduce the number of hard bounces to an acceptable level.

2. *Reader rate*, more commonly referred to as the Open or View rate, based on number of readers, and calculated as

$$\textbf{\textit{Reader rate} = \textit{nReaders/nRecipients}}$$

For HTML e-mails, we can get an indication of the reader rate according to whether a marker graphic contained within the e-mail has been downloaded.

This rate compares to the proportion of people who evaluate the contents of the mailer and then open it in a traditional campaign. We have much better visibility about this process when we are using HTML e-mails. However, we don't know how many delete the e-mail immediately – the equivalent of dispatching it to the bin. As we will see in Chapter 6, open rates have dropped significantly over the last few years as more e-mail readers have used image-blocking software to avoid notifying spammers that an address is live.

3. *Clickthrough rate* (CTR), calculated as

Clickthrough rate = nClick on Links/nReaders or nRecipients or nSent

The clickthrough rate is a key measure, since it indicates the quality of the creative and offer; if you get good clickthrough, the campaign will be a success provided the landing page or microsite is of good quality. The CTR can be reported in different ways, as shown in Figure 3.14. It is common to report it as a percentage of those who open the e-mail (nReaders), which is useful for assessing the effectiveness of the creative and the offer, but for overall campaign success it is better to use a percentage of those received or sent.

Remember that since you may have multiple hyperlinks in the e-mail, using *total clicks* for calculating clickthrough rates may be misleading because some recipients may click more than once. Some e-mail marketers therefore use *unique clicks*, which determine clicks from unique visitors to the microsite. Alternatively, for newsletters in particular, which have many links, you will want to report CTRs for the different hyperlinks in the message.

4. *Conversion rate of completing landing page form*, calculated as

Conversion rate = nComplete form/nClickthroughs

Where appropriate, this refers to the number of people who clickthrough and complete a form, such as a registration page for a prize draw. The conversion rate can refer to converting to any outcome, whether it is completing the form, subscribing to a newsletter or catalogue or actually buying a catalogue. The response rate, described below, refers to those that act on the initial registration.

The completion of reply form rate is not known for a traditional direct mail campaign.

5. *Response rate* (based on number of responses), calculated as

Response rate = nAct/nRecipients

Here, the response rate from the e-mail campaign is exactly the same as the information obtained from a traditional direct mail campaign. It will be useful to monitor the rate at which responses are received also. The majority of responses are received within 2 or 3 days from an e-mail campaign.

Great care has to be taken when quoting the response rate because, as you can see from Figure 3.14, it can be formulated in a number of ways:

- Response rate 1 is the number of readers who clickthrough as a proportion of the number who open the e-mail. This response rate will often be used by agencies or managers to describe the success of their campaigns, since it is the biggest number!

- Response rate 2 is the number of readers who clickthrough as a proportion of those who received e-mail (i.e. it excludes bounce). It is a better indication of the overall rate of success than response rate 1.

- Response rate 3 is the number of readers who clickthrough as a proportion of those who were sent e-mail (number broadcast).

- Response rate 4 is the number of readers who complete an action as a proportion of those who sent e-mail. This action is usually responding to the form, but it may also include making a sale (i.e. becoming a customer). This is the most meaningful indication of the overall success of the campaign, although, as we will see in the next section, each can be useful for understanding particular strengths and weaknesses of the campaign.

6. *Rejects rate* (more commonly referred to as the unsubscribe rate), calculated as

   Opt-out rate = nUnsubscribe/nRecipients

   It is useful to monitor the unsubscribe rate of each campaign against the average unsubscribe rate. If the campaign unsubscribe rate is much higher, it indicates a problem with the content or tone of the campaign.

7. *Referrals rate* (based on number of referrals of new prospects), calculated as

   Referral rate = Number of referrals/number of respondents

   This refers to the viral element of an e-mail campaign, if used. If a campaign has involved generating additional leads through providing an offer to encourage disclosure of other e-mail addresses, then the referral rate can be measured as the number of referrals per respondent. This capability is not always provided by e-mail broadcasters, so it is worth checking when selecting an e-mail broadcaster. A review of questions to ask with regard to measurement is presented in Chapter 6. Perhaps the most important capability is being able to assess who is responding to specific offers or links at an *individual customer* level, since this is an important capability for follow-up targeting.

More detailed measures are also available, including number of clickthroughs per e-mail and which calls-to-action were responded to – for example, those in the bottom, middle or top of the e-mail.

CONTINUOUS IMPROVEMENT OF CAMPAIGNS

We have seen how it is possible to target according to the past responses to e-mails – whether they are opened or there is clickthrough. In a similar way, it is also possible to take corrective action by reviewing the results of a campaign. This is particularly important in a multi-message campaign.

It is difficult to give industry averages of the value of metrics which may indicate a problem with the campaign, but I give estimates based on different campaigns of which I have knowledge.

Hard bounces >5–10 per cent (Don't receive)

For good quality lists, hard bounces should not exceed 5 per cent. From 5 per cent and into double figures, this suggests a problem that should be resolved. Possible alternative solutions to reduce the number of bounces involve exploring different reasons for the problem:

1. If the list has aged (sometimes referred to as attrition), then cleaning is required. Indeed, the addresses giving hard bounces should be removed after three mailings, when we can be sure they are no longer valid. It is vital to follow up bounces where appropriate,

to recapture valid addresses – for instance, a postcard reminder can be sent, or when customers are talking to the contact centre they can be reminded to give their new address.

2. A high level of hard bounces may indicate a problem with the verification of e-mail addresses when they were originally collected. Methods for verifying e-mail addresses include asking the customer to enter the e-mail twice (entry confirmation), double opt-in, and a check that the e-mail is in a valid format (such as a@b.com or a@b.co.uk). E-mail Vision uses 'intelligent forms' which check for the existence of a SMTP mail server at the domain.

3. There may have been poor-quality control of manual data entry – for example, e-mails captured at point of sale or by sales representatives. This can be improved through training which stresses the importance of valid e-mail addresses and shows how to check validity.

Soft bounces

These are usually in the range of 1–2 per cent. No action is required, since most mail servers will keep trying until the message is successfully delivered.

A section on managing the different types of bounces is included in Chapter 6.

Open rate <10–30 per cent (Don't open)

The open rate will depend on how many users have a preview pane open. If a high proportion of users have the preview pane open, then this will increase the open rate; however, this is offset by image-blocking functionality in the e-mail reader which will prevent the image being recorded. Despite many consumers using the preview pane, the open rate can fall to below 10 per cent – particularly for rented lists in a competitive category. This suggests a problem with the subject line, since recipients will only click on the e-mail to open it if the subject line is relevant to them. The obvious action to improve the open rate is to consider alternative subject lines. Practical alternatives for improving the subject line are covered in Chapter 6 – for example, personalizing the subject line to refer to a particular product or person in the subject line is likely to improve open rates. There may also be something more fundamentally wrong with the e-mail – it may be poorly targeted, or the offer referred to in the subject line not be relevant or strong enough. Different types of appeals and copy in subject lines can also be tested to improve this.

As well as problems in the subject line, other factors will affect the open rate. A From address that is unknown or confusing may decrease the open rate (see Chapter 6). For B2B mailings the time of day may have been inappropriate (first thing on Monday morning, for example, may be a bad time), so consider testing and changing the time of day the e-mail is sent.

Clickthrough <5–10 per cent (Open, don't click)

If the clickthrough rate from e-mails that have been opened is below 5–10 per cent, this suggests a problem with different aspects of the creative or the relevance of the message and offer – i.e. it is not sufficiently personalized. Improving these aspects of a campaign is discussed in Chapter 6. Remember that we may also have different hyperlinks for different calls-to-action, so we will need to assess the success of each of these. In summary, different issues to review to improve the clickthrough rate are:

- *Position of the call-to-action hyperlink.* If it is at the bottom of long copy, then recipients may not scroll down to it – can the call-to-action be duplicated, higher in the e-mail?

- *Prominence of the call-to-action.* In text e-mails, the call-to-action hyperlink should be placed on a separate line for prominence. In HTML e-mails, the call-to-action can use specific copy, bold text or an image to increase its prominence. Images must look 'clickable'.

- *Multiple calls-to-action.* Combining different types of call-to-action, including images and text-based, will increase response, since different users will respond better to each. Often, simple hyperlink-based calls-to-action in the body-text can help.

- *Structure of the calls-to-action.* Perhaps you have used multiple calls-to-action, but how are these structured? Are they crafted in a logical sequence or flow for the selling process? It may be helpful to think of traditional direct mail, with a range of copy for each of the details of offer/product, link to page, testimonials, additional offers and main call-to-action.

- *Length and size.* The e-mail may be too long or, if it is a rich media e-mail or contains graphics that have not been optimized for the web and takes a long time to download, then the clickthrough may be decreased.

- *The offer.* If the e-mail is well designed and you don't think it is the factors above that are causing the problem, then poor clickthrough is likely down to the offer. If the offer (or the way it is described in the e-mail) is not sufficiently appealing to the target audience, then this needs improving. Perhaps a secondary offer will increase clickthrough.

- *The message.* The content or style of the message may simply not be relevant for the target audience. If you don't connect with the recipients' individual mindset, then they won't respond.

Landing page form completion <40–60 per cent (Click, don't act)

Once recipients have clicked through, this shows a high level of interest in the offer – they have already committed time to reading and evaluating the e-mail. Given this investment in time, they are pre-disposed to complete the landing page, provided it does not form too high a barrier. It should be possible to achieve over 40 per cent of respondents completing the form. If the proportion falls below this, then the main issues to consider are:

- Changing the number of questions asked or number of screens required if the campaign involves an extensive research component.

- Perhaps the offer does not appeal as much as was thought from the subject line or body copy.

- Perhaps there is a problem with the privacy options – does the landing page reassure respondents that their details will not be shared with third parties, for instance?

- Perhaps the tone and design of the landing page is not consistent with the campaign or brand, which again will not help to reassure respondents.

TESTING

There are two main types of testing required for e-mail marketing. The first, which is essential, is efficiency testing, to make sure the campaign reaches as many people as possible and that they can view it. The second is effectiveness testing, which allows you to change the variables of the campaign (such as creative elements, targeting and media integration), which helps make sure the campaign objectives are met.

Campaign efficiency or platform testing

This is one type of testing that can't be omitted, because when using technology to deliver different campaigns there are lots of things that can go wrong due to different ISP and user set-ups for hardware and software. A well-established procedure and management enforcement of this is necessary for this to work.

Here is a checklist of things that could apply to an e-mail campaign. We cover how to improve renderability or display of creative in Chapter 6, and deliverability in Chapter 8.

CAMPAIGN CHECKLIST: TYPICAL TESTING VARIABLES FOR AN E-MAIL CAMPAIGN

Campaign features
- List ☐
- Segment targeted ☐
- Offer ☐
- Subject line ☐
- Content – copy, style, tone, structure ☐
- Best day of week ☐
- Best time of day ☐
- 'From' address ☐
- Different forms of personalization ☐
- Landing page (microsite) characteristics ☐

The basics
- Spelling/grammar ☐
- Effectiveness of creative, offer ☐
- Prominence of call-to-action(s) ☐
- Data protection compliance ☐

Technology features
- Are images available on the server? ☐
- Do links go to the right landing page when clicked? ☐

- Are landing pages present – does response mechanism such as online forms work? ☐
- Deliverability – check whether spam filters reject message because of subject line and body copy; you should check with a tool such as www.lyris.com/contentchecker or use test accounts on Hotmail and Yahoo!Mail which have their own spam filters (this is covered in more detail in Chapter 7) ☐
- Do you have both Text and HTML versions for Multipart/MIME messages (see Chapter 6)? ☐
- For e-mail, test appearance for different:
  - reader platforms – Hotmail, Yahoo!Mail, AOL, Lotus Notes, MS Outlook ☐
  - reader display options such as preview panes and the first two lines of messages ☐
- Do you use HTML without graphics (NB Outlook 2003)? ☐
- Do you use the most popular screen resolutions of 800 × 600 and 1024 × 768? ☐

Campaign effectiveness testing

The need for testing the different variables of an e-mail campaign would seem obvious, particularly since both agencies and clients are learning about this evolving media. Here are 12 ideas for you regarding tests that could help you improve your e-mail marketing. How many of them are you doing or should you be doing?

1. Test copy in e-mail headers – different subject lines and From addresses

2. Check different offers – does 10 per cent discount or £50 off work best? It is usually the latter. Are secondary offers useful in elevating the overall response?

3. Time broadcasts on different days of the week

4. Assess text vs HTML, embedded versus linked images (see Chapter 6)

5. Use integration with other media (e.g. e-mail teaser before DM or response mechanism after DM)

6. Consider tone of voice

7. Test long vs short copy

8. Assess calls-to-action (number and location of links)

9. Use personalization for different targeting approaches and dynamic messaging

10. Check which newsletter template is most effective

11. Assess which frequency interval for a newsletter maximizes revenue (while avoiding perceptions of spam)

12. Use a touch strategy for triggered e-mail – which sequence of offers and intervals between them works best?

While testing sounds like a great, logical idea, the reality is that testing is time consuming. Some may see it as an extra cost, since responses rates are currently high. Others may see it as delaying a campaign that has to hit a deadline. We will look at several different forms of testing, some of which have a relatively low cost.

Pre-testing campaign variables

Pre-testing refers to trialling the campaign, varying different elements with a subset of our audience, before rolling it out to a wider audience having selected the best combination of campaign variables. For example, you mail two cells with 5 per cent each of your list to find which offer works best. Pre-testing can also refer to running focus groups from the audience to determine their opinions and response about different proposed creative treatments.

Let's take the example of pre-testing an e-mail campaign, which is done in the same way as for direct mail. The outline procedure for pre-testing, which is summarized in Figure 3.16, is as follows:

1. Split the list into at least two parts or cells, including *test* and *control*; the control cell is similar to previous communications

2. Vary *one feature* in each of the cells – the offer, creative, copy or subject line; it is vital that only one feature or variable is changed for each test cell

3. The groups used are of course smaller in size than the list, but must be sufficiently large for differences in response to be significant – for example, if you have 10 000 e-mail addresses, a test group of 250 and a control group of 250 is appropriate (statistical tables must be consulted to determine this)

4. The groups must be taken randomly from the list, and should contain a range of segments and length of subscription to e-mail; taking the first 200 in a list will often just give those who have been on the list the longest

5. Test the responses by tagging links in the creative (although separate landing pages could be created, this is more straightforward).

The best combination of variables according to response is then used when mailing to the remainder of the list.

When testing, each test should be marked with key codes so that responses to it will be clear from studying the web analytics tool. For example, these codes can be used to highlight the characteristics of each test:

- List = L1
- Segment targeted = S1
- Date/time broadcast = D1
- Offer = O1
- Subject line = SL1

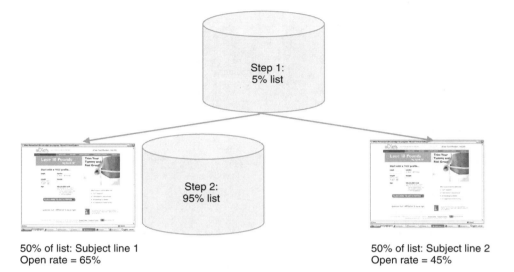

50% of list: Subject line 1
Open rate = 65%

50% of list: Subject line 2
Open rate = 45%

Figure 3.16   Methodology for pre-testing an e-mail broadcast

- Content = C1
- Hyperlink = H1 (e.g. first hyperlink in message)
- Format = FT, FH
- Call-to-action = CA1

These codes can then be combined into the hyperlink that is the call-to-action within the e-mail. A question mark '?' is used to separate the testing key codes from the landing page for the clickthrough. The following is an example of what might appear in a text e-mail: http://www.company.com/promotion.htm?SL1O2

Tagging in such a way can be used to test different interactive ads and different calls-to-action on a web site, as well e-mail marketing.

E-MAIL MARKETING INSIGHT

Develop a standard set of key codes early on which can be used to test the response to different campaigns.

Live split-testing or A/B testing

In this approach, we test the success of different creative treatments during the campaign in order to change the style later in the same campaign or in future campaigns. This approach works well for e-mail marketing, Pay-per-click advertising, display ads and alternative response pages. It is also one of the best testing methods, since it is relatively fast and cheap.

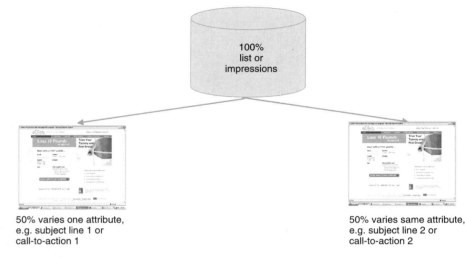

Figure 3.17 Methodology for live split testing of a campaign broadcast

Here, there is again a control group and one or more test cells where different variables can be tested. A common approach is to do a simple split test, as shown in Figure 3.17. Half of the list receives one subject line (e.g. newsletter plus the month) and another receives a different subject line (perhaps with a theme for the newsletter). The highest open rate can then be determined. Check how easy it is to do this type of test with your e-mail management software.

You can see how this approach works equally well for online ads or landing pages, where the different alternatives can be automatically displayed in real-time.

Example of results of live split testing

Site intelligence wanted to invite IT and marketing managers to an executive briefing to showcase their new web analytics product. Before sending out to the bulk of the rented list, they tested three different alternative subject lines: A, B and C. The results are shown in Table 3.1. You can see that there are substantial differences, and changing the subject line changes not only the open rate but also the response rate, since it can expose a different audience to the e-mail body or change how recipients are conditioned to respond to the message.

Table 3.1 Alternative subject lines

Batch	Subject line	Open rate (%)	Registration rate (%)
A	Web-site performance	45	5
B	News from site intelligence	48	4
C	Executive briefing invitation	32	1

Advanced cross-campaign testing

Advanced testing is used to improve effectiveness when there is a large list; this type of testing is often involved because the list can't be tested within a single campaign. Examples include testing:

- *Segmentation approaches* – for example, delivering messages with a particular offer or tone or style to a particular audience type.

- *Offer response approaches* – assessing which types of offer yield the best response at different times in the customer lifecycle.

- *Touch strategy approaches* – deciding what is the best interval for e-mails and how this is combined with different offer types. Testing the best frequency (i.e. balancing the danger of too many e-mails, leading to unsubscribes and brand damage, against lower sales owing to too few e-mails) has to be completed over a period of several months.

- *Newsletter content and offers* – it is often not possible to make major improvements to e-newsletters in a single e-blast.

Multivariate testing can be used to test different creative elements of an e-mail. We look at this further at the end of Chapter 6.

E-MAIL MARKETING CHECKLIST: TOP TEN E-MAIL EVALUATION DOS AND DON'TS

Do:

1. Measure!

2. Set SMART objectives for campaigns, based on previous campaign performance

3. Try to isolate the successful elements of a campaign by considering both views and clicks

4. Test clicks for different creative elements, e.g. text hyperlink vs image hyperlink

5. Benchmark against other e-newsletters for your audience

6. Use tracking that works both for e-mail and web-site landing page(s)

7. Plan follow-up messages based on the four response options – don't open, open don't click, click don't respond, and do respond

8. Review how the profile of those who do view or click differs from the overall list profile and those who don't

9. Use a spreadsheet to compare performance of campaigns over time if your e-mail tool doesn't permit this

10. Pre-test or conduct live split testing to learn for the future.

Don't:

1. Forget the importance of bounces – these must be followed up to regain permission to e-mail

2. Just measure total views or opens – unique views or clicks are often more effective

3. Just look at total clicks; look at how clicks vary for different link positions/types

4. Forget the financial metrics (costs and outcomes); build an ROI model

5. Rely just on the hard measures – ask customers for their views, too

6. Forget the need to measure deliverability for different ISPs (problems with spam recognition)

7. Forget to model likely results based on previous campaigns, to set more realistic goals

8. Forget to measure referrals – how many people pass along the message (a 'viral' effect)?

9. Assume a low unsubscribes shows interest – many recipients delete rather than unsubscribe

10. Just concentrate on the e-mail metrics – also consider responses on the landing page or web site.

Consumers' suggestions on how to improve permission e-mail

Of course, there is a limit to what you can determine through control tests of response, and qualitative surveys and secondary research are useful too. eMarketer (2002) reported on a survey of 1250 US e-mail users and asked them for their opinions on how e-mail programmes could be improved. The results highlight the importance of the campaign planning variables that we have mentioned. From the most to the least important changes suggested (two choices per respondent), the results were:

- Less frequent messages (42%)

- Better prices and offers (35%)

- More relevant, targeted messages (24%)

- More control over e-mail options (18%)

- Time savers and convenience (18%)

- Exclusive e-mail offers (17%)

- More self-personalized content (9%)

- More entertaining messages (6%)

- More timely messages (6%)
- More reminders (2%)
- More frequent messages (1%).

CAMPAIGN MANAGEMENT AND RESOURCING

Approaches to managing the whole campaign process in terms of which suppliers to use are covered in Chapter 7.

REFERENCES

Chaffey, D., Mayer, R., Johnston, K. and Ellis-Chadwick, F. (2006). *Internet Marketing: Strategy, Implementation and Practice*, 3rd edn. Financial Times-Prentice Hall.

eMarketer (2002). Consumers want more from e-mail marketing. eStatNews from eMarketer, 20 May.

Farris, J. and Langendorf, L. (2001). Engaging customers in e-business: how to build sales, relationships and results with e-mail. White paper, available at www.e2software.com.

Kotler, P., Armstrong, G., Saunders, J. and Wong, V. (2001). *Principles of Marketing*, 3rd edn. Financial Times-Prentice Hall.

Nitsche, M. (2002). Developing a truly customer-centric CRM system: Part two – analysis and campaign management. *Interactive Marketing*, **3(4)**, 350–366.

Pickton, A. and Broderick, D. (2000). *Integrated Marketing Communications*. Financial Times-Prentice Hall.

Sargeant, A. and West, D. (2001). *Direct and Interactive Marketing*. Oxford University Press.

Seybold, P. (1999). *Customers.com*. Century Business Books, Random House.

Smith, P. R. and Chaffey, D. (2005). *eMarketing eXcellence – At the Heart of eBusiness*, 2nd edn. Butterworth-Heinemann.

Smith, P. R. and Taylor, R. (2002). *Marketing Communications*, 3rd edn. Kogan Page.

van Doren, D., Flechner, D. and Green-Adelsberger, K. (2000). Promotional strategies on the world wide web. *Journal of Marketing Communications*, **6**, 21–35.

WEB LINKS

ClickZ (www.clickz.com/experts) channels on e-mail marketing.

Conversion marketing objectives spreadsheet (www.davechaffey.com/Spreadsheets).

E-marketing best practice and buyers guides (www.e-consultancy.com).

Chapter **4**

Using e-mail for customer acquisition

CHAPTER AT A GLANCE

Overview

This chapter discusses how to use online marketing to acquire new customers and migrate existing offline customers online. Capture of e-mail addresses and profiling information is key to this, so a large part of this chapter is about building a house e-mail list. We will also explore how to use e-mail as part of online customer acquisition.

Chapter objectives

By the end of this chapter you will be able to:

- devise different approaches to building a house e-mail list
- evaluate the quality of rented e-mail lists
- assess the use of e-mail sponsorship or advertising
- use e-mail to convert leads to sales.

Chapter structure

- Introduction
- Building a house e-mail list
- Using e-mail marketing to support customer acquisition
- Web-based customer acquisition strategy
    1. Devise incentives(s)
    2. Use online and offline communications to drive traffic to the web site
    3. Revise web-site design to emphasize offer
    4. Define profiling needs and capture form
    5. Select permission levels – what does opt-in really mean?
    6. Draw-up privacy statement
    7. Define the opt-out
    8. Follow-up registration
- Measuring acquisition effectiveness
- References

INTRODUCTION

Customer acquisition means gaining new customers, right? Of course, but for success in online marketing we need to look at separate strategies for gaining new *online* customers. This means

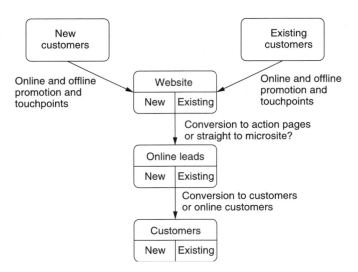

Figure 4.1   Two routes to customer e-mail acquisition

strategies for acquiring prospects and converting these leads to customers, but also strategies for migrating existing customers to online customers who either buy or self-serve online, or with whom we can communicate via e-mail. Figure 4.1 shows that the first stage of customer acquisition varies depending on whether new visitors or existing customers are being targeted, with different online and offline promotion campaigns being used to attract first-time visitors to the web site. Use of all touchpoints between company employees and potential or new customers should also be used to encourage them to visit the web site and capture e-mail addresses. Such touchpoints include the salesperson, point of sale, support enquiry and so on.

Once the first-time visitor is on the web site, we ideally need to convert these visitors to action or, at least, create a favourable impression and awareness of our services. If we fail to achieve either of these, then the first-time visitor will never be seen again. For a new potential customer, we want to start a dialogue by capturing an e-mail address and profile. For an existing customer, we also want to acquire an e-mail address if we don't already have it. We may already have some profile information which we could link to through a customer reference or account number. To convert as many of the first-time visitors to action as possible, think about where the promotion directs them. If it directs them to the home page, then they will have to find the offers to acquire them; however, if they are directed to a particular landing page or microsite, then the proposition will be clearer and there will be fewer distractions – so the conversion rate will be higher. For example, CRM vendor Siebel uses search-engine marketing to drive visitors to hundreds of different landing pages, each specific to a particular product and audience need. If the first-time visitor arrives on the home page, then think about using different offers for new customers and existing customers. Many organizations use a 'one-size fits all' offer. Once we have converted our visitors to action, the final stage is to change the potential customers from leads to customers, and the existing customers to online customers or repeat customers. E-mail can help to remind and inform the prospect, and encourage them to go online, but this final stage is not always most effectively achieved online. Phone calls, direct mail or visits from sales people are often best to help achieve this.

Since both types of acquisition share much in common, in this chapter we will look at a generic process for customer acquisition; however, do consider different strategies for each type of acquisition. In this chapter, we will cover these stages:

1. Devise incentive(s).

2. Use online and offline communications to drive traffic to the web site.

3. Revise web-site design to emphasize offer.

4. Define profiling needs and capture form.

5. Select permission levels – what does opt-in really mean?

6. Draw up privacy statement.

7. Define the opt-out.

8. Follow-up.

Stage 2, using online and offline communications to drive traffic to the web site, is one of the most important aspect of this process. This is because if we can gain visitors to the web site, we have an excellent chance of converting them to customers if the offer, design and privacy options on the site are also right. We will therefore explore this in some detail. Different types of communications that we will describe include online communications techniques such as:

*   search-engine registration and optimization

*   using a rented list of e-mails to acquire customers via e-mail

*   placing banner advertising on other web sites

*   placing advertising in other e-mail newsletters.

Offline communications techniques we will look at briefly include:

*   direct mail promotions

*   advertising

*   PR.

BUILDING A HOUSE E-MAIL LIST

Maximizing opportunities for capturing e-mail addresses from your current customers is a key part of customer acquisition using e-mail, so we begin here. A simple starting point to establish how well this is working is to assess the current figure for the proportion of current customers for whom you have e-mail addresses. You can then set targets for this metric and devise techniques to increase this figure. When devising these techniques, don't only think quantity but also quality. What procedures can you use to maximize the number of valid e-mail addresses? E-mail addresses that have just one character wrong are no good to anyone, since you won't usually know which the miscreant character is. A further aspect of quality is opt-in. Just because you have obtained an e-mail address from the customer doesn't necessarily mean it is opt-in; it is only opt-in if the customer has proactively agreed and expects to receive e-mail communications. Perhaps there is a range of e-mail communications available to the customer, such as different e-newsletters or e-mail alerts. Which have they agreed to receive, or is there the expectation that they will receive all of them?

As explained in the previous chapter, it is useful to have an *allowable cost of e-mail address acquisition*. This is a notional figure for addresses from new prospects, since it is difficult to put a precise value on an address when this depends on its quality – how well it is likely to convert to sale. However, it is useful to help control spend on media such as paid search. Examples include a B2B software company that places an allowable cost of e-mail acquisition of $0.40 per e-mail, and a recruitment company that places an allowable cost of e-mail address (as part of a job application) at $0.70.

E-MAIL MARKETING INSIGHT

Estimate an allowable cost of e-mail address acquisition (for non-customers) to help control the costs of list-building.

Examples of objectives for list-building include:

- *List size* – to increase the size of the list over a particular time period (e.g. add 5000 subscribers to an e-newsletter in a year).

- *E-mail address coverage* – to increase coverage of the e-mail addresses in the customer base – you may have 15 per cent of customers who have opted in to an e-newsletter, but you want to increase this to 35 per cent over the next year.

- *E-mail address quality* – to increase the proportion of valid or active e-mail addresses on your list (i.e. those that don't bounce back, or the percentage of customers who are 'e-mail active' – i.e. who open or clickthrough on e-mails within a defined period).

- *E-mail permission quality* – to increase the proportion of e-mail addresses with permission. Although you may have collected e-mail addresses, you may not have explicit permission to use them, which is required by laws in many countries; also, you may only have permission to send some e-communications (e.g. alerts and e-newsletters) rather than the full range.

- *List value* – to increase the value generated per 1000 list members in terms of sales/leads in a time period.

- *Targeting quality* – to increase the proportion of subscribers qualifying for your products about whom you have collected profiling information.

- *Data quality* – to increase the proportion of specific profile fields held about individuals.

This section describes a range of offline and online techniques to increase e-mail address capture and make sure that the accuracy is a high as possible.

E-MAIL MARKETING INSIGHT

When improving your coverage of e-mail addresses, think quality as well as quantity. Devise techniques to increase the accuracy of e-mail addresses collected.

Touchpoints for collecting and updating e-mail addresses

It is important to have a structured approach to collecting and maintaining customer data. A good way to review all the possible methods of capturing e-mail addresses is for marketers to brainstorm alternative methods of doing this by thinking about opportunities for capture:

- online
- offline
- of existing customers
- of new customers

E-MAIL MARKETING INSIGHT

Use all customer touchpoints as opportunities for gaining e-mail addresses.

The matrix in Figure 4.2 provides a good way for a company to review all the possible methods of capturing e-mail addresses and other profile information. Some examples are shown.

Here, we will consider online and offline opportunities for e-mail capture separately. Many of these apply equally to potential and existing customers.

Here are eight *online* methods to help build a house list:

1. *Direct from web site* – permanent incentives to capture leads should be one of the main aims of a web presence, particularly for a B2B organization. Design, structure and content should be devised to maximize conversion to sign-up.

2. *Web response from offline communications* – here, an offer is publicized offline and respondents are referred to a web site to sign up – for example, Dell offered a monthly notebook prize draw (www.dell.co.uk/winanotebook), and Mars ran the now discontinued Chocollect promotion (www.chocollect.com), which was featured in TV ads).

3. *Renting an e-mail list from a third party* – here, recipients who clickthrough to a landing page are encouraged to opt-in to your house list.

4. *Placing an ad in a third party e-newsletter* – this has the same aims as (3) above, but may be more cost-effective and can often be tightly targeted.

	New customers	Existing customers
Online touchpoints	*Examples:* • Online incentive such as prize draw (B2C) or white paper download (B2B) • Viral marketing • E-newsletter opt-in on site • Registration to view content or submit content to a community forum • Renting list, co-branded e-mail or advertising in third party e-newsletter to encourage opt-in • Co-registration with third party sites	*Examples:* • Capture e-mail when customer first registers or purchases online • E-newsletter and other methods given on left
Offline touchpoints	*Examples:* • Direct mail offer perhaps driving visitor to web • Trade show or conference • Paper response to traditional direct mail communication • Phone response to direct mail or ad	*Examples:* • Paper order form, customer registration/product warranty form • Sales reps – face-to-face • Contact centre – by phone • Point of sale for retailers

Figure 4.2 Matrix showing customer touchpoints for collecting and updating customer e-mail contact and other profile information

5. *Using a third-party site* – a third-party site, sometimes referred to as an 'acquisition' centre, can be used to provide offers with a view to sign-up (for example, MyOffers – www.myoffers.co.uk).

6. *Campaigns with viral elements* – viral elements where a friend or colleague is referred can also increase the size of the house list. Here, permission marketing and data protection law require you to send an e-mail offering the referred person the option to opt in before further communications are sent.

7. *Any other forms of online traffic-building not mentioned above* – examples include graphical online ads or pay-per-click text search engine ads.

8. *E-mail appending services* – US companies such as Acquirenow (www.acquirenow.com/append.asp) and Freshaddress (www.freshaddress.com) can be used to identify likely e-mail addresses from existing customers who have not yet supplied their address, e.g. John Smith at IBM is John.Smith@ibm.com. Similar services can also attempt to correct e-mail addresses with typos.

Offline opportunities for capture are the full-range of customer touchpoints. Here are eight more:

1. *Any form of paper registration or order form* – but be sure to check the form of wording such that an opt-in to all forms of future communications is achieved.

2. *Visits from sales representatives* – visits can be used for opt-in either on paper, or through subscribing online.

3. *A phone contact at a call centre* – for example, a bank might ask customers whether they have an e-mail address during a routine phone enquiry.

4. *Telemarketing* – this can be specifically to capture e-mail addresses, but is more cost-effective if it is part of a telemarketing campaign.

5. *Point-of-sale* – in a retail context.

6. *Trade show or conference* – for example, from a prize draw collecting business cards (but care with the opt-in).

7. *Paper response to a direct mail offer* – a traditional direct response.

8. *Phone response to direct mail or ad* – again, a traditional direct response.

When e-mail addresses are captured offline, a common problem is the level of errors in the address – this can often reach a double-figure percentage. Plan to control this – staff should be trained in the importance of getting the e-mail address correct and in how to check for an invalid address format. Some call centres have even incentivized staff according to the number of valid e-mail addresses they collect. When collecting addresses on paper, some practical steps can help, such as allowing sufficient space for the e-mail address and asking for it to be written in capital letters.

Techniques for list maintenance

As with any customer database, maintaining a list can be a major headache. For e-mail or mobile-related lists the headache can be more intense, because:

- with permission-based e-mail, the customer can opt-out or unsubscribe at any time

- e-mail addresses tend to change more frequently than postal addresses

- multiple e-mail addresses are held, often to counter spam

If your e-newsletters or e-mail campaigns are of good quality, then the unsubscribe rate shouldn't be too much of a problem. A typical rate for unsubscribes is 1 per cent, or less for a house list.

The main problem lies with the second point – people changing addresses. A MercerMC (2001) report highlighted the extent of this problem. This found that, on average, 20 per cent of US customers in a typical database change their contact information over the course of a year. Changes were 16 per cent (address), 17 per cent (job), 25 per cent (e-mail address) and 33 per cent (cell-phone number). There is nothing to suggest this is much better today. Furthermore, the report estimated that the cost of updating or re-consenting these databases could run into tens of millions of dollars for a large database, not to mention the opportunity costs owing to lost sales from contacts who cannot be contacted!

All the forms of collecting e-mail addresses online and offline that were mentioned in the previous section can also be used to keep e-mail addresses fresh, since the most recent e-mail address can be collected. This particularly applies to the offline methods, where employees talk directly to customers and prospects. Since it is annoying for customers constantly to be asked 'is your e-mail contact address still correct?', it is best if this is only done when an address becomes inactive (see section below).

Direct mail promotions also provide opportunities for gaining e-mail addresses. In fact, whenever a prospect or customer has to fill in a form there is an opportunity. Collecting the e-mail address should be an inbuilt part of the sales process.

A further technique for high-value customers is to research their e-mail address. Case study 4.1 shows how one B2B company employed research to gain e-mail addresses. Costs of acquisition are in low single figures.

CASE STUDY 4.1 E-MAIL MARKETING EXCELLENCE – BLUE SOLUTIONS USES PHONE RESEARCH TO BUILD ITS HOUSE LIST

Blue Solutions Limited, a trading software distributor, wanted to increase the number of people who received its e-mail newsletter and to replace fax broadcasting as its marketing method. Rather than employing a temporary staff member it decided to enlist the help of data supplier Corpdata to research the e-mail addresses by phone and obtain an e-mail address, which was then used for additional research using a questionnaire. Mark Charleton of Blue Solutions said:

> *A high percentage of all e-mail questionnaires were received within a few days of the original contact. We received a 56% conversion rate from call to completion and, as a result, were able to capture an additional 788 e-mail addresses to add to our database of 6,500 records. The four day turnaround time was impressive especially when compared to the usual turnaround time of approximately three months.*

(Source Caroline Redfern, Corpdata Press Release, 17 May 2002, with kind permission of Corpdata (www.corpdata.co.uk) and Blue Solutions)

USING E-MAIL MARKETING TO SUPPORT CUSTOMER ACQUISITION

There is a vast range of approaches in using e-mail to support customer acquisition. These techniques are summarized in Table 4.1.

We will now review the six e-mail marketing techniques shown in Table 4.1 in more detail. For each of them we will review the communication from the point of the view of the recipient, since the recipient's perception of the source of the message is critical in affecting the response.

1. Cold or rented-list e-mail campaign

Here, the recipient receives an opt-in e-mail from an organization which has rented an e-mail list from a consumer e-mail list provider such as Experian (www.experian.com), Claritas (www.claritas.com) or IPT Limited (www.myoffers.co.uk); a business e-mail list provider such as Mardev (www.mardev.com), Thomson (www.thomson.com) or Corpdata (www.corpdata.co.uk);

Table 4.1 Summary of methods of using e-mail marketing for customer acquisition, and their advantages and disadvantages

Option	Application	Benefits	Issues
1. Rented list	Acquisition	Reach	List source; high typical cost of acquisition; low responsiveness
2. Co-branded list	Acquisition	Leverage brands	Exclusivity
3. Third-party e-newsletter ad/sponsorship	Acquisition and relationship building	Responsiveness; reach	Prime position; clutter; cost
4. Viral e-mail	Acquisition and list building	Potentially low cost and high reach.	Achieving cut-through; negative brand impact
5. Event-triggered e-mail	Conversion of leads	Automated – just sit back and relax	Optimizing creative, offer and frequency
6. House e-newsletter	Acquisition and retention	Helps build a relationship with recipient over time	Achieving balance between informing the list-member and selling to them

or a trade publisher/event provider such as VNU. Although recipients have agreed to receive offers by e-mail, the e-mail is effectively cold. For example, a credit card provider could send a cold e-mail to a list member who is not currently one of its own members. It is important to use some form of 'statement of origination', otherwise the message may be considered to be spam. Cold e-mails tend to have higher CPAs than other forms of online marketing, but different lists should still be evaluated.

Rental of a list provides a more rapid method, but is a more expensive method of gaining customers via e-mail compared to gradually building a house list. Here, a list of e-mail addresses is purchased and then sent to potential customers with an offer that is again intended to obtain permission to contact prospects in the future. Sub-sets of lists are usually purchased according to different criteria, such as age, sex or income. These sub-sets are chosen through applying 'selects' against the database. This term derives from the Structured Query Language (SQL) query that is performed, for example:

SELECT * FROM list WHERE Sex = "MALE" AND Income > 50 000

The Virgin Atlantic Fly Free for Life campaign referred to in Case study 1.1 used these lists, selects and numbers:

- The Mutual.net – HTML & text   10 000   30+, £40k+, have clicked on travel offers
- Doubleclick – HTML & text   15 000   Economy, professional
- Claritas – HTML & text   15 000   Economy travellers, non-European destinations
- Guardian newsletter – Text   5 × 35 000   Long-haul travellers
- Virgin Wines database – HTML & text   90 000

Of the 190 523 e-mails delivered there was a clickthrough rate of around 30 per cent, resulting in over 50 000 visits to the microsite. Thus, buying good quality lists with the right selects to produce a targeted audience, combined with the right offer and creative buying lists, can be a very effective method of building the house list.

Remember that with e-mail lists you usually pay for a single contact with the customer – you don't actually own the list or have a physical copy. The e-mail list is carefully controlled by the list owner so that unsubscribes can be managed, it remains opt-in and is not used to contact customers too frequently with similar offers. It is important that the steps above are followed, to maximize collection of e-mail addresses when the customers visit the microsite intended to capture their details.

Consider a multi-message campaign where you send two messages to a rented list, the second of which is dependent on the response to the first – i.e. there is a different follow-up for those who don't clickthrough to a web site and for those that do. Also, if the budget allows, consider purchasing additional profile information that enables you to make a phone call or use direct mail. Indeed, some B2B organizations don't rent e-mail lists; rather, they rent or buy lists of phone numbers and gain e-mail opt-in through telemarketing.

E-MAIL MARKETING INSIGHT

By negotiating purchase for two broadcasts, the overall campaign may be more cost-effective.

Of course the list that is rented must be opt-in, otherwise it is nothing less than spam. Therefore, when looking to purchase a list from a broker or the list owner, the first question should always be 'is it an opt-in list?' Unfortunately the answer will usually be 'yes', whether this is the case or not, so a follow-up question should always be used to ascertain the exact opt-in mechanism.

Even if consumers have agreed to receive e-mails by opting in, there is a risk (particularly if time has elapsed) that they will not recall doing this. This presents a danger, because if the consumer receives an e-mail as part of this list they may perceive it to be spam – particularly if the name of the sender is different to that of the the party that originally collected the data. For this reason, it is vital to use a *statement of origination* in the body of the e-mail when dispatching e-mails. The statement of origination, or 'why am I receiving this message? statement', highlights the list owner (who collected the data) and on whose behalf the list has been sent. A typical statement of origination is:

> *This e-mail is sent to you using opt-in contact information that you supplied to <list owner>. It is sent on behalf of <company name renting list>. For more information please visit <www.listowner.com>.*

The statement of origination should appear at either the top or the bottom of the e-mail. Many prefer the top, to avoid the perception of spam and encourage the reader to read on. Figure 4.3 gives an example of this approach. It can be argued that such a statement of origination should

Figure 4.3 Opt-in e-mail campaign to a rented list

be included in all e-mail, even if it is to a house list, since prospects or customers may have forgotten that they opted in to receiving the e-mail.

E-MAIL MARKETING INSIGHT

When sending e-mails to an opt-out list, a statement of origination should always be used to highlight the list owner (who collected the data) and on whose behalf the list has been sent.

List management

You should also check who manages opting out from the list. Opt-outs can only realistically be managed by a single party. This means that the e-mail addresses on an opt-in list will not typically be provided to you when you rent or purchase; rather, when you rent an opt-in e-mail list it will be for a broadcast (or series of broadcasts) controlled by the list owner, who will manage all the opt-outs or unsubscribes. Managing unsubscribes would be difficult or impossible if the list were rented or provided to different purchasers for a period.

More questions to ask when purchasing an opt-in list

When purchasing an opt-in list, many of the questions to ask a list vendor or list broker will be similar to those for a traditional list. Typical questions include:

- *Type of list* – is the list opt-in, and what form of opt-in was used?

- *Location of e-mail capture* – which particular site was used to collect e-mails and profile information? Was it an independent site set up for this purpose (see section below on acquisition centres), or is associated with a particular content site such as an online magazine?

- *Invalid e-mail addresses* – how often is the list cleaned of duplicates and out-of-date e-mail addresses, and what mechanism is used for this? Is there a straightforward opt-out mechanism which will lead to higher responses? What is the typical bounce rate on past campaigns (as explained in Chapter 3, a bounce occurs when the e-mail is returned because it is no longer valid)?

- *Recency* – when were the e-mails on the list added? How long have e-mails been on the list? (This is important, because the more recent the e-mails, the higher the response.) What is the profile of the ages of e-mails on the list – for instance, what proportion are less than a year, six months or three months old? Is it possible to select according to age of e-mails on list? Some list owners send out what is known as a *probe* e-mail to detect which e-mail addresses are still valid.

- *Targeting options* – what selects can be used to target consumers more closely? For consumer lists, age, sex and postcode would be expected, but is further lifestyle information available?

- *Exclusivity* (i.e. previous use of the list) – how many times will prospects on the list have received e-mails? A particular concern is competitor use of the list – have there been similar offers, or offers from competitors? If so, when was this?

- *Responsiveness* – what were the results from previous campaigns using the list? You may be met with a 'how long is a piece of string?' answer, saying that (of course) it will depend on the quality of the creative, offer, timing and targeting, as we reviewed in the last chapter. However, what about the best campaigns using the list – what response did these achieve?

Testing lists

Purchasing an unknown or unproven list can result in disappointing quality, in terms of both bounces from the list and response rate, so always test if the list is unproven. As well as testing the quality of the list, the effectiveness of different selects can also be evaluated. Typically 1000 addresses may be used for a test, and if successful these will be scaled up. In addition to list quality and selects, testing can also be performed for the subject, creative and offer. However, if you do the full range of tests with 1000 addresses you might soon use up all of the targeted members on the list you are considering. Another method is to test aspects such as the offer and creative in other online forms, such as banner advertising.

Cost-related questions

It will be apparent that the questions above mainly relate to the quality of the list. If you are happy that the list is of suitable quality, we can turn to the cost questions. The main question is the cost per thousand. The rate card costs can expect to vary between £100 per thousand and £300 per thousand. Some vendors will charge according to the number of selects, so closer targeting, using more selects, may add a cost of £50 per additional select.

Other cost questions concern how much is charged for additional services. These costs will depend on how the cost is split between the list owner, broker and those broadcasting the e-mail. Assuming you are talking to a single supplier, check whether the following will cost extra:

- testing – can you sample the list by sending one e-mail to 1000 list members?

- transmission – is there an additional cost for transmission? The typical cost is between 1p and 5p per thousand

- tracking – is there an additional cost for measuring and reporting? Some vendors charge for this separately, but it is an inclusive cost for most.

Today, most reputable e-mail list vendors will only charge for e-mails that are delivered – so always ask for 'payment by guaranteed response'. It is important to achieve this, since there is often a high bounce rate on third-party lists.

A description of all the costs of an e-mail campaign was included in the budgeting section of Chapter 3.

2. Co-branded e-mail

Here, recipients receive an e-mail with an offer from a company which they have a reasonably strong affinity. For example, a credit card company might partner with a mobile service provider such as Vodafone and send out the offer to its customers (who have opted-in to receive e-mails from third parties). Of course, this list owner must have received permission to send e-mails offering third-party products. Although this approach can be considered a form of cold e-mail, it is warmer since there is a stronger relationship with one of the brands and the subject line and creative will refer to both brands. An example is shown in Figure 4.4. Co-branded e-mails tend to be more responsive than are cold e-mails to rented lists, since the relationship exists and fewer offers tend to be given. I know some e-mail marketers who have found that rented lists never give them the required return on investment, so instead use co-branded e-mails.

E-mail acquisition centres

The Internet has proved a nirvana for 'compers' – consumers who love to enter competitions and prize draws. Thanks to the hyperlink, such consumers can now visit a single site which links to a range of competitions, and enter more competitions than ever before. For example, Loquax (www.loquax.co.uk) offers a directory of the latest links. Demand for such sites has provided the impetus for many companies to build very large lists of consumer e-mails. They have created portals that offer compers and other Internet users the chance to sign up to competitions and other offers, but only on an opt-in basis.

Other examples of these companies include Acxiom E-mail inform (www.emailinform.co.uk) and My Offers (www.myoffers.co.uk) from IPT Ltd. The Mutual.net (www.mutual.net) is another approach to e-mail acquisition, based on rewarding shopping.

For B2C organizations, these acquisition centres offer tremendous potential for customer acquisition through combining the B2C brand with the established data collection brand. Why focus all your efforts on trying to drive traffic to your own site when you can also partner with other sites with established traffic levels? Companies that offer promotions such as a prize

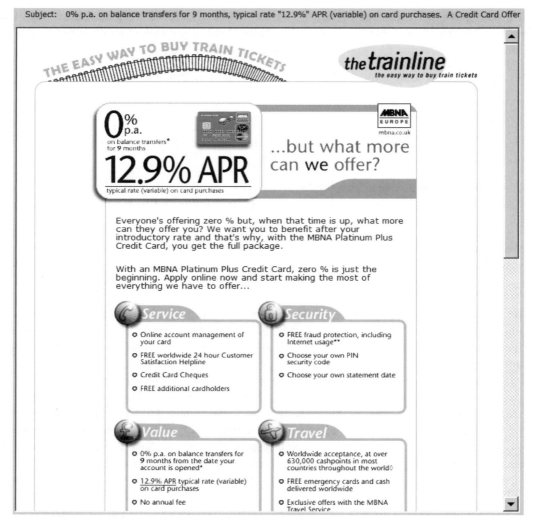

Figure 4.4 Example co-branded e-mail

draw on one of these sites can then add all entrants to its house list for future use in campaigns that aim to convert these prospects into customers.

3. Third party e-newsletter ads or sponsorship

In this visitor acquisition option, which is a form of interactive advertising, a company publicizes itself in a third-party e-newsletter. This could be in the form of an ad, sponsorship or PR (editorial) which links through to a destination site. Good examples are the ads placed by sponsors in the E-marketing newsletters from Clickz (www.clickz.com) and E-consultancy (www.e-consultancy.com; see Figure 4.5).

Such placements may be set up as part of an interactive advertising ad buy, since many e-newsletters also have permanent versions on the web site. Since e-newsletter recipients tend to

Subject: [E-business Briefing] Interview with Nick Burne of Christian Aid

In my experience the key things are having a cohesive design, message and brand. The only way this happens is if everyone is on the same page at the beginning. If more than one agency is involved, one has to take creative lead. Otherwise you are in danger of having a URL on an advert and people visiting that URL thinking they have gone to the wrong site. It sounds funny but I see it all the time.

Sponsor's message: ProAgency - Email Marketing for Agencies

ProAgency Solutions - Email Marketing and Online Survey Solutions for Marketing Agencies

Looking for a solution which enables you to...

-   *Generate recurring revenue by providing a variety of email marketing and online survey services to your clients?*

-   *Service all of your clients' email marketing and market research needs with a single solution?*

-   *Join an established network of over 50 resellers and agencies world-wide with clients such as Leading Hotels of the World, Coty and EA Games?*

-   *Choose flexible payment options including a highly competitive on-demand model?*

For further information, visit www.proagency.co.uk or contact Mike Broomfield at +44 1386 849 241

6. What percentage of visitors convert / donate immediately?

I would love to know this! We are currently redesigning our corporate site and conversion tracking is a top priority. No doubt it depends on the site, marketing campaign and appeal.

7. What other online marketing tools and techniques do you employ to boost fundraising, over the long-term?

Email segmentation is something we are working on. Sending out different emails to different people based on what we know about them.

For example, we may send an email during an emergency appeal to those people who have donated to previous appeals and separate one to those that haven't donated before. You can go into ridiculous detail but it is important to keep it simple. Another thing we are looking at is tracking. By knowing how people donate online we can improve conversions.

8. Have you experimented with viral marketing? What do you think constitutes a viral campaign?

Christian Aid has actually done some award winning viral sites. **Lifeswitch.org** was nominated for a Bafta and won a Gold Cyber Lion. More recently **MailOrderChickens.org** won a Bronze Cyber Lion.

We have found viral marketing to be a very cost effective way to reach new audiences. However, I do think the concept

Figure 4.5   Ad within E-consultancy e-newsletter (© E-consultancy.com Ltd, 1999–2006)

engage with them by scanning the headlines or reading them if they have time, e-newsletter placements can be relatively cost-effective.

Placing advertising in a third-party e-mail newsletter may be a favourable option compared to traditional banner advertising. If the content of the newsletter is well targeted for the audience, then engagement will be high – and it is arguably less easy to avoid an advert in an e-mail newsletter. Combined with the right creative and offer, the clickthrough should be significantly better than traditional banner advertising at single digits.

Banner ads will vary in format according to the newsletter format. Ads in text e-mails are generally less easy to ignore than those in HTML e-mails, where the ads are more consistent with traditional banner ads. This depends, however, on the impact of the banner ad, which is in turn dependent on its size, animation and colour contrast with the remainder of the e-mail. E-mail newsletters with informative content are also often printed for reference, so consider the impact of the ad in the printed version as well. Other factors that will affect the impact will be the number of advertisers, your position in the newsletter, and the ratio of copy to ads. If there are more than three advertisers in a newsletter, you are bound to have less impact than in a newsletter with just one!

To consider your options for positioning and costs of advertising, view the media kit for one of the main opt-in list suppliers. The following are typical options for advertising in an e-newsletter and on a site hosting the content:

1. *Feature ad position (skyscraper vertical web banner)* – ad placed to left or right of a range of content on the site

2. *HeadsUp* – each ad includes a headline, six lines of text, URL and logo or image; options are top, middle and bottom, with rate card rates declining according to position

3. *Banner ads* – typically at the top or bottom of a site

4. *Advertorial* – a 200–300 word article by the editorial staff relevant to the list reader, often a case study featuring the companies services

5. *E-mail text ads* – used for reaching the audience when they are scanning through text e-mail newsletters, before they have clicked through on the links to receive the richer content and ads described above; these are typically four to eight times 60 characters, including the URL.

When considering which newsletter to advertise in, there will typically be a choice between the more expensive high-reach newsletters and the less expensive options with a smaller reach. Your budget may only allow you one placement in a newsletter if it is to an audience of, say, 50 000. For a list to a smaller, niche audience of, say, 5000, it may be possible to afford a placement each month throughout the year. Repeated exposure should lead to greater recall of the advert, and the overall number of leads may be higher. You can also experiment with different offers and creative. However, if you have a great offer, and you get the creative right first time, the high-reach newsletter may be the best option.

As for traditional banner advertising, you will have a choice of cost per thousand, cost per click or cost per customer acquisition. Since the number on the list is known, there is usually a single fee for an advert, related to its position in the e-mail. If possible, you should negotiate a cost-per-click deal.

E-mail sponsorship

Sponsorship can be an effective method of gaining visitors via e-mail. A great business-to-business example of online sponsorship is offered by WebTrends, which sponsors the marketing analytics channels on Clickz.com (www.clickz.com/experts). WebTrends combined this sponsorship with different ads each month, offering e-marketers the opportunity to learn about different topics such as search marketing, retention and conversion marketing through detailed white papers and 'Take 10' online video presentations by industry experts, which could be downloaded by registered users. The objective of these ads was to encourage prospects to subscribe to the WebTrends WebResults e-newsletter and to assess purchase intent at sign-up, enabling follow-up telemarketing by regional distributors. WebTrends reported the following results over a single year of sponsorship (2004):

- List built to 100 000 WebResults total subscribers

- 18 000 'Take 10' presentations

- 13 500 seminar attendees.

4. Viral marketing

Viral marketing harnesses the network effect of the Internet and can be incredibly successful in reaching a large number of people rapidly, in the same way as a computer virus can infect many machines in minutes. Viral marketing is word-of-mouth delivered, and enhanced on line. It doesn't only refer to online marketing, it can also be used as a broader term referring to word-of-mouth marketing over a range of media, as explained by Kirby and Marsden (2005).

In practice, viral e-mails can work well in that 'Friday afternoon moment' when people are unwinding or simply can't face any more work. If you have such a moment, go to www.viralbank.com to see the latest virals spreading through the digital neighbourhood.

Viral marketing is often thought of as a 'campaign', but virals can be designed to work over a much longer period. For example, the Relief Race site (www.reliefracer.com) viral game to support the Nurofen brand has succeeded in achieving many plays and e-mail registrations over a three-year period.

For rapid transmission, the e-mail has to have a WOW factor – it has to have a big entertainment impact on the recipient, which usually doesn't mean news, but sex, humour or even violence. Rapid transmission happens because, if we have the WOW factor, it is easy to encourage recipients to pass on the e-mail to friends or colleagues by typing their name into the box (conveniently provided in all viral campaigns) on the form. Transmission can therefore occur by:

- *Word-of-Web* – the viral content is passed on by typing into a web-based form, which is converted into an e-mail, which is sent to recipients and contains a link to the web site containing the viral web site. Owners of other sites may blog about the viral, encouraging their visitors to go through to the site.

- *Word-of-e-mail* – some viral content, such as jokes or amazing sexual exploits, is transmitted by e-mail only. It is easy to forward to other like-minded individuals in your address-book. Often word-of-e-mail works in combination with Word-of-Web. Pepsi used e-mail to deliver e-mails containing links to streamed video footage of punditry from players and managers, which linked through to a web site. Having large video clips as attachments to e-mails is impractical.

- *Word-of-mouth* – traditional word-of-mouth is also important: if the WOW factor is large, people will speak about the campaign and seek it out via the search engines. So again your campaign should be registered on the search engines. If the campaign is featured on mainstream media, such as print or TV, this can also enhance the effect.

Types of viral

It is common for marketers to ask an agency to 'make a campaign viral' or add a viral element, but there are different types of viral, and some are more viral than other. These are common types of viral:

1. *Pass-along viral*. Towards the end of an e-mail it does no harm to prompt the recipient to pass the e-mail along to interested friends or colleagues. Even if only 1 in 100 responds to this prompt, it is still worthwhile.

2. *E-mail-a-friend viral*. This is the tried and tested viral technique, the five-minute viral referred to in more detail below. It is another form of pass-along viral which is achieved on the web site by having a form to forward information about a particular page. Many of these fail in the implementation – they are annoying for the recipient because they only pass along a link, and the recipient thinks, I know the marketers are trying to get me clickthrough to the site, but a bit more information such as an introduction to the article gives me the chance to decide whether it worth it or not.

3. *Incentivized viral*. This is what we need to make virals really take-off, and is what most people mean when they talk about 'making it viral'. By offering some reward for providing someone else's address, we can dramatically increase referrals. Remember the Virgin Atlantic case from Chapter 1 (Case study 1.1); more responses were received from the viral element than from those initially sent, and this isn't an uncommon scenario.

A common offer is to gain an additional entry for entry into a prize draw. This was the approach used by Virgin Atlantic. Marketers have to decide how many names they can get away with, given the offer – the respondent may need to provide one, two, three, four or even five friends to get that additional entry. As well as limiting the offer according to the number of referrals, marketers should also think about limiting it by action. This is encouraging the person transmitting the virus – the 'sneezer' – to further encourage the friend to take part, perhaps by phoning. For instance, there could be an extra entry for each friend that actually takes part in the prize draw, and not just for providing their address. In this case it may be possible to get some permission from the referred person. Other ways of encouraging action are to provide the extra entry only if the friend registers for a site or newsletter, orders a catalogue or even makes a purchase. Legal guidance should be sought about incentivized viral marketing, since consent to receive messages is not given by the recipient of an e-mail, but by their friend or colleagues. Best practice is to send the friend a single e-mail containing the link, which encourages him or her to opt in.

Challenges of viral marketing

Designing creative with the WOW factor is 99 per cent of a successful viral campaign, but there are blunders that will kill the campaign even with the best creative. For the virus to propagate it needs to be seeded to the right people, the influencers that are connected to the target market. For viruses with a fantastic general appeal, it may be sufficient just to seed to employees and encourage them to send to friends and colleagues. Generally, more specific targeting may be used. B2B store location consultancy Geo-business introduced an up-to-the-minute e-mail circular of store openings, closures and relocations which was first sent to managers amongst their clients. In this specialist field, the information proved of such value that it quickly spread round several hundred of the specialists in this area – excellent PR for the company. This virus was sustainable, since those interested could register to a newsletter form of the virus.

Seeding may also occur to a house list. The band Oxide & Neutrino ran a campaign where an 'eFlyer' containing video and sound clips was sent to the house list, and referrals were encouraged using entry into competitions.

The viral effect of a campaign can be augmented by PR. If it is a dramatic campaign, media mentions (whether web, TV, radio or print) can help to drive it. A viral campaign based on Christmas Cracker cards found that the largest single source of traffic to the site was a mention on a radio show with millions of listeners.

Mark Cridge, of agency Glue London, speaking at the IDM Digital Marketing Conference in 2004, presented a great summary of the viral marketing concept, saying:

- Viral is not a new concept;

- It used to be called 'word of mouth';

- It makes the sender look good;

- People will share what they are interested in.

I think the key to success factor with viral marketing, which is sometimes overlooked and is certainly difficult to achieve, is that 'it makes the sender look good'. But how is this achieved? Mark went on to talk about the creative challenges – viral typically has to be unconventional (or at least have clear benefits) to succeed, so companies must be prepared to challenge convention. This sits uneasily with some brands or organizations which traditionally seek to portray themselves as serious, trustworthy and professional.

Other challenges are that if the creative is too commercial this will restrict the spread, but if it is not commercial it may not do much for your brand. One of the most widely viewed virals ever, www.subservientchicken.com, is an example of this. The concept is fantastic – the dancing person dressed as a chicken in suspenders is certainly unconventional and creative – but its impact on the brand may be limited because it is not overtly commercial.

The type of creative can include a video clip, game or a competition, or simply valuable information. The challenge is to select the right viral creative for the brand and its audience. Some business-to-business or not-for-profit companies feel that viral marketing is not for them, for this reason. However, all audiences are human, and quizzes and competitions can be devised that work for these particular audiences. Business professionals often want to prove their skill or knowledge, so the viral concept can appeal to this desire.

Barriers that may kill the viral effect include:

- *Size*. If the viral content is a video clip or streaming video, if it is too large (over a megabyte) then this will reduce referrals, particularly for those who have to download it across a modem.

- *Media format.* Using a non-standard format for the viral content if it is rich media can kill viral. The majority of users will have Windows Media Player to play AVI.files, but may not have the facility for the latest Shockwave animation. However, for a young audience this is less of a problem, since their street cred. is low if they are not up-to-date.

- *Attachments.* If the viral content is in the form of an attachment such as a video clip or Flash animation, then this may reduce transmission since some company firewall software will not allow such large attachments to penetrate.

- *Cumbersome referral mechanisms.* Most virals are not seen as profiling and data collection exercises, as this will kill the impulse of forwarding to a friend. As a result, most virals just require your e-mail and those of friends. Fields to make it easy to forward to several friends should be included. With games, the referral mechanism is best immediately after the game is played, and if it is not mandatory but an option before further plays.

Legal issues in viral marketing

E-mail marketing always involves careful assessment of the legal consequences, as described in Chapter 2, but nowhere is this more true than for viral marketing. Viral marketing typically involves collecting two main pieces of information, first the e-mail address of the recommender or referrer, and secondly the e-mail address of the recipient. The difficulty is that the law requires consent by the recipient, yet here consent is given by the friend or colleague on the recipient's behalf.

Typically, the way the e-mail addresses collected in such a way are employed is as the basis for a single future communication to pass on the message, and this is used convert the recipient to a site visit and then registration. A humorous viral campaign with an additional offer such a prize draw can be used to target both referrers and recipients.

The law on the use of viral marketing is often not clear, and at the time of writing is being revised. Some of the codes, such as the UK Advertising Standards Authority (ASA) CAP code, are also likely to incorporate more guidelines on viral marketing. In 2005, the ASA upheld a complaint against a film supplier who used a viral campaign that used torture as the theme of the e-mail. With advertisers pushing the envelope of what is acceptable, it is inevitable that there will be more cases such as this.

In late 2005, The IPA Direct Marketing Group (DMG) signatories agreed that they should avoid creating and distributing web-site material that's likely to cause offence or distress and also give users advance warning about viral material. The code states:

> ***In those cases where it's considered that offence or distress may be caused, we regard it as best practice to alert users to this fact prior to access to the relevant Web site material.***

To summarize, tread with care when using viral marketing ...

Incentivized viral marketing

A different form of viral marketing to that above, one that doesn't just rely on standout content for transmission, is to use incentives to achieve referral. We have all received e-mails that offer us a free mobile phone of our choice if we send the e-mail to 10 others. Of course this type of viral marketing is in all likelihood a scam, but it has a legal and effective relative. An incentive is used to encourage the recipient to forward an offer to friends – for example, an e-tailer might offer a 10 per cent discount on future purchases if the e-mail is forwarded to five friends. The mechanism for viral referral is usually a landing page rather than manual forwarding, as is the case with the scam. Using the landing page for referral enables the e-mail marketer to send a tailored message to the referees; it also enables capture of the referred addresses and monitoring of the campaign.

A viral campaign is most effective when the offer not only requires provision of the friend's name, but is also dependent on them taking some action. Brewer (2001) gives the example of a campaign where not only did five names have to be provided, but also three of them actually had to subscribe to a catalogue or e-mail. Better still, the offer was true 'member get member', and one of the friends had to become a customer. Brewer (2001) warns of the problem of not capping viral incentives such as a $5 credit for every five friends referred. He says this can end up causing a marketer financial, customer-service and privacy-related problems.

Godin (2001a) writes about the importance of what he terms 'the ideavirus' as a marketing tool. He describes it as 'digitally augmented word-of-mouth'. What differences does the ideavirus have from word-of-mouth? First, transmission is more rapid; secondly, transmission tends to reach a larger audience; and thirdly, it can be persistent – reference to a product on a service such as Epinions (www.epinions.com) remains online on a web site and can be read at a later time. Godin emphasizes the importance of starting small by seeding a niche audience he describes as a 'hive', and then using advocates in spreading the virus – he refers to them as 'sneezers'. Traditionally, marketers would refer to such a grouping as customer advocates or brand loyalists.

The viral campaign is started by sending an e-mail to a targeted group that is likely to propagate the virus.

The speed of transmission and impact of the message must be balanced by naturally negative perceptions of viruses. A simple yet elegant method of customer acquisition is the 'e-mail a friend' facility, where a form is placed on an article that enables a customer to forward the page to a colleague. Other techniques include forwarding particular information, such as a screensaver or an online postcard.

Five minute viral marketing

A rapid, cheap but effective form of viral marketing is simply to include an 'e-mail a friend' or 'e-mail a colleague' form on a page. This works for B2C, where product information can be sent round to members of a family – 'this is what I am looking for, for Christmas please'. This also works well for B2B, where product information or information about events such as seminars can be shared between different members of the buying unit.

Technically and in terms of page design, this is straightforward. All that need to be added to the page are:

- an 'e-mail a friend caption' and box to highlight the option

- a box for the contact's e-mail

- a box for the sender's e-mail and name (so the recipient knows where the e-mail has come from)

- an explanation of the privacy implications (usually in a pop-up window or separate page, so as to not confuse the matter)

- a freeform text field to add an optional short message (this is sometimes omitted, but is crucial)

- HTML code to post the form to a script which will forward the e-mail and message and also populate the house list with these e-mails.

OK, so maybe not a five-minute job, but a day should do it. Once set up for one page, however, it will only take five minutes to add it to other pages, since it is generic code and design. Think of the locations where you could use this code:

- as part of a viral campaign

- in an e-mail newsletter template or subscription page

- in product catalogue pages

- in sales promotion web pages

- for events such as seminar registration.

In terms of return on investment, this has to be the most cost-effective e-marketing possible. Once set up the form needs no maintenance, and even if it is not used frequently it is still helping with acquisition, conversion and retention.

5. Event-triggered e-mail

Event-triggered e-mails are automated follow-up e-mails that can be sent out to persuade the recipient to sign up for a service or make a first or subsequent purchase. I think they are really underused by many companies that are still in a campaign mindset. The benefit of event-triggered e-mails is that once set up and tested for effectiveness, they are a low-cost method of boosting response. You can let the technology take the strain, since there are too many triggers to manage manually.

They work when someone visits a web site and expresses interest in a product or service by registering or by requesting a quote. They provide their e-mail address and some profile information, but they do not buy. For example, betting company William Hill found that automated follow-up e-mails converted twice as many registrants to place their first bet compared to registrants who did not receive an e-mail. This is a powerful technique; once the rules have been set up and the message, offer and timing optimized, they provide a relatively low-cost, but efficient, method of converting interest to sale. Figure 4.6 provides an example of an event-triggered e-mails. An example of a plan to determine the objectives, suitable sequence and interval between triggered e-mails for acquisition and retention is shown in Table 4.2.

Figure 4.6 Event-triggered e-mail from More Than aimed at converting quote to sale

6 Regular e-newsletter

An e-newsletter is typically thought of as a customer retention tool, and we cover them in detail in the next chapter. However, they can also be used to convert to sale. Lastminute (www.lastminute.com) is an example of a company that uses e-mail in this way. In the next chapter, we explore key decisions regarding defining and refining an e-newsletter.

Table 4.2 An example of a plan for event-triggered messaging

Message type	Interval and trigger condition	Outcomes required	Medium for message/sequence
1. Welcome message	Immediate; guest site membership sign-up	• Encourage trial of site services • Increase awareness of range of commercial and informational offerings	E-mail, post-transaction page
2. Engagement message	1 month; inactive (i.e. <3 visits)	• Encourage use of forum (good enabler of membership) • Highlight top content	E-mail, home page, side panels deep in site
3. Initial cross-sell message	1 month; active	• Encourage membership • Ask for feedback	
4. Conversion	2 days after browsing content	Use for range of services for guest members or full members: • membership • qualification • training • event	Phone or e-mail
5. Reactivation message	6 months or 1 year active	Give option to re-engage through: • feedback – tell us what you think/satisfaction survey • offer-related products based on profile • if no response, reduce message frequency	E-mail or direct mail
6. Annual message	6 months or 1 year active; active >6 visits per year	• Feedback – tell us what you think/satisfaction survey; ask for preferred communications channels for future use • Offer-related products based on profile	

WEB-BASED CUSTOMER ACQUISITION STRATEGY

Having established objectives for building lists and acquiring customers as explained above, a strategy can be developed to maximize the number of visitors to the site and those that convert to online customers. In this chapter, we present an eight-step approach:

1. Devise incentives(s)

The first step in acquisition is to devise incentives that will be used to encourage disclosure of the e-mail address and profile details when an existing or potential customer visits the web site. For other contact points, such as point-of-sale, different forms of offer may be needed. The alternative types of offers that can be used were covered in Chapter 3. As a reminder, these are:

- information value
- entertainment value
- monetary value
- transaction value
- privilege value
- service value

We summarized the combination of offers as 'free, win, save'. We also said that identifying different levels of offers will help conversion, so provide a primary offer and a secondary offer to encourage the clickthrough or visit to the web site. Think about the combination of offers. Web sites that have creative, well thought-through acquisition strategies have a combination of offers. Look at Figure 4.7, which has a wide range of offers available for different decision-makers.

Finally, as we mentioned at the start of the chapter, it is also worth considering how different incentives will appeal to existing customers and potential customers visiting the web site.

2. Use online and offline communications to drive traffic to the web site

There is a range of communications that can be used to drive visitors to a web site where they will be made aware of the permission-based incentives. For a description of these techniques, refer to Smith and Chaffey (2005). Note, though, that the best techniques change rapidly, so the techniques you invested in last year may not be the best techniques this year. Figure 4.8 summarizes the range of online and offline techniques that are available, and we will consider these in this section, starting with the online techniques.

The six main types of digital communications tools shown in Figure 4.8 are:

1. Search-engine marketing – placing messages on a search engine encouraging clickthrough to a web site when the user types a specific keyword phrase. These targeted campaigns are particularly important for generating quality visitors who will give their e-mail addresses.

2. Online PR – maximizing favourable mentions of your company, brands, products or web sites on third-party web sites which are likely to be visited by your target audience.

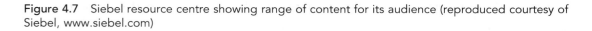

Figure 4.7 Siebel resource centre showing range of content for its audience (reproduced courtesy of Siebel, www.siebel.com)

3. Online partnerships – creating and managing long-term arrangements to promote your online services on third-party web sites or e-mail communications. Different forms of partnership include link building, affiliate marketing, online sponsorship and co-branding.

4. Interactive advertising – using online ads such as banners and rich media ads to achieve brand awareness and encourage clickthrough to a target site.

5. Opt-in e-mail – renting opt-in e-mail lists, placing ads in third-party e-newsletters, making deals with third parties for co-registration or co-branding of e-mails, or building your own in-house e-mail list.

6. Viral marketing (effectively, online word of mouth) – messages are forward to help achieve awareness and, in some cases, drive response.

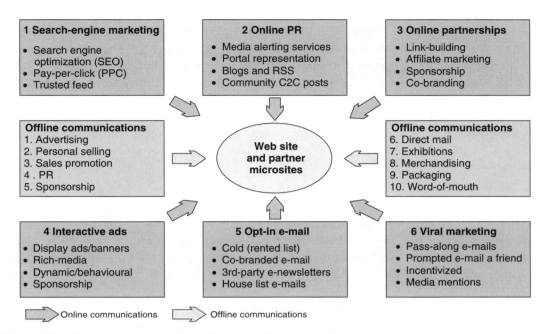

Figure 4.8 Alternative options for online and offline promotion

Since most of us spend more time in the real world than the virtual world, and because established communications tools and media work, the role of offline communications techniques should not be underestimated. Often, in large organizations, however, the e-marketers do not have control of the advertising budget, so the opportunity may be missed.

Advertising

Much offline advertising of a company's online presence is incidental rather than specific. By 'incidental', I mean that the web address is added as an afterthought to the print, outdoor or TV ad. This is often deliberate. If we are advertising insurance, for example, we would prefer viewers to phone up rather than using the Internet, where they may easily get diverted from our offer. It is not surprising that much direct response advertising still uses the phone to generate leads – it works best. There may be some circumstances, though, where the web can be used to manage direct response. For example, a Mastercard prize draw to win tickets to the 2002 World Cup used TV advertising to drive site traffic as means of gathering e-mail addresses. Alternatively, if we are serious about using offline media to drive traffic we can use more than a web address to appeal. Print advertising can readily feature an Internet value proposition as part of a strap-line related to the web address. Regardless of the form of advertising, if its aim is to capture e-mail addresses, do try and use a URL which helps you track the campaign and avoids the need for the customer to try to find the relevant offer on the home page. It is still common to see ads with the URL www.company.com, but for user convenience www.company1.com/<insert campaign name here> is better, and best of all for tracking ad effectiveness is www.company1.com/<insert campaign name here> + referrer digit (e.g. 1).

PR

PR is a powerful and relatively low-cost form of offline communication. There is still demand amongst the general and specialist media for stories about e-everything, providing it is fresh news. PR can leverage events such as site launches and re-launches with new services, particularly when they are first in a sector. Press releases can be issued through normal channels, but using e-mail linked to the full story on the web site to get information to the journalists faster. Options for getting mentions on the new online-only news sources and listings should also be explored.

Direct mail

Physical reminders about web-site offers are important because, as we said before, most of our customers spend more time in the real world than in the virtual world. What is in our customers' hands and on their desk top will act as a prompt to visit your site and overcome the weakness of the web as a pull medium. Examples include brochures, catalogues, business cards, point-of-sale material, trade shows, direct mail sales promotions, postcards (in magazines), inserts (in magazines) and password reminders (for extranets).

3. Revise web site design to emphasize offer

When your web site was first designed, how important a criterion would you say was the visual prominence of offers to acquire customers? Judging by many current sites, the answer is that this was low priority. Yet one of the main aims of a web site has to be converting visitors to customers. This isn't going to happen unless it is a design objective. In *The Big Red Fez*, Seth Godin shows many examples where visitors are not encouraged to action (Godin, 2001b). He says:

> *I imagine the web as a series of offer pages, all competing for us to click. And if those sites make it really clear and obvious where's the monkey's banana, then the time-starved, not very bright consumer (that's you and me folks!) will go for it. Some people might object to the characterization of web surfers as monkeys. After all, they say, we are smarter than that. No actually, we're not ... we're busy or distracted, or we have never been to a particular site before and we're not mind readers.*

E-MAIL MARKETING INSIGHT

Maximize lead generation from your web site through evaluating site design and offers.

Common approaches to increase the conversion rate include the following:

1. Try to increase the prominence of calls-to-action, by:

   - an improved position on screen – are calls-to-action above the fold, or do visitors have to scroll down to reach them?

   - an increased size – can you see the acquisition wood from the brochureware trees? Use of graphical banners can assist.

- colour – is a distinctive colour (in keeping with the design of the site) used to highlight the call-to-action?

- animation – can movement be used to draw attention to the call-to-action?

2. Increase the range of calls-to-action on the home page.

3. Don't neglect text-based calls-to-action. If your graphical calls-to-action look too much like banner advertisements, then some site visitors may naturally filter them out. Try different forms of words for the calls-to-action in headings or within the body text.

4. Look at consumer concerns. Think about the barriers that may stop consumers giving their details. Is your privacy statement prominent enough? Is it clear, or impenetrable? Have you explained why you are asking them to provide their details?

5. Don't forget the big picture. If the design, style and content of the site don't suggest credibility of your organization to deliver, then it doesn't matter how prominent the calls-to-action are. The visitor will more likely hit the back button.

Finally, experiment with these variables. One of the benefits of web-based marketing is that you can 'suck it and see'. Try changing headings and offers, and count the leads and use the site statistics to monitor the traffic patterns. One approach is to use different URL parameters for different forms of wording to monitor their effectiveness. For example, we could have three links from graphical or text hyperlinks each linking the landing page 'register.htm' as follows:

> *http://www.company.com/register.htm?l1*
> *http://www.company.com/register.htm?l2*
> *http://www.company.com/register.htm?l3*

The number of visitors that have clicked on these three types of links are then highlighted in the referring URLs report of WebTrends or similar packages.

Tailored landing pages

For the purposes of permission marketing and e-mail acquisition, many companies now drive visitors straight to a simplified custom landing page, which includes the registration form, rather than the home page. Figure 4.9 gives an example of this.

4. Define profiling needs and capture form

In a similar way to that described in the last section, we can monitor the effectiveness of the landing page in converting those who have expressed an interest to action. You can compare how many leads you receive to how many click on the links and go through to the page. There are several steps that can be taken to maximize the response rates:

1. *Information requested on forms should be kept to a minimum.* Make it short. Early practice on information collection through online forms seemed to be to collect as much information as possible to help build up profiles of customers. There was a backlash against this, with users refusing to fill in too much information. Some companies then went to the other extreme and captured the minimum information – usually just an e-mail address.

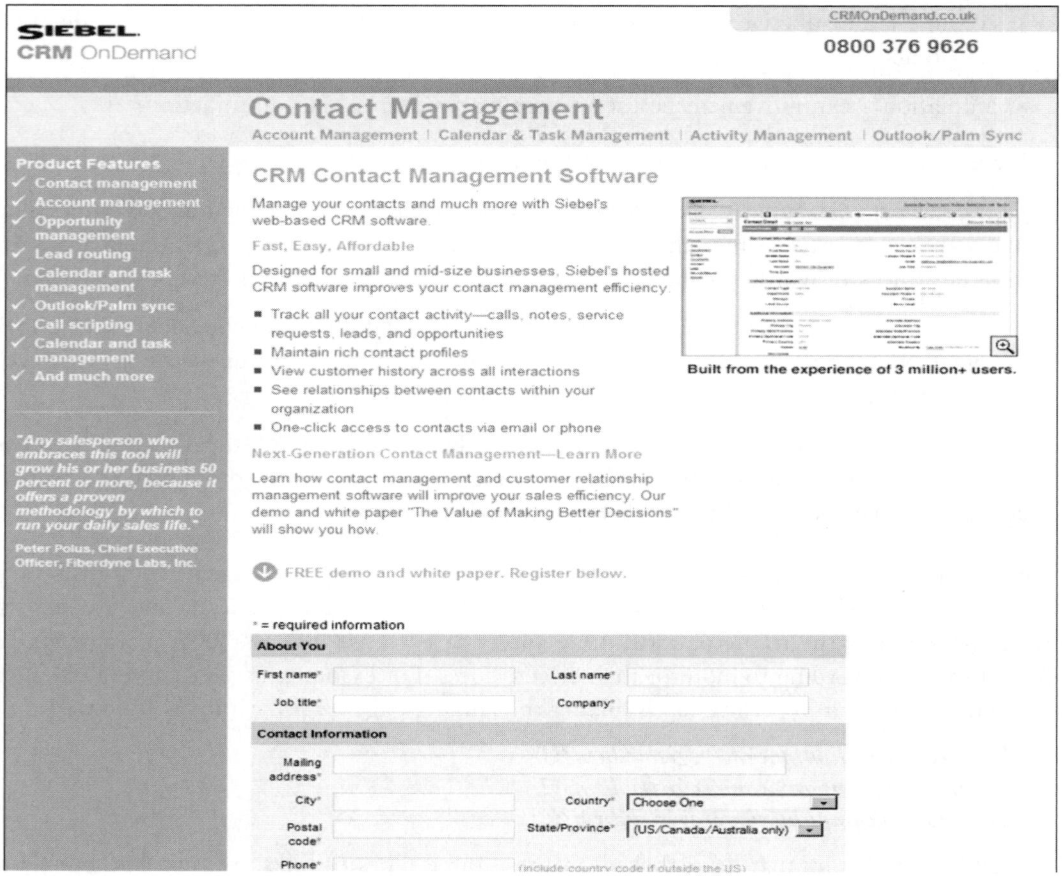

Figure 4.9 Siebel custom landing page to encourage opt-in to generate leads (reproduced courtesy of Siebel, www.siebel.com)

Each company has to decide on a realistic minimum for its purposes. Remember that you can gain more information on the customer as the relationship develops. We suggest the following minimum information for B2C organizations:

- e-mail address (of course)

- first and last names

- age

- sex

- geography

- product interest

- preferred means of communication (opt-in and whether HTML – with pictures for simplicity – or text).

And for B2B:

- e-mail address
- first and last names
- company name
- company size (employees or turnover)
- company sector/product if applicable
- role of individual in buying decision (job title is usually a proxy for this)
- number of staff individual is responsible for
- preferred means of communication.

Remember that we also need to record time on list, so another field can automatically be added to the database for the date when first added. Yesmail research shows that someone who has opted in within 30 days is more likely to respond than is someone who has opted in within the last 90 days.

E-MAIL MARKETING INSIGHT

Limit attrition from profiling questions by asking minimum number of questions.

It will be possible to keep in contact with the customer via an e-mail, and work back to other information such as company name and position.

2. *Explain the reason why information is being collected.* Customers will more readily give up personal information and spend time filling in a form if they know the reason why the information is being collected. Explain how it will benefit them by the proposition of communications such as a newsletter.

3. *Explain clearly the use to which data will be put.* This is required by law in a privacy statement, but if the data will not be shared with third parties this should be highlighted since it may encourage opt-in.

4. *Make it easy.* Use the features of HTML to ease data entry. For example, use drop-down lists where appropriate. These improve data quality by giving consistent data in the database. However, don't you hate those lists of 137 countries with Afghanistan at the top? Surely prospects can enter their own country? In the Siebel example, the main menu options are removed to increase focus.

5. *Indicate mandatory fields.* Extra information can be collected from customers if they have time by marking essential fields in a suitable way (perhaps through an asterisk or highlighting in bold).

6. *Validate*. Checks should be performed after the form is filled in to check that the user has filled in all mandatory fields. Fields should also be checked for validity – has the customer entered a valid e-mail address with the '@' symbol, is the postcode or zip code valid? The user should be clearly prompted regarding what information is wrong and why. Such validation can be performed using scripts such as Javascript.

7. *Provide 'opt-in'*. Check-boxes should be made available that users can select if they do not want to receive further information through e-mail or communications through other media. As explained in Chapter 2, however, a tick-box is not a legal requirement – just a clear form of consent which could be clicking a button.

8. *Provide prompt confirmation*. After a user has filled in a form, a company should respond to acknowledge confirmation of receipt as soon as possible and describe what the follow-up actions will be. For example, if a customer has ordered a product, the confirmation note should thank the customer for shopping with the company and state clearly when he or she can expect to receive the product by courier.

5. Select permission levels – what does opt-in really mean?

This is important. We have covered the merits of opt-in and opt-out as part of the introduction to permission marketing in Chapter 2, but what does opt-in mean in practice, at the level of boxes on forms and associated wording? In selecting permission levels, we have to achieve a balance between obtaining as many quality profiles as possible, and legal and ethical constraints. Many e-mail marketing gurus and legal advisers will say that e-mail *must* be opt-in, and this is the received wisdom. However, when faced with the reality of designing a form for collecting prospects, the reality is not this simple. Despite the opt-in mantra, many companies are not practising true opt-in – it all depends on how the forms are designed.

True opt-in requires potential customers *proactively to agree* that they are prepared to receive future communications, by selecting the option using a tick-box or ratio-button. Alternatively, it can increase sign-up if the box is pre-checked or simply requires a button to be pressed on a web form. Opt-out is where the person completing the form has *proactively to decline* the offer of receiving further communications. Consider the alternatives in Figure 4.10. Which is opt-in? Figure 4.10(a) is clearly an opt-in form, whereas Figure 4.10(b) is an opt-out design, but what about Figure 4.10(c)? Figure 4.10(c) is a good approach. In order to register, you have to give your e-mail address and then confirm opt-in using a button. The implication, from the way the form is structured, is that it is agreed that future information can be received.

Permission marketing is a matter of degree, and in the same way spam is a matter of degree. So how can you make the decision as whether to offer opt-in or opt-out? There are several factors involved, but the most important are the number of responses and the brand perception. Proponents of opt-out argue that more targets can be added to the database using this approach, since some people filling in the form will not notice or care about this option. However, such members of the list are probably less likely to respond to any offers in subsequent e-mails than those who consciously decided not to opt-out, although there will be some targets who do. As a result a greater number of responses will be achieved, although the overall response rate will be lower. Proponents of opt-in argue that if the action is not proactive, then recipients of e-mail

(a) Would you like to receive information via email?

   ⦿ Yes ○ No

Your Request (Optional):

Would you like to receive information via email?

   ○ Yes ⦿ No

Your Request (Optional):

SUBMIT →   SUBMIT →

(b)

Your Name & Address   To enter you in the £10,000 prize draw, please make sure you enter your name and email address on this page and your contact address on the next page.

The questions in bold are obligatory fields.

Title: Select answer ▾

Surname:

First Name:

Phone No:

Mobile No:

Email:

Is this email address your:

○ Home   ○ Business   ○ Both

Which is your preferred format for receiving email offers?

(c)   ○ HTML   ○ Plain text

Figure 4.10 Options for obtaining opt-in

will not recall agreeing to receive information. They also argue that the future of legislation is not known and, with many proposing a strict opt-in regime, it is safest to collect only opt-in addresses now as part of planning for the future. Some may view the e-mails received as spam, and the perception of the brand will be damaged. However, if a statement of origination is included this damage may be ameliorated. An example of a statement of origination is as follows:

> *This e-mail is sent to you by / using data supplied by <Company X>*

It has been said that 'spam is in the eye of the beholder', so to minimize damage e-mail marketers should view e-mails as a spectrum ranging from pure opt-in to pure spam. This is an example of how a business person reacted on receiving an unrecognized e-mail:

> *No request was made to me nor permission given to use my personal data and it is therefore an offence under UK and European Data protection legislation.*
>
> *I am copying this correspondence to the Information Commissioner with a request to initiate action against you.*

In this case, the prospect had received an e-mail from a rented list but had no recollection of granting permission. It indicates the need for careful checking with the list provider about the form of opt-in, signing an agreement with the provider that the data are legal following data protection law, and the provider is using a clear statement of origination.

An example of what can happen when a company contacts customers who believe they have opted out is provided by Boots The Chemist. Boots gave applicants for their loyalty card the option to opt out of further (paper-based) mailings. According to a report at Marketing Law (www.marketinglaw.co.uk), over half a million customers did this. When Boots contacted them after some time to explain new promotions, there were 28 complaints to the Advertising Standards Authority. In this case, sending out the mailing to those who had opted out was a breach of the data protection law and the complaints were upheld.

Delving a bit deeper, there are two further options available which are both variants of opt-in. *Double opt-in* is where a confirmation e-mail is sent to recipients after completion of the initial form. Recipients have to reply to confirm that they wish to receive information. This approach is often required by e-mail list servers (Chapter 7) since, historically, this is the way they operate. While this technique has the benefit of making doubly sure that the sender wants to receive the information, there is a nuisance factor involved. *Notified opt-in* is a more common approach, which involves sending a standard autoresponse e-mail explaining that the subscription has been received, and giving details of how to unsubscribe if the e-mail has been sent in error. Both of these forms of message can also be used for marketing purposes.

One final approach for opt-in is to differentiate whether communications are desired between the organization hosting the web site and third-party companies. If there is no intention of generating revenue from selling the e-mail list to third parties, it is worth stressing that 'your details will not be passed to third-party companies'. Receiving unexpected e-mail is a common cause for complaint and fear amongst consumers, so explicitly excluding the possibility of undesired third-party e-mails can help in increasing the number of customers that opt-in.

So, which approach to collecting e-mail addresses on online forms is best? We can say that opt-out is best for size of list, but worst for responses and because it will annoy those who can't recall agreeing to receive information. We can also say that opt-in is best for quality, since it will have higher response rates and is less likely to damage the brand. What is less easy to say, however, is which is best for the overall number of responses. Opt-out is likely to give more responses, since some who didn't register that they had the choice of opt-out are likely to respond.

6. Draw-up privacy statement

Many companies have a privacy statement on their web site, but does it cover the right areas? The E-mail Marketing Association developed the following guidelines for privacy statements as part of its charter for best practice by its members. This is an abbreviated version of what it suggests should be presented in the privacy statement:

1. *Identity of the list owner* – the company name and address of the list owner for data that have been collected.

2. *Uses of data* – the uses to which the personal data will be put and the choices the user has regarding the use of the personal data.

3. *Third-party use of data* – the categories of third parties to whom the personal data may be disclosed, including (but not limited to) any list manager, service bureau or database manager.

4. *Nature of data* – the nature of the personal data collected.

5. *Data collection methods* – this refers to collection by techniques which will not be immediately evident to the user; such techniques include *cookies*, which are necessary to identify repeat visitors and to reconcile site visitors with information held about them in a database. It also includes *clear-gifs*, which can be used to record site visits. It is recommended that the privacy policy should explain that the data collected by such techniques do not constitute personal data and are only used for the purposes of analysing the effectiveness of e-mail marketing material. There should also be links to the opt-out sections in relation to use of such techniques.

6. *Combined data sources* – the possibility that the list owner may acquire information about the user from other sources and add such information to its house files. For example, lifestyle data or credit references could be obtained from another source.

7. *Opt-in policies* – whether the requested personal data are necessary to the transaction between user and list owner, or are voluntary. The consequences of failing to provide the requested information should also be explained.

8. *Security of personal data* – the steps taken by the list owner to ensure the technical and organizational measures taken to protect the security of the personal data.

9. *Opt-out procedures* – an explanation of how the opt-out process will work.

10. *Access to data* – this describes the processes for users to be provided with a copy of their personal data, and to contest and correct inaccuracies or request that their personal data be deleted.

You may also want to consult the latest data protection legislation in your country. For the UK, the legislation is at www.informationcommissioner.gov.uk.

Remember also to try to capture the consumers's primary e-mail address. The *Doubleclick Sixth Annual Consumer E-mail Survey* (Doubleclick, 2005) showed that almost half of all consumers reported maintaining at least three e-mail accounts, an increase from 2004. Nearly 95 per cent consider one of their e-mail addresses to be a 'primary' account; 72 per cent use a single address specifically for making purchases. This shows the importance of gaining the primary e-mail address for opt-in, particularly for an e-newsletter. To help with this, make sure you explain the proposition in detail and give examples of previous e-newsletters. If the frequency is relatively low, this may also help with primary e-mail addresses.

7. Define the opt-out

The opt-out should be a prominent notice, usually at the end of the e-mail, which allows the user to unsubscribe by e-mail (typically with the word 'UNSUBSCRIBE' in the subject line) or by clicking through to a web page. As noted previously, it is often better to take customers to a communications preferences page where they can selectively opt-out. This usually decreases unsubscribe. Defining the procedure for opt-out is part of the privacy statement. You may know from personal experience that opting-out in practice is often difficult. In fact, spammers use the opt-out reply as a means of checking that yours is a valid e-mail; you are then likely to receive yet more spam. Many opt-out procedures simply do not work. Whether this is deliberate or due to a problem with implementation is unclear.

The opt-out should not necessarily be viewed as a bad thing; it is part and parcel of permission marketing and it will save you the expense of targeting someone who is not predisposed to your service. It will even help increase your response rates. As we said in Chapter 3, the level of opt-outs or unsubscribes should be monitored through time since a rapid increase in opt-out highlights a problem with a campaign. The opt-out can even be viewed as an opportunity. Perhaps customers may prefer information about other services they were unaware of, so offer them alternatives. Perhaps you can use it to research problems with different aspects of the marketing mix or the e-mail marketing itself. Prompt with a short questionnaire or a free-form field to obtain feedback. The BBC Alert site (www.bbc.co.uk/alert) is a good example of best practice in this area.

E-MAIL MARKETING BEST PRACTICE

Perform the opt-out on the web site and use it as an opportunity to communicate.

8. Follow-up registration

Many organizations seem only to plan their acquisition up to Step 7. In this way they are losing potential from the follow-up. Using carefully executed follow-ups, a company can encourage conversion, show it is responsive, and educate the customer further about its services.

The nature of follow-up will vary according to the type of offer. For some applications, a simple automated response may be sufficient. For example, on subscribing to a newsletter it is conventional to receive a notification message, 'thank you for subscribing, you will receive the next newsletter shortly'. To me, this is a lost opportunity. At the very least, there should be a link back to the archive or web site. But better still, why not add content to the e-mail notification about current promotions on the site or topics from the last newsletter?

Following a lead generation offer, there should be a hard-hitting e-mail to reinforce the benefits of the service and the next stages. Giving a personal touch and combining the e-mail with a phone call is a great benefit here.

E-MAIL MARKETING INSIGHT

Don't neglect the opportunity provided by the follow-up to registration.

Multi-step messages

Multi-step or multi-stage e-mails are a more sophisticated form of follow-up. Here, a sequence of e-mails follows initial registration. The beauty of this approach is that the conversion process can be automated, as Case study 4.2 shows.

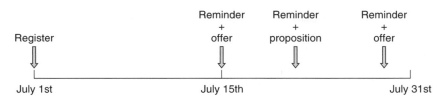

Figure 4.11   Automated multi-stage messages to encourage magazine subscription at MAD

CASE STUDY 4.2 E-MAIL MARKETING EXCELLENCE – MAD USES MULTIPLE E-MAILS TO ENCOURAGE SUBSCRIPTION

Marketing publications from MAD (www.mad.co.uk) are available on a trial 30-day basis. MAD makes use of automated multi-step or sequenced messages to encourage subscription. Figure 4.11 shows the sequence of messages. Note how the offer is escalated through the month, with additional carrots dangled to encourage registration. Such a sequence of messages is also used to encourage subscription renewal.

Multi-step messaging can be applied to many events in the sales cycle. For example, if an annual insurance renewal is due, e-mail can be used, in combination with other media, to encourage the customer to renew. If there is a major seminar event or product launch, a series of e-mails can be sent leading up to the event.

MEASURING ACQUISITION EFFECTIVENESS

To finish this chapter where we started, how should companies monitor the success of their acquisition campaigns? The metrics we looked at at the start of the chapter were the percentage coverage of all customer e-mails in the database, together with an indication of quality – how many are valid, current e-mail addresses?

To control e-mail acquisition on a monthly basis, reporting should also be in place to assess:

● the number of new e-mail addresses and complete profiles captured each month

● the percentage of site visitors who contribute e-mail addresses

● the conversion rates from qualified leads captured to customers.

For a fuller picture of the success of acquisition, these measures should be recorded for visitors referred from different sources. Successful referrers with a relatively low cost of acquisition and a high conversion rate can then be built on in future site promotion.

REFERENCES

Brewer (2001). Tips for optimising viral marketing campaigns. Clickz newsletter (www.clickz.com), 22 February.

Doubleclick (2005). *Doubleclick Sixth Annual Consumer E-mail Survey*. Doubleclick,

Godin, S. (2001a). *Unleashing the Ideavirus*, available online at www.ideavirus.com.

Godin, S. (2001b). *The Big Red Fez: How to Make Any Web Site Better*. Fireside (an imprint of Simon and Schuster).

Kirby, J. and Marsden, P. (2005). *Connected Marketing: The Viral, Buzz and Word of Mouth Revolution*. Butterworth-Heinemann.

MercerMC (2001). Making CRM make money. *A Mercer Management Consulting Commentary*, available at www.mercermc.com.

Smith, P. R. and Chaffey, D. (2005). *eMarketing eXcellence – At the Heart of eBusiness*. Butterworth-Heinemann.

Chapter **5**

Using e-mail for customer retention

CHAPTER AT A GLANCE

Overview

This chapter shows how e-mail can be best used for customer retention and to generate return visitors to a site who have subscribed to e-mail communications.

Chapter objectives

By the end of this chapter you will be able to:

- decide on an approach to develop an integrated e-mail retention campaign
- understand how to segment your e-mail list to target existing customers better
- take the key decisions to develop an effective e-newsletter.

Chapter structure

- Introduction
- Success factors for online retention
- Planning retention
- Targeting approaches
- RFM analysis
- E-newsletters – defining and refining
- References
- Web links

INTRODUCTION

E-mail is primarily a retention medium – the majority of e-mail marketing activity and expenditure is focused on retention. To be successful, retention e-mail marketing requires careful targeting of customers to deliver relevant, timely communications to customers. Yet different research studies have shown that often the same message is broadcast to everyone on the list. A JupiterResearch (2005) report has suggested that around 24 per cent of permission-based marketing e-mails are broadcast mailings with undifferentiated identity, 65 per cent have a limited degree of targeting, and just 11 per cent have context relevance – i.e. they are sent at the best time with the most appropriate offer. Meanwhile, Marketing Sherpa (2005) has suggested that many retention campaigns are only personalized to a certain degree. I have summarized this research in Table 5.1, which again shows that undifferentiated campaigns are still common, with advanced segmentation and targeting based on product profiling or behavioural targeting surprisingly rare.

The relative lack of targeting is surprising, since it is well known that a comparatively small increase in customer retention can generate large increases in profitability. Reicheld and Sasser (1990) estimated, in a cross-industry study, that by reducing customer

Table 5.1 Targeting techniques used in e-mail campaigns according to Marketing Sherpa (2005)

Personalization technique used	Usage in B2C mailings (%)	Usage in B2B mailings (%)
None	26	24
Name	47	55
Demographics (age, gender, etc.)	29	18
Product profiling (time and type of product purchased)	26	26
Behavioural (length of relationship, campaign response)	32	27

defections by just 5 per cent, profitability could be increased from 25 per cent to 85 per cent. In this chapter we therefore look at how, once we have acquired a customer's e-mail address and converted to the first sale, we can use e-mail to develop the relationship, to build loyalty and encourage further sales.

We start this chapter by looking at success factors which can help you to improve retention. We review a range of approaches for targeting according to the customer's position in the lifecycle, and explain how more sophisticated behavioural targeting techniques such as RFM analysis can be used. We then look at two different vehicles for retention marketing: regular e-newsletters and standalone (or solus) e-mails. Newsletters are covered by looking at the different types of decisions needed to launch an e-newsletter for the first time, or refine an existing e-newsletter.

Remember that retention can have different meanings according to context. For most companies it begins at the point of the first sale, when a prospect becomes a customer. Online, though, we may have prospects who are visiting the web site and who we want to convert to customers. To achieve this, we have to retain them as visitors and prospects for long enough, through ongoing communications such as e-newsletters. This distinction is important, since when designing e-newsletters, for example, the intended audience is not solely existing customers but also prospects. For some media sites, such as portals or online newspapers, we will also have site visitors who return to the site and use it as a free service. The media owner may be looking to convert them to a paid-for subscription, but in the meantime they are still a source of revenue, since their eyeballs help to bring advertising to the site.

SUCCESS FACTORS FOR ONLINE RETENTION

A useful approach to reviewing how to improve all aspects of digital marketing, or indeed any marketing activity, is success factor mapping. You may know this as 'cause and effect analysis' or 'fishboning'. With this approach, the ultimate objective is placed at the right of the diagram and the success factors or performance drivers that will help to achieve this outcome are placed on the left of the diagram. Figure 5.1 shows my success factor map for online retention marketing.

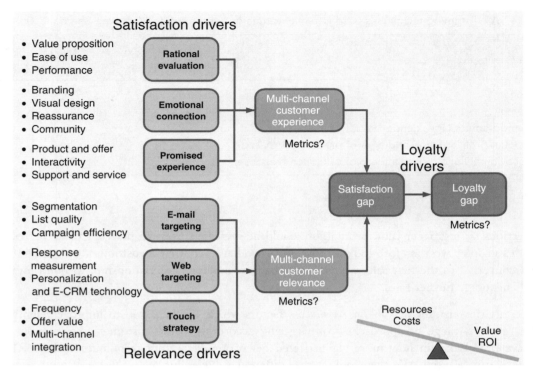

Figure 5.1 Success factor mapping for online retention

In the case of online retention marketing, our ultimate goal, on the right of Figure 5.1, is customer loyalty. The factors on the left help to deliver two facets of loyalty. The first is emotional loyalty, where loyalty to a brand is demonstrated by favourable perceptions, opinions and recommendations. The success factors in the upper half of the diagram, which are all related to the customer experience of using an online service, tend to influence emotional loyalty the most, and these are important in determining customer satisfaction. Of course, a favourable customer experience is very important to achieving repeat purchases – how many online sites have you continued to use after a poor level of service was delivered? This is to remind us that, no matter the quality of our e-mail marketing, there are some basic hygiene factors in the experience of the first purchase that have to be right in the first place.

Reicheld and Schefter (2000) suggest that it is key for organizations to understand what determines not only service quality and customer satisfaction, but also loyalty or repeat purchases. From their research, they suggest five primary determinants of loyalty online:

1. Quality customer support

2. On-time delivery

3. Compelling product presentations

4. Convenient and reasonably priced shipping and handling

5. Clear, trustworthy privacy policies.

Of course, the precise nature of these loyalty drivers will differ between companies. Reicheld and Schefter (2000) reported that Dell Computer had created a customer experience council that researched key loyalty drivers, identified measures to track these, and put in place an action plan to improve loyalty. The loyalty drivers and their summary metrics were:

Driver	Metric
Order fulfilment	Ship to target – percentage that ship on time exactly as the customer specified
Product performance	Initial field incident rate – the frequency of problems experienced by customers
Post-sale service and support	On-time, first-time fix – the percentage of problems fixed on the first visit by a service rep. who arrives at the time promised

The second type of loyalty is behavioural loyalty, where loyalty translates to repeat sales and response to marketing campaigns. To achieve these repeat sales, companies work hard to deliver relevant marketing communications either through e-mail or web-based personalization, or through direct mail.

Figure 5.1 also stresses the importance of delivering and measuring experience and relevance across different channels according to the customers' preferences for these different channels. Some web-savvy customers will prefer the web as a communications medium, but others are likely to be more responsive to traditional communications such as direct mail. Finally, the balance at the bottom-right corner of Figure 5.1 suggests another significant challenge – that there are many advanced targeting approaches and technology that can be deployed, but putting in place the right processes, technology and people is far from straightforward. The biggest challenge of all is selecting and implementing the best approaches to deliver the return on technology investment, which we turn to in Chapter 7.

PLANNING RETENTION

Producing a plan for retention encourages a long-term view of the aims for our campaigns, and enables them to reinforce each other rather than their being isolated. To build a retention plan, work towards building a communications timeline for the next 6, 12 or 18 months, such as that shown in Figure 5.2. This helps to form a picture that shows the different forms of communication and their frequency. These issues are considered in the next section. It also helps to develop an editorial calendar that shows the different incentives and promotions which will be used at different times. In the case of B2B, these may be different white papers that need to be produced to highlight an issue of concern to the audience. For a B2C marketer, they may be new product launches or promotions planned for different times in the year.

Developing a 'sense and respond' system

For effective retention e-mail marketing which delivers timely, relevant messages, the appropriate infrastructure must be in place. Such a system needs to deliver the customer insight to identify

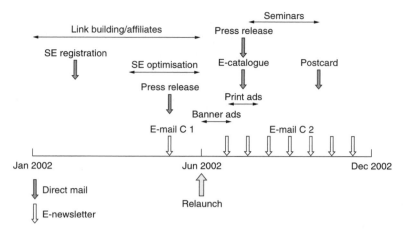

Figure 5.2 Retention planning timeline

specific customer types for whom we can develop different marketing treatments to encourage retention and extension. For example, we can target:

- the most valuable customers
- the most growable customers
- the most responsive customers
- the most vulnerable customers.

At the same time we have, of course, a limited marketing budget, so need to prioritize campaigns on those that will give the best returns. As Jim Novo in Novo (2003) puts it:

> ***Don't spend until you have to . . . Spend at point of maximum impact.***

Digital marketing provides us with the knowledge about customers to more readily identify those who fall into the four categories above. It also provides us with a more efficient way of targeting these customers, since:

- customers can be continuously monitored to assess their status – for example, customers identified as valuable may exhibit behaviour that suggests they are likely to become the most vulnerable
- specific campaigns do not have to be developed for each customer – contact strategies can be developed where an e-mail, mail or phone communication can be triggered when the customer changes status
- communication costs can be reduced – where we think it will be effective, we can send out e-mail communications that are lower cost both for the initial e-mail and the follow-up
- increased intelligence about customer behaviour – we can identify recipients of e-mail opening or clicking through on particular content or offers, and can see what web-site visitors view and how far they develop through the buying process. We can also interact with them, asking them directly what their interest is.

To be able to identify customers in the categories of value, growth, responsiveness, or vulnerability to defection, we need to characterize them using information about the customers which indicates their *behaviour*. This is because the past and current actual behaviour is often the best predictor of future behaviour. We can then seek to influence this future behaviour. This goes beyond e-mail marketing, to combine response behaviour to e-mail, on web-site visits and in other channels such as in-store or phone.

Online marketing enables marketers to create a cycle of:

- monitoring customer actions or behaviours and then ...

- reacting with appropriate messages and offers to encourage desired behaviours

- monitoring response to these messages and continuing with additional communications and monitoring

  or, if you prefer, simply:

  - sense

  - respond

  - adjust.

TARGETING APPROACHES

There are different levels of sophistication in targeting, some of which may not be worthwhile according to the size of your list. However, it is useful to review the segmentation and targeting approach used by the top e-retailers to deliver relevance. Typically, these are based upon five customer-centric elements that are, in effect, layered on top of each other for effective targeting. These approaches are based on identifying and targeting according to:

1. Customer lifecycle groups

2. Customer profile characteristics (demographics)

3. Customer behaviour in response and purchase

4. Customer multi-channel behaviour (channel preference)

5. Customer tone and style preference.

Customer lifecycle groups

As visitors use online services they can potentially pass through seven or more stages, as shown in Figure 5.3, as their relationship with a company evolves. This approach is widely used by online retailers.

Once you have defined these groups and set up the customer relationship management infrastructure to categorize customers in this way, you can then deliver targeted messages, either by personalized on-site messaging or through e-mails that are triggered automatically

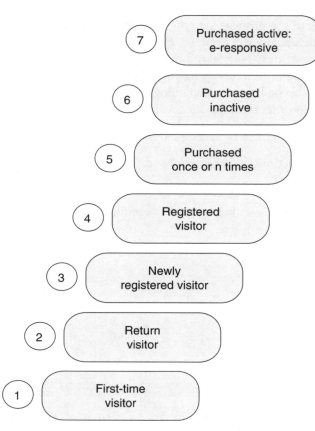

Figure 5.3 Typical lifecycle segmentation for e-retailer customers

due to different rules. First-time visitors can be identified by whether they have a cookie placed on their PC, and their computer set-up or user agent settings. Once visitors are then registered, they can be tracked through the remaining stages. Two particularly important groups are customers who have purchased one or more times. For many e-retailers, encouraging customers to move from the first purchase to the second purchase and then onto the third purchase is a key challenge. Specific promotions can be used to encourage further purchases. Similarly, once customers become inactive – i.e. they have not purchased for a defined period such as three months – further follow-ups are required.

An example of the lifecycle segmentation approach is given by Humby and Hunt (2003), who describe how e-retailer Tesco.com uses what it calls a 'commitment-based segmentation' or 'loyalty ladder' which is based on recency of purchase, frequency of purchase and value; this is used to identify six lifecycle categories:

1. Logged-on

2. Cautionary

3. Developing

4. Established

5. Dedicated

6. Logged-off (the aim here is to win back).

These are then further divided to target communications.

Tesco then uses automated event-triggered messaging to encourage continued purchase. For example, Tesco.com has a touch strategy which includes a sequence of follow-up communications triggered following different events in the customer lifecycle. In the example given below, communications after event 1 are intended to achieve the objective of converting a web-site visitor to action; communications after event 2 are intended to move the customer from a first-time purchaser to a regular purchaser, and after event 3 to reactivate lapsed purchasers.

E-MAIL MARKETING EXCELLENCE: TARGETING COMMUNICATIONS

Trigger event 1: Customer first registers on site (but does not buy).

Auto-response (AR) 1: Two days after registration, e-mail sent offering phone assistance and £5 discount off first purchase to encourage trial.

Trigger event 2: Customer first purchases online.

AR1: Immediate order confirmation.

AR2: Five days after purchase, e-mail sent with link to online customer satisfaction survey asking about quality of service from driver and picker (e.g. item quality and substitutions).

AR3: Two weeks after first purchase, direct mail sent offering tips on how to use service and £5 discount on next purchase, intended to encourage re-use of online services.

AR4: Generic monthly e-newsletter sent with online exclusive offers encouraging cross-selling.

AR5: Bi-weekly alert sent with personalized offers for customer.

AR6: After two months, £5 discount for next shop.

AR7: Quarterly mailing of coupons sent, encouraging repeat sales and cross-sales.

Trigger event 3: Customer does not purchase for an extended period.

AR1: Dormancy detected – reactivation e-mail sent with survey of how the customer is finding the service (to identify any problems) and a £5 incentive.

AR2: A further discount incentive is used in order to encourage continued usage to shop after the first shop after a break.

Customer profile characteristics (demographics)

This is a traditional segmentation based on the type of customer. For B2C e-retailers this will include age, sex and geography. For B2B companies, this will include size of the company and the industry sector or application they operate in.

It is worth trialling different forms of segmentation and targeting. These may not have previously been possible with direct mail because of the cost of different executions, but the beauty of e-mail marketing is that different forms of targeting and testing can be conducted at lower cost (but only if the resource and culture within the organization supports it). For example, many B2B companies target according to industry sector, but do not also look at job roles. Different messages can be developed for people with more strategic interest (for example, for a senior manager the benefit of a new printer may be reduced costs, while for an IT manager it may be ease of administration or throughput). Similarly, many B2C companies may conduct national campaigns, but with e-mail can add a regional element – perhaps using the postcode to determine different parts of the country and then, for a travel company, giving different messages according to the region or airport they will fly from.

E-MAIL MARKETING INSIGHT

Use the lower cost of e-mail creative and broadcast to test different targeting forms.

Customer behaviour in response and purchase

As customers progress through the lifecycle shown in Figure 5.3, by analysis of their database it will be able to build up a detailed response and purchase history. A relatively simple method of showing behaviour is to develop an *activity score*. Here, customers are each scored according to their response, whether it is the number of opens, clicks, leads or purchases. Different communications can then be sent to list members depending on their historical level of activity. Customers who don't seem to be responsive to online messages can be targeted through other approaches, such as direct mail or phone.

A more sophisticated method of understanding behaviour is to categorize customers according to the details of their recency and the frequency, monetary value and category of products purchased (RFM analysis). The RFM technique is quite involved, so we will cover that in more detail in a moment.

Using these RFM techniques in combination with the other targeting techniques, it becomes possible to use predictive modelling to identify the 'Next Best Product' for particular customer types. With the right system of tracking and web analytics, it should be possible to see not only which types of links in an e-mail a customer has clicked upon, but also which types of web pages they have visited recently. For example, a select on the database for a wine promotion could be used to target customers who have been to the wine section of the website in the last three months, but have not purchased wine.

Customer multi-channel behaviour (channel preference)

Regardless of the enthusiasm of the company for online channels, some customers prefer using online communications channels and others prefer traditional channels. This will, to an extent, be indicated by RFM and response analysis, since customers with a preference for online channels will be more responsive and make more purchases online. Customers can also be asked direct through surveys. It is useful to have a flag within the database indicating the customers channel preference and, by implication, the best channel to use to target them. Customers that prefer online channels can be targeted mainly by online communications such as e-mail, while customers who prefer traditional channels can be targeted by traditional communications such as direct mail or phone.

Customer tone and style preference

In a similar manner to channel preference, customers will respond differently to different types of message. Some may like a more rational appeal, in which case a detailed e-mail explaining the benefits of the offer may work best. Others will prefer an emotional appeal based on images and with warmer, less formal copy. Sophisticated companies will test for this in customers, or infer it using profile characteristics and response behaviour, and then develop different creative treatments accordingly. Companies that use polls can potentially use these to infer style preferences.

To deliver relevance also requires a plan specifying the number, frequency and types of online and offline communications and offers. This is a contact or touch strategy, described in Chapter 2.

To summarize the approaches described, the example of Euroffice is a good one – see Case study 5.1.

CASE STUDY 5.1: E-MAIL MARKETING EXCELLENCE – EUROFFICE DEVELOPS A FUNNEL-BASED APPROACH TO TARGETING

Euroffice (www.euroffice.co.uk) is a large online office supplies company which targets small and mid-sized companies. This description is adapted from the company web-site press releases and *Revolution* (2005). According to George Karibian, Euroffice CEO, 'getting the message across effectively required segmentation' to engage different people in different ways. The office sector is fiercely competitive, with relatively little loyalty, since company purchasers will often simply buy on price. However, targeted incentives can be used to reward or encourage buyers' loyalty. Rather than manually developing campaigns for each segment, which is time consuming, Euroffice mainly uses an automated event-based targeting approach based on the system of identifying the stage at which a consumer is in the lifecycle – i.e. how many products they have purchased, and the types of product within their purchase history. Karibian calls this a 'touch marketing funnel approach', i.e. the touch strategy is determined by customer segmentation and response. Three main groups of customers are identified in the lifecycle, and these are broken down further according to purchase category. Also layered on this segmentation is breakdown into buyer type – are they a small home-user, an operations manager at a mid-size company or a purchasing manager at a larger company? Each will respond to different promotions.

The first and largest group, at the top of the funnel, 'Group 1: Trial customers', who have made one or two purchases. For the first group, Euroffice believes that creating impulse buying through price promotions is most important. Promotions will be based on categories purchased in the past. The second group, 'Group 2: The nursery', consists of customers who have made three to eight purchases. A particular issue, as with many e-retailers, is encouraging customers from the third to the fourth purchase; there is a more significant drop-out at this point, which the company uses marketing to control. Karibian says: 'When they get to group two, it's about creating frequency of purchase to ensure they don't forget you.' Euroffice sends a printed catalogue to Group 2 separately from their merchandise, as a reminder about the company.

The final group, 'Group 3: Key accounts', consists of customers who have made nine or more orders. They also tend to have a higher basket value. These people are the 'Crown jewels', and will spend an average of £135 per order compared to an average of £55 for trial customers. They have a 90 per cent probability of re-ordering within a six-month period. For this group, tools have been developed on the site to make it easier for them to shop. The intention is that these customers find the tools help them in making their orders and they become reliant on them, so achieving 'soft lock-in'.

We can target the five segments through using fields within the database to identify which segment customers belong to, and then using mass customization and personalization to tailor offers to customers, as described in the following section.

Design personas

Related to the five targeting approaches above, it is also useful to consider using *design personas* for typical customer types. This is a powerful web-design technique used to improve the usability and customer-centricity of a web site. It has the benefit that it characterizes segment types in the context of the targeting options mentioned above, such as stage in lifecycle, demographics and style preferences. The concept can also potentially be used for e-newsletters.

A design persona is a summary of the characteristics, needs, motivations and environment of typical web-site users. Personas are essentially 'thumbnail' descriptions of a type of person. They have been used for a long time in research for segmentation and advertising, but in recent years have also proved effective for improving web-site design by companies who have applied the technique. In a web context, *customer scenarios* are developed for different personas. Patricia Seybold, in her book *The Customer Revolution* (Seybold and Marshak, 2001), explains them as follows:

> *A customer scenario is a set of tasks that a particular customer wants or needs to do in order to accomplish his or her desired outcome.*

Customer scenarios (user journeys) are therefore alternative tasks or outcomes required by a visitor to a web site, and are typically accomplished in a series of stages of different tasks involving different information needs or experiences. You will see that scenarios can be developed for each persona. For an online bank, scenarios might include:

1. New customer – opening online account

2. Existing customer – transferring an account online

3. Existing customer – finding an additional product.

How, then, does this translate to targeting for e-mail? Well, the model is slightly different in that web-site visits are often a pull medium, where people have a particular intent to shop and will then visit a web site via a search engine. I have not heard about personas being used that much in an e-mail context, but I think they could be usefully applied, particularly for e-newsletters. One example where they have been used is by the American National Football League (NFL, http://www.nfl.com/nflnewsletter), which has identified three types of scenarios – one of a customer following a particular team and who wants to check upcoming games, one of a customer who is very interested in the statistics associated with the fantasy league, and another of a customer who tends to be more interested in the position in the league. In Figure 5.4, you can see how the design reflects this.

These are some guidelines and ideas on what can be included when developing a persona. The start or end point is to give each persona a name. The detailed stages are as follows.

1. *Build personal attributes into personas*:

   - demographic – age, gender, education, occupation and, for B2B, company size, position in buying unit

   - psychographic – goals, tasks, motivation

   - webographics – web experience (months), usage location (home or work), usage platform (dial-up, broadband), usage frequency, favourite sites.

2. *Remember that personas are only models of characteristics and environment*:

   - design targets

   - stereotypes

   - three or four usually suffice to improve general usability, but more are needed for specific behaviours

   - choose one *primary persona* (a representation of the typical site user) who, if satisfied, means others are likely to be satisfied.

Figure 5.4 Example e-newsletter using scenario-based design (reproduced courtesy of National Football League)

Once different personas have been developed who are representative of key site-visitor types or customer types, a primary persona can sometimes be identified. Wodtke (2002) says:

> *Your primary persona needs to be a common user type who is both important to the business success of the product and needy from a design point of view – in other words, a beginner user or a technologically challenged one.*

She also says that secondary personas can be developed, such as super-users or complete novices. Complementary personas are those that don't fit into the main categories and which display unusual behaviour. Such complementary personas help with 'out-of-box thinking', and require choices or content that may appeal to all users.

RFM ANALYSIS

As is well known by catalogue retailers, knowledge about customer purchase behaviour typically falls into three key areas:

1. Recency of last purchase, e.g. three months ago

2. Frequency of purchase, e.g. twice per quarter or twice per year

3. Monetary value of purchase(s), e.g. average order value of £50, total annual purchase value of £5000.

Assessing these behavioural characteristics is known as RFM, or a similar equivalent, FRAC, representing:

- Frequency

- Recency

- Amount (obviously equivalent to monetary value)

- Category (types of product purchased – not always included within RFM).

These approaches have not been limited to retailers, though; they have been a staple approach for many years for some marketing applications, for example for catalogues and mail-order companies, for grocers and other retailers with loyalty schemes, for charities (which can track donations) and for car manufacturers (which can track car purchases or services through time).

However, for many other organizations they have proved less relevant. With the advent of web and e-mail marketing, there are many more opportunities for applying this behavioural customer information and using RFM in virtually every market. This is possible because recency and frequency of purchase can be used to understand and respond to other types of digitally recorded transactions and interactions – for example, visits or log-ins to a website, or interaction with e-mails such as opens or clicks. These types of interactions apply not only to e-retail sites but also to relationship-building websites, brand-building sites and portals.

We will now give an overview of how RFM approaches can be applied in online marketing, with special reference to e-mail marketing.

Recency

Recency shows the number of days since a customer completed an action, and is compared to the current time as shown in Figure 5.5. The dark arrow nearest to the present has a higher recency to the present day than does the light arrow nearest to the present.

Novo (2003) stresses the importance of recency when he says:

> *Recency, or the number of days that have gone by since a customer completed an action (purchase, log-in, download, etc.), is the most powerful predictor of the customer repeating an action ... Recency is why you receive another catalogue from the company shortly after you make your first purchase from them.*

Of course, this applies in particular to catalogue-style purchases.

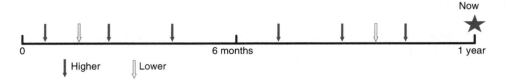

Figure 5.5 Diagrammatic representation of recency and frequency

Online marketing examples: online, we can measure a lot more than days elapsed since last purchase. We can assess

- purchases
- visits to site or particular type of content (using cookies)
- log-ons to a site (more accurate than cookies, provided user ID is not shared)
- opening of or clickthroughs on an e-mail or e-newsletter.

Applications: online applications of analysis of recency include

- monitoring through time to identify vulnerable customers
- scoring customers to preferentially target more responsive customers for cost savings.

Frequency

Frequency refers to the number of times an action is completed in a period, as shown in Figure 5.5. Dark arrows indicate events that occur more closely together, i.e. they have a higher frequency.

Online marketing examples: examples are similar to those for recency, but with reference to a time period – for example

- five purchases per year
- five visits per month
- five log-ins per week
- five e-mail opens per month
- five e-mail clicks per year.

Applications: online applications of analysis of include combining frequency with recency for RF targeting.

Monetary

Monetary value is the amount spent in a period – for example, per month, per quarter or per year, depending on the type of application. For an e-retailer, average order value would also be appropriate.

Online marketing examples: generally, customers with higher monetary values tend to have a higher loyalty and potential future value, since they have purchased more items. Assessing the characteristics of these customers on the database to understand factors which may make them more valuable is often insightful; the customers could also be surveyed to find out these factors.

Applications: an application might be to exclude these customers from special promotions if their RF scores suggest that they are actively purchasing.

Frequency is often a proxy for monetary value per year, since the more products purchased, the higher the overall monetary value. It is possible, then, to simplify analysis by just using recency and frequency. Monetary value can also skew the analysis with high-value initial purchases.

The next section describes how values can be assigned to each customer.

Dividing customers into different RFM groups

The rigorous approach to RFM analysis is to place an equal number of customers in each quintile of 20 per cent (10 deciles can also be used for larger databases). This approach is shown in Figure 5.6.

Figure 5.6 also shows one application of RFM with a view to using communications channels more effectively. Lower cost e-communications are used for the most loyal customers, and more expensive communications are used for the less loyal customers.

It is also possible to place each division for recency, frequency and monetary value in an arbitrary position. This approach can be useful, as marketers can set thresholds of value relevant to their understanding of their customers' behaviour – for example:

Recency:

0	Not known
1	Within last 12 months
2	Within last 6 months
3	Within last 3 months
4	Within last 1 month

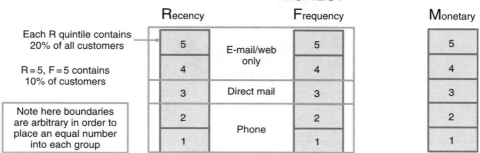

Figure 5.6   RFM analysis showing possible application

This could be purchase recency or, as here, recency of a visit to the web site.

Frequency:
0   Not known
1   Every 6 months
2   Every 3 months
3   Every 2 months
4   Monthly

This could be purchase frequency or, as here, frequency of visits to the web site.

Monetary value:
0   Less than £10
1   £10–£50
2   £50–£100
3   £100–£200
4   More than £200

This could be total purchase value through the year or, as here, average order value.

An example using real world data is shown in Figure 5.7.

You can see that plotting customer numbers against recency and frequency in this way for an online company gives a great visual indication of the health of the business and of groups that can be targeted to encourage greater repeat purchases.

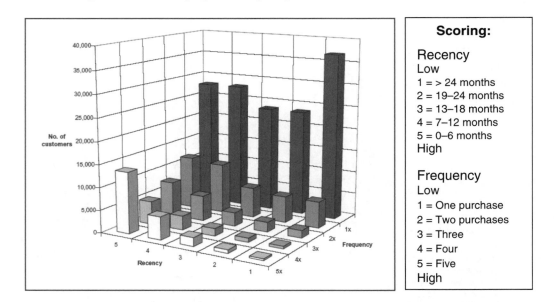

Figure 5.7 Example of RF analysis (source: *Interactive Marketing Journal*, January–March 2004, SilverMinds music catalogue)

Another example, showing how RFM can be applied in non-retail settings, indicates how a theatre group uses these categories for its direct marketing:

Oncers (attended theatre once)

Recent oncers	attended <12 months
Rusty oncers	attended >12, <36 months
Very rusty oncers	attended 36+ months

Twicers:

Recent twicer	attended <12 months
Rusty twicer	attended >12, <36 months
Very rusty twicer	attended 36+ months

2+ subscribers:

Current subscribers	Booked 2+ events in current season
Recent	Booked 2+ last season
Very rusty	Booked 2+ more than a season ago

This approach shows how the full RFM analysis approach doesn't have to be applied; three or four RF groups can be sufficient. A final example is shown in Figure 5.8, where online community provider Magicalia has categorized its audience to assess the volume of members in different categories (denoted by the size of the circles). Triggered e-mail communications and on-site personalized messages are then developed for each group to encourage customers to migrate to higher recency/frequency categories.

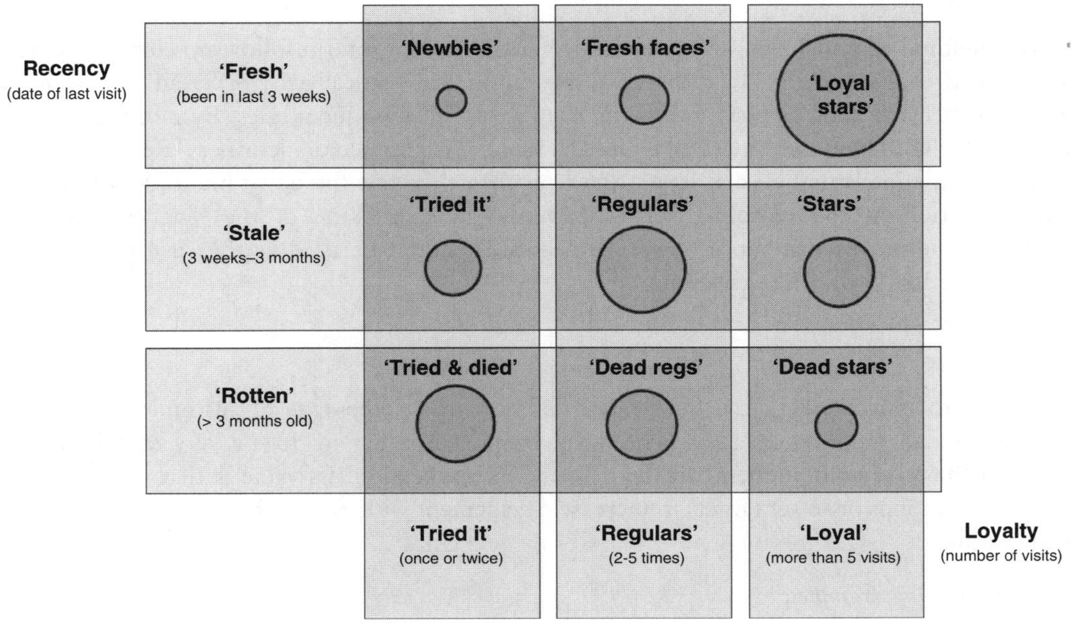

Figure 5.8 Segmentation scheme used by Magicalia

Additional measures of online customer behaviour

Novo (2003) also suggests two additional measures that can be used to understand customer behaviour and also to set targets for retention marketing. These are the *latency* and the *hurdle rate*.

Latency

The latency is the average time between customer events in the customer lifecycle.

Online marketing examples: latency can be applied to these events

- web-site visits

- second and third purchases

- e-mail clickthroughs.

Applications: online applications of analysis of include

- putting in place triggers that alert you to behaviour outside the norm – increased interest or disinterest, then . . .

- managing behaviour using e-communications or traditional communications.

For example, a B2B or B2C organization with a long interval between purchases might find that the average latency increased for a particular customer, but the customer may be investigating an additional purchase (recency and frequency would likely increase also). E-mails, phone calls or direct mail could then be used to target this person with relevant offers according to what he or she is searching for.

A great method of visualizing average latency and using it to inform follow-up communications is indicated in Figure 5.9. This diagram shows, on the vertical axis, different stages in the customer lifecycle, such as registration and then first and subsequent sales. By plotting intervals of time which different customers take for each stage, it is possible to identify a 'latency envelope' of typical time intervals for each stage. Marketers can then test the best time to do a follow-up communication as the customer moves towards the right side of the 'latency envelope'. RedEye recommends that more powerful incentives should be used as the customer looks at risk of defecting beyond the envelope.

Hurdle rate

According to Novo (2003), the hurdle rate refers to the percentage of customers in a group (such as in a segment or on a list) who have completed an action. It is a very useful concept, although the terminology doesn't really describe its application. Its value is that it can be used to compare groups or to set targets to increase engagement with online channels, as the examples below show.

Online marketing examples:

- 20 per cent of customers have visited in past six months

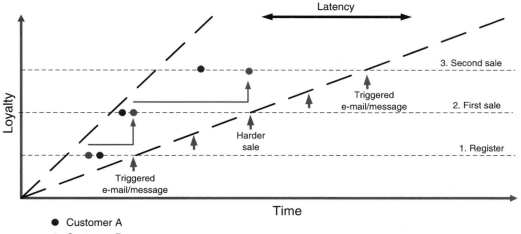

Figure 5.9 Plot showing how latency can be used to plan retention marketing activities

- 5 per cent of customers have made three or more purchases in the year
- 60 per cent of registrants have logged on to the system in the year
- 30 per cent have clicked through on e-mail in the year.

Applications: online applications of analysis of include

- use for objectives, to deepen the relationship
- use for targeting communications on particular groups, e.g. to reactivate those who are less engaged
- use for monitoring the impact of communications, i.e. how many change hurdle rates as a result of tactics.

A related approach to RFM analysis is *propensity modelling*, which is one name given to the approach of evaluating customer characteristics and behaviour – in particular, previous products or services purchased – and then making recommendations for the next suitable product. However, it is best known as recommending the 'next best product' to existing customers. A related acquisition approach is to target potential customers with similar characteristics through renting direct mail or e-mail lists, or advertising online in similar locations.

Lifetime value calculations

An appreciation of lifetime value (LTV) is key to the theory and practice of marketing and customer relationship management. However, while the term is often used loosely, calculation of LTV is not straightforward, so many organizations do not in fact do it. Lifetime value is defined as the total net benefit that a customer or group of customers will provide a company over their total relationship with that company. Modelling is based on estimating the income

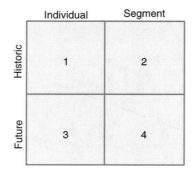

Figure 5.10 Different representations of Lifetime value calculation

and costs associated with each customer over a period of time and then calculating the net present value in current monetary terms using a discount rate value applied over the period.

There are different degrees of sophistication in calculating LTV. These are indicated in Figure 5.10. Option 1 is a practical way or approximate proxy for future LTV, but the true LTV is the future value of the customer at an individual level.

Lifetime value modelling at a segment level (4) is vital within marketing, since it answers the question: how much can I afford to invest in acquiring a new customer?

If online marketers try to answer this from a short-term perspective, as is often the case – i.e. by judging it based on the profit from a single sale on an e-commerce site – there are two problems:

1. We become very focused on short-term return on investment (ROI) and so may not invest sufficiently to grow our business

2. We assume that each new customer is worth precisely the same to us and we ignore differentials in loyalty and profitability between differing types of customer.

Lifetime value analysis enables e-mail marketers to:

- plan and measure investment in customer acquisition programmes

- identify and compare critical target segments – strategies usually involve preferentially targeting the most profitable customers and minimizing communications with the least profitable customers

- measure the effectiveness of alternative customer retention strategies

- establish the true value of a company's customer base

- make decisions about products and offers

- make decisions about the value of introducing new E-CRM technologies.

To illustrate another application of LTV and give an example of how it is calculated, consider the e-mail marketing challenge in Case study 5.2.

CASE STUDY 5.2: E-MAIL MARKETING EXCELLENCE – CHARITY USES LTV MODELLING TO JUSTIFY INVESTMENT IN E-MAIL MARKETING

A charity is considering implementing a new e-mail marketing system to increase donations. The charity's main role is as a relief agency which aims to reduce poverty through providing aid, particularly to the regions that need it most. Currently, its only e-mail activity is a monthly e-newsletter received by its 200 000 subscribers, which features its current campaigns and appeals. It hopes to increase donations by using a more targeted approach based on previous customer behaviour. The e-mail system will integrate with the donor database, which contains information on customer profiles and previous donations.

The company is considering three solutions, which will cost between £50 000 and £100 000 in the first year. In the charity, all such investments are assessed using lifetime value modelling. Table 5.2 shows the model for lifetime value with the current system.

Based on preliminary tests with improved targeting, it is estimated that with the new system retention rates will increase from 50 per cent to 51 per cent in the first year, increasing by 5 per cent per year as currently. It is estimated that in Year 1 donations per annum will increase from £100 per annum to £102 per annum, increasing by £20 per year as currently. The modelling of the returns from the new system in Table 5.3 show that the £50 000 investment will become profitable within 2 years and the payback period for the £100 000 investment will be 3 years. Over 5 years, both deliver a good Return on Investment.

Therefore:

Increase in NPV for new system	£40 000	£78 184	£108 584.5	£131 773	£149 515.8
Return on investment at £50 000	−20.0%	56.4%	117.2%	163.5%	199.0%
Return on investment at £100 000	−60.0%	−21.8%	8.6%	31.8%	49.5%

Touch (contact) strategy

Another key aspect of retention planning closely related to targeting is to think about your options for the range of e-mail and traditional communications, and the frequency that you plan to use. To deliver relevance also requires a plan specifying the number, frequency and type of online and offline communications and offers. This is a contact or touch strategy. Getting the frequency right is particular important, since if you get it too low you will miss out on your maximum potential for sales or leads but if you get it too high the recipient will stop paying attention to your communications or, worse still, will perceive them as spam. We have said several times previously in this book that spam is in the eye of beholder, and this is also

Table 5.2 Lifetime value model for customer base for current system

		Year 1	Year 2	Year 3	Year 4	Year 5
A	Donors	100 000	50 000	27 500	16 500	10 725
B	Retention	50%	55%	60%	65%	70%
C	Donations per annum	£100	£120	£140	£160	£180
D	Total donations	£10 000 000	£6 000 000	£3 850 000	£2 640 000	£1 930 500
E	Net profit (at 20%)	£2 000 000	£1 200 000	£770 000	£528 000	£386 100
F	Discount rate	1	0.86	0.7396	0.636	0.547
G	NPV contribution	£2 000 000	£1 032 000	£569 492	£335 808	£211 196
H	Cumulative NPV contribution	£2 000 000	£3 032 000	£3 601 492	£3 937 300	£4 148 496.7
I	Lifetime value at net present value	£20.0	£30.3	£36.0	£39.4	£41.5

A *Donors* – this is the number of initial donors; it declines each year dependent on the retention rate (row B)

B *Retention rate* – in lifetime value modelling it is usually found that this increases year on year, since customers who stay loyal are more likely to remain loyal

C *Donations per annum* – likewise, the charity finds that the average contributions per year increase through time within this group of customers

D *Total donations* – this is calculated through multiplying rows A and C

E *Net profit (at 20% margin)* – LTV modelling is based on profit contributed by this group of customers; column D is multiplied by 0.2

F *Discount rate* – since the value of money held at a point in time will decrease due to inflation, a discount rate is applied to calculate the value of future returns in the terms of current day value

G *NPV contribution* – this is the profitability after taking the discount factor into account to give Net Present Value in future years; it is calculated by multiplying row E by row F

H *Cumulative NPV contribution* – this adds the previous year's NPV for each year

I *Lifetime value at net present value* – this is a value per customer, calculated by dividing row H by row A.

suggested by the *Doubleclick Sixth Annual Consumer E-mail Survey* (Doubleclick, 2005) where Doubleclick asked consumers what they rated as spam. Table 5.4 lists the results of the survey.

The e-mail contact strategy should combine communications that coincide with different customer lifecycle stages, as defined in Figure 5.3, and also planned campaign activities and e-newsletters.

We also have to discover at which frequency the customer will become annoyed. Clearly if e-mail communications are too frequent, then the customer is less likely to have the time or inclination to open them. One approach is therefore to monitor the response for

Table 5.3   Lifetime value model for new system

After system installed	Year 1	Year 2	Year 3	Year 4	Year 5
Donors	100 000	51 000	28 560	17 422	11 498
Retention	51%	56%	61%	66%	71%
Donations per annum	£102	£122	£142	£162	£182
Total donations	£10 200 000	£6 222 000	£4 055 520	£2 822 299	£2 092 683
Net profit (at 20%)	£2 040 000	£1 244 400	£811 104	£564 459.8	£418 536.5
Discount rate	1	0.86	0.7396	0.636	0.547
NPV contribution	£2 040 000	£1 070 184	£599 892.5	£358 996.5	£228 939.5
Cumulative NPV contribution	£2 040 000	£3 110 184	£3 710 076.5	£4 069 073	£4 298 012.5
Lifetime value at net present value	£20.4	£31.1	£37.1	£40.7	£43.0

e-mail communications. However, higher frequencies will likely lead to higher response – which helps to explain the high volume of e-mails sent by Tesco.com to its consumers, although Tesco.com has recently been exposed by the BBC as 'bombarding UK consumers with a massive e-mail marketing campaign' (BBC, 2005). Based on the e-mail tracking service E-mail Monitor (www.e-mailmonitor.co.uk), from Interactive Prospect Targeting Services, the BBC said that Tesco was blitzing the nation with 16–20 million e-mails per month and reported that in September 2005 it issued 44 separate e-mail campaigns – more than Sainsbury's, Asda, Waitrose and Somerfield put together. Part of this activity can be explained by Tesco's market share. A Tesco spokesman was reported as saying:

> *More people shop with us online than with anyone else and we do communicate with a lot of them by e-mail. We know that customers hate junk mail so we try to target them as much as possible and make it easy for them to stop receiving e-mails if they don't want them.*

In 2005 Tesco was dealing with about 170 000 orders per week, compared with its nearest rival, Sainsburys.co.uk, which was receiving about 38 000.

The alternatives to a high touch frequency, particularly for non-retail brands, are to research customer preferences or to offer a choice of frequencies at the point of initial opt-in. This may well suit the customer better, although it will probably lead to reduced sales compared to when the company has the choice of frequency.

Table 5.4 What do consumers rate as spam?

What is spam?	Replies (%)	Notes
E-mails that intend to trick me into opening them	94	Take care with clever teaser subject lines
E-mails from senders who are unknown to me	90	Make sure the From is a well-known brand, company or, exceptionally, person
E-mails of an offensive subject matter	90	
E-mails from a company I have permission with offline but no permission online	57	Use a statement of origination or 'why am I receiving this?' message section explaining how you gained permission
E-mails from a company I have done business with but that come too frequently	49	Permission-based marketers can be perceived as spammers if they get the frequency wrong
E-mails that I gave permission for at one time, but I no longer wish to receive	49	If your unsubscribe process doesn't work you will be viewed as a spammer, or even if the relevance of your communications decreases
Any e-mails that try to send me a product or service, even if I know the sender	29	I guess there's no pleasing some people; however, if relevance isn't there the beauty of permission marketing is that unsubscribe is possible

A contact strategy should indicate:

1. Communications targeting

2. Communications frequency

3. Communications interval

4. Communications content and offers

5. Links between different forms of e-mail marketing, such as e-newsletters and campaign e-mails

6. Links between online communications and offline communications

7. A control strategy

8. Communicaitons flexibility.

Communications targeting

In the previous section, we have described in detail different options for targeting. Particularly important in the case of the touch strategy is customer-lifecycle based targeting.

The section on targeting in Chapter 3 also reviewed a wide range of choices when targeting, including:

1. Demographics (age, sex, geography B2C characteristics)

2. Lifestyle or psychographic (B2C characteristics)

3. Company or individual role in decision-making unit (B2B characteristics)

4. Product (categories of purchase)

5. Purchase history (recency, frequency and monetary value analysis)

6. Customer value

7. Customer loyalty

8. E-mail preference

9. Time on list (in months)

10. Responsiveness to e-mail campaigns.

Communications frequency

This defines the minimum frequency (e.g. once per quarter) and maximum frequency (e.g. once per month) of communications. Remember that we will often e-mail too infrequently. It may be useful to set communications targets such as 'at least four e-mails per year'.

A key point in planning retention campaigns is getting the frequency of campaigns right. We are looking to achieve the right balance between overexposure and underexposure. With overexposure, recipients receive e-mail from the same supplier so frequently that they don't have the time to read it. Underexposure is where opportunities are lost because the customer does not receive e-mails sufficiently frequently, perhaps due to problems in resourcing this campaign. In terms of metrics, we are looking to maximize clickthrough and minimize unsubscribes, so these metrics should be monitored (as for newsletters) to get the frequency right. Some companies have regular monthly competitions, but these will tend to have less impact than irregular promotions. Such irregular promotions include event-based tie-ins.

E-MAIL MARKETING INSIGHT

Plot the response rate and unsubscribe rate of your e-marketing campaigns through time. Try to maximize clickthrough and minimize unsubscribe rates.

If messages are received too frequently from an organization, their effectiveness will fall. Frequency options include:

- *regular newsletters* (for example, daily, weekly, monthly) – let customers choose the frequency

- *event-related messages* – these messages tend to be less regular, but give a higher impact; they are sent out perhaps every three or six months, when there is news of a new product launch or an exceptional offer

- *multi-stage messaging* – e-mails automatically sent out before a renewal to encourage re-subscription.

Frequency options are discussed further with respect to newsletters later in this chapter.

Communications interval

Some companies may seek to set limits on the communications interval – for example, there must be a gap of at least one week or one month between communications. This may be overtly restrictive, which brings us to the next point...

Communications content and offers

We may want to limit or achieve a certain number of prize draws or information-led offers.

The types of offer we can use in retention campaigns were reviewed in Chapter 3. We summarized the main types of offers as 'free–win–save'. The type of offer used with sales promotions will also vary according to the type of site. Promotion campaign options include:

- *retail sites* – loyalty schemes, discounts, buy one get one free, free shipping or free gift

- *B2C bricks and clicks sites* – prize draws, competitions

- *B2B sites* – competitions, and seminars (webinars) about new products, new content or new services.

Links between different forms of e-mail marketing, such as e-newsletters and campaign e-mails

Often the link between e-mails and campaign e-mails is overlooked in communications planning. This can lead to missed opportunities where the e-newsletter could be used to reinforce messages in campaigns, or sometimes the e-newsletter itself may be the main vehicle for explaining an offer but it may get diluted amongst the other items.

Options for e-mail marketing include:

- regular newsletter e-mails to keep customers informed about industry, company or product news

- an e-mail discussion list, perhaps related to customer support or a user group

- e-mail promotions – special offers, competitions and discounts to encourage repeat visits to the company web site and then convert the visit to a sale (these are explored in the next section)

- viral e-mails, for example where customers on the house list are encouraged to enter the e-mail addresses of friends or colleagues to forward information or entertainment to them (this is combined retention and acquisition covered in the previous chapter)

- promotions to encourage renewal. Where the product involves renewing a contract, as is the case for insurance or mobile phones, for example, promotions should be planned to achieve this. The timing of these will vary according to when the customer originally signed the contract, so this is an automated approach and may involve several reminder messages (multi-stage messaging) and different media (telesales may also be used).

A further issue to consider is the balance between e-newsletter communications and standalone or solus e-mails. Some companies seem to focus most of their e-mail marketing on e-newsletters (Figure 5.11a) and others on solus e-mails (Figure 5.11b). If all of the communications are focused on e-newsletters, there is a danger that major news about key promotions or product launches might be diluted. I have seen tests done where the same offer performs much better when in a solus e-mail than when in an e-newsletter. On the other hand, e-newsletters are great at engaging an audience and offering value. For each type of communication, there is also the choice of two alternative forms of targeting – sending a different creative treatment to different segments, or using dynamic content pods or panels within the message to appeal to different segments.

Links between online communications and offline communications

Again, synergies between online and offline communications may be missed, or there may be mixed messages.

A control strategy

A mechanism to make sure these guidelines are adhered to is essential. One method is to use a 'focal point', or single person, who checks all communications for one group of customers before creation or dispatch.

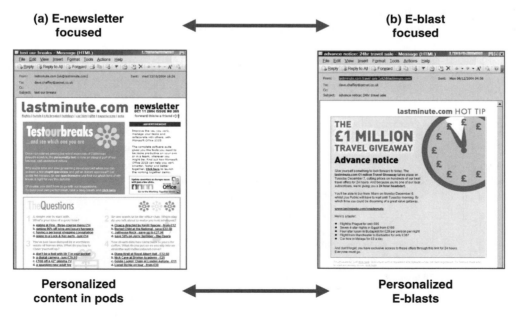

Figure 5.11   Getting the right balance between (a) e-newsletters and (b) solus e-mail communications

Communications flexibility

It is impossible to create rules to cater for all occasions, and some companies have limited their opportunities by creating such rules. For example, a rule to limit intervals to greater than one week or month will restrict multi-message campaigns where a reminder is sent out to boost response.

Enhancing customer insight

Planning retention strategy should also specify approaches to learning more about the customer. There should be a plan to gradually understand more about the customer in terms of their characteristics, preferences and opinions. Figure 5.12 shows a plan for increasing knowledge about the customer through time. While it is good to have such a plan for data collection, the methods for storing and integrating this data are not straightforward – for example, information on customer preferences, e-mail response behaviour and buying behaviour may all be held on different systems. Retention planning therefore also involves an approach for integrating data from all these different sources. Moreover, it needs to consider methods of keeping customer information fresh – encouraging customers to update their e-mail address if it changes, or their preferences. This should be built in to retention campaigns. All such campaigns and newsletters should have the option to update the customer preferences or profile. Indeed, periodically this should be one of the main aims of a campaign – to learn more about customers and keep their information up-to-date.

Customer surveys

Campaigns intended to develop customer satisfaction surveys should also be incorporated within the retention plan. These show that the company is not just exploiting the relationship, but also looking to find ways to improve its services. A good resource for best practice for developing online surveys is Virtual Surveys (www.virtualsurveys.com).

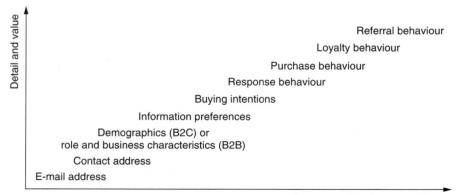

Figure 5.12 Plan for increasing detail of customers through time

E-MAIL MARKETING INSIGHT

Give customers access to their profile (via web site and e-mail) to enable them to update it.

E-NEWSLETTERS – DEFINING AND REFINING

Many web sites now have a prominently placed 'Sign-up to our newsletter' box. But is this enough?

How many e-mail newsletters do you subscribe to? If you're anything like me, the number is well into double figures – and most weeks I will opt in to yet another. The trouble is, the more I subscribe to, the less likely I am to have time to look at them, so some are never opened. I think we all have a mental list of 'must read', 'maybe read' and 'only if I have time' e-newsletters. Typically, I don't unsubscribe, since I may have a chance one week to look at them.

Thus, for organizations to make their e-newsletters successful, they have to work really hard to get them into the '*must read*' category of their subscribers. This is a big challenge because, in any sector, many companies have already seized the opportunity provided by e-mail newsletters to build relationships with potential customers and develop relationships with their existing customers. However, it is certainly possible – in the UK, consumer newsletters from online brands such as lastminute.com, dabs.com and Tesco.com get great open rates and deliver a substantial amount of business. Many business-to-business e-newsletters have also found the secret of success within their niche.

When devising an e-newsletter, there are many decisions that must to be made for it to be effective. This section is about the decisions you take as you plan the launch of an e-newsletter, and also decisions regarding how to gain subscribers and keep them. Use these lists of decisions to plan an e-newsletter or to improve on your current e-newsletter.

Decision 1 – organization objectives

The starting point for planning an e-newsletter has to be to examine (or re-examine) why you are publishing it. You will probably have a primary objective, such as boosting sales on a site through clickthrough, or building a brand by providing value to customers, but what about other objectives? The 5 Ss of Smith and Chaffey (2005), originally applied to a corporate web site, provide a good way to think about e-newsletter objectives:

1. *Sell* – grow sales (the e-newsletter often acts as both a customer acquisition tool and a retention tool)

2. *Serve* – add value (give customers extra benefits online, such as online exclusive offers or more in-depth information about your products or industry sector)

3. *Speak* – get closer to customers by creating a dialogue, asking questions through online research surveys, and learning about customers' preferences through tracking (that is, what type of content are people most interested in)

4. *Save* – save costs (of print and post); if you have a traditional offline e-newsletter, can you reduce print runs or extend its reach by using e-mail?

5. *Sizzle* – extend the brand online; a newsletter keeps the brand at 'front-of-mind' and helps reinforce brand values, and added value can also be delivered by the e-newsletter in informing and entertaining customers.

All the newsletter design decisions we discuss below should, of course, also be controlled by the main objectives of the e-newsletter.

Decision 2 – measuring success

When thinking about the objectives, consider how you will judge the success of your newsletter.

The following metrics are commonly used to assess the effectiveness of e-newsletters through time:

- open rates (for HTML e-newsletters)
- clickthroughs to more detailed content or promotions
- number of unsubscribes
- number of new subscribers.

While it is easy to automate collection of these metrics, think about whether they really relate to the goals in Decision 1. Think also about whether the automated measures give you the full story. Some companies also conduct surveys to determine softer measures related to how the customer perceives the newsletter and how it impacts on the brand. This is also covered in Decision 19 – tracking and assessing satisfaction.

Decision 3 – resourcing

For an e-newsletter to be categorized as 'must read' by its subscribers, you will need to allocate the resources. It will usually take at least a day of one person's time to compile the newsletter; this will involve going to the people in the company who know the customers best and asking them to contribute copy or develop offers. The newsletter may not be perceived as a priority by these content providers, but a way has to be found to communicate the importance of the newsletter to the brand, to ensure that high-quality content is contributed.

Costs of broadcasting must also be considered. If an external provider is used there is wide variation in cost and capabilities for targeting and tracking, so it is worth making sure you get the best balance of cost and performance.

Decision 4 – audience

Before deciding on the proposition, content and structure of the newsletter, you will have to think about readership. This is a tricky problem for newsletters, since many will try to accommodate both existing and potential customers. If you are refreshing your e-newsletter, assess the proportions of subscribers who are existing customers or potential customers.

For some, the majority of subscribers are not in fact customers, so one of the main measures of newsletter success is the conversion rate achieved from e-newsletter subscriber to customer. For some organizations, separate newsletters for prospects and existing customers are justified.

For both existing and potential customers, providers should analyse the subscriber base to assess whether subscribers fit into existing 'segments' – for example, by interest, geographic, life stage or product ownership categories.

Building up subscriber profiles in order to benefit from segmentation necessitates asking customers questions, such as requesting their postcode, and also analysing their preferences by seeing how they 'read' your newsletter – for example, a subscriber may mainly click through to the theatre section.

Remember that there are non-customer audiences, too. A business-to-business company may have press, students, consultants and, of course, competitors subscribing.

Refer to the text on targeting and design personas earlier in this chapter to get ideas about how you can make your e-newsletter more customer-centric.

Decision 5 – proposition

The proposition defines how value will be delivered to the main audiences. The proposition will need to be carefully formulated and then communicated online and offline to encourage and keep subscribers. The proposition will show how your e-newsletter will deliver value to subscribers through:

- saving time by providing a single, up-to-date source
- learning – increasing knowledge and solving day-to-day problems
- saving money – for instance, through exclusive offers or offering new ways of working through a company's products
- being entertaining – all newsletters can and should be fun for their audiences; this is not only the preserve of consumer newsletters
- growing trust – you will also need to demonstrate that you are a reliable, knowledgeable source, and that the customer's data are safe.

For business-to-business e-newsletters, think about how you could add value by acting as a filter for information about your market sectors. Your e-newsletters can potentially alert, aggregate and distil information through market alerts, industry trends and in-depth best-practice case studies. However, delivering this information-based value will not be cheap, as the content will have to be up-to-date, relevant, accurate, concise and clearly presented.

Decision 6 – content

As with any printed publication, the e-newsletter will live or die according to its content. Think carefully about the type of content that will lead to regular reading by subscribers and stop them unsubscribing. What special offers or nuggets of information can be provided that are indispensable?

Existing newsletter providers can assess which type of content receives the greatest number of clickthroughs. *What's New in Marketing?* (www.wnim.com) conducted a survey six months after its launch to ask for readers' views of the content – what was good, bad or missing?

The details of content provided should be driven by the objectives, audiences and proposition described above, and the proportion of content should be driven by the balance between these. Often it won't be possible to accommodate all these in a single e-newsletter or communication.

The sell/inform balance

Achieving the correct balance between using your newsletter as a sales tool and as a value-adding information supply tool is key to success of a newsletter.

Remember that this relates to the structure, too – the most enticing content needs to be 'above the fold' when the e-mail is opened. Start with what you feel are the strongest articles for your audience. Have regular features plus new, topical articles separate in each issue.

As well as the different types of feature, think about how you can use your e-newsletter to give a sense of community and engage the audience. A good example of this is the Bank of Scotland 42° e-newsletter, shown in Figure 5.13.

Community

Since the publication of the article by Armstrong and Hagel entitled 'The real value of online communities' (Armstrong and Hagel, 1996) and John Hagel's subsequent book (Hagel, 1997), there has been much discussion about the merits of using the web for virtual communities. The potential of virtual communities, according to Hagel (1997), is that they exhibit a number of positive feedback loops (or 'virtuous circles'). Focused content attracts new members, who in turn contribute to the quantity and quality of the community's pooled knowledge. Member loyalty grows as the community grows and evolves.

Behind the hype, what virtual communities offer at a basic level is group conversations about topics of interest to members of the group. Contributions or postings are added using an e-mail package or through fields on a web-based interface. These conversations are mediated by servers which either distribute messages through e-mail or as listings on a web page. For discussing the latest in Internet marketing, one of the leading discussion groups is UK Netmarketing (www.chinwag.com). This uses e-mail as the main communications mode. Contributions are posted by e-mail and received by e-mail, either as one message per post or as a daily digest. An archive of posted messages is available on the site and can be searched using Google. Other groups include the forums of E-consultancy (www.e-consultancy.com) and *The Wall of Revolution* magazine (www.revolutionmagazine.com). These both use a web-based interface for posting and reading messages. E-mail based discussion groups seem to be most popular since most of us spend more time in our e-mail package than web browser, and also we do not need to remember to visit the site to make a post.

If you are considering using discussion groups as part of your retention strategy, the main choice is whether you should host the discussion group on your web site or form a partnership with an independent site. For example, Boots The Chemist has created Handbag.com as

Figure 5.13 *42°* e-newsletter (reproduced courtesy of Bank of Scotland Corporate)

a community for its female customers rather than using the main Boots site. Another, less costly, alternative is to promote your products through sponsorship or co-branding on an independent community site or portal, or to get involved in the community discussions. If not, you may be better contributing to independent communities. When posting to groups, it is important to contribute to the groups by adding insights that will help group members. Simply posting messages that are thinly veiled product plugs will cause offence and anger.

Restrict your comments to insights, and add your web address and proposition in a short signature to your e-mail. If it sounds as though you know what you are talking about, potential customers will check out your site.

Since many successful communities thrive on their independence from suppliers and vendors, this makes it difficult for a B2B supplier to get its own community to reach critical mass. However, if you already have an active user group for your products and the products are complex in terms of installation and usage, then support-related interest may maintain a discussion group.

Depending on market sector, an organization has a choice of developing different types of community for B2C – communities of purpose, position and interest – and communities of profession for B2B.

- *Communities of purpose* are for people who are going through the same process or trying to achieve a particular objective. Examples include those researching cars (for example at Autotrader, www.autotrader.co.uk) or stocks (for example at the Motley Fool, www.motleyfool.co.uk) online. Price or product comparison services such as MySimon, Shopsmart and Kelkoo serve this community. At sites such as Bizrate (www.bizrate.com), The Egg Free Zone (www.eggfreezone.com) or Alexa (www.alexa.com), companies can share their comments on companies and their products.

- *Communities of position* are for people who are in a certain circumstance, such as suffering a health disorder or in a certain stage of life – for example, young people or old people. Examples include Dobedo (www.dobedo.co.uk), the teenage chat site; Cennet (http://www.cennet.co.uk), New horizons for the over 50s; www.babycenter.com and www.parentcentre.com for parents; and The Pet Channel (http://www.thepetchannel.com/) for pet owners.

- *Communities of interest* are for people who share an interest or passion such as sport (www.football365.com), music (www.pepsi.com), leisure (www.walkingworld.com) or any other interest (www.magicalia.com).

- *Communities of profession* are important for companies promoting B2B services. For example, Vertical Net has set up over 50 different communities to appeal to professionals in specific industries, such as paints and coatings, the chemical industry or electronics. These B2B vertical portals can be thought of as 'trade papers on steroids'. In fact, in many cases they have been created by publishers of trade papers – for example, EMAP Business Communications has created Construction Plus for the construction industry. Each has, as expected, industry and company news and jobs, but also offers online storefronts and auctions for buyers and sellers, and community features such as discussion topics. Of course, the trade papers (such as EMAP's *Construction Weekly*) are responding by creating their own portals.

What tactics can organizations use to foster community? Despite the hype and potential, many communities fail to generate activity – and a silent community isn't a community. Parker (2000) suggests eight questions that organizations should ask when considering how to create a customer community:

1. What interests, needs or passions do many of our customers have in common?

2. What topics or concerns might our customers like to share with each other?

3. What information is likely to appeal to our customer's friends or colleagues?

4. What other types of business in our area appeal to buyers of your products and services?

5. How can we create packages or offers based on combining offers from two or more affinity partners?

6. What price, delivery, financing, or incentives can we afford to offer to friends (or colleagues) that our current customers recommend?

7. What types of incentives or rewards can we afford to provide customers who recommend friends (or colleagues) who make a purchase?

8. How can we best track purchases resulting from word-of-mouth recommendations from friends?

A good approach to avoiding problems is to think about the difficulties you may have with your community-building efforts. Typical problems are:

1. *Empty communities.* A community without any people isn't a community. Traffic-building techniques need to be used to communicate the proposition of the community.

2. *Silent communities.* A community may have many registered members, but a community is not a community if the conversation flags. This is a tricky problem. You can encourage people to join the community, but how do you get them to participate? Here are some ideas:

    -   seed the community

    -   use a moderator to ask questions, or have a weekly or monthly question written by the moderator or sourced from customers

    -   have a resident independent expert to answer questions

    -   visit the communities on Monster (www.monster.co.uk) to see these approaches in action and think about what distinguishes the quiet communities from the noisy ones

    -   make your community select – limit it to key account customers or set it up as extranet service that is only offered to valued customers as a value-add; members may then be more likely to get involved.

3. *Critical communities.* Many communities on manufacturer or retailer sites can be critical of the brand. Think about whether this is a bad thing. It could highlight weaknesses in your service offer to customers and competitors, but enlightened companies use a community as a means to better understand their customers' needs and failings with their services. Community is a key market research tool. Also, it may be better to control and contain these critical comments on your site rather than having them voiced elsewhere in newsgroups where you may not notice them and can less easily counter them. The computer-oriented newsgroup on Monster shows how the moderator lets criticisms go so far and then counters them or closes them off. Particular criticisms can be removed.

Finally, remember the *lurkers* – those who read the messages but do not actively contribute. There may be ten lurkers for every active participant. The community can also positively influence these people and build brand.

Decision 7 – format

Options to consider that are related to format are as follows:

1. MIME – the normal approach to be used is to send out a multi-part MIME e-mail which will be displayed according to the capabilities of the e-mail package used. If resources permit, HTML e-newsletters should be used; these not only get the highest response rates, they also provide options for a multi-column layout – which is a much better way of delivering the sell vs inform balance.

2. Text only – this may be best option for a technical audience, particularly if the e-mail is brief and limited to alerts. Often, limited resources will be the only reason for a text-only newsletter option.

3. Give choice – despite the benefits of HTML, readers may prefer text or their e-mail client may not support HTML well. In both these cases, readers should be given the choice of HTML or text, and the text version should be given the attention it merits.

These issues are discussed in more depth at the start of Chapter 6.

Decision 8 – layout and structure

A strong layout that helps to deliver the right content to the right audience to meet the right objectives is important (see Figure 5.14). If you look at a range of newsletters, you will see that they have common features. These are some of the characteristics to consider.

1. *Header block*. This graphical area at the top of the e-mail is used to brand the e-mail and can also be used as a navigation element. It can also include a varying headline that indicates the theme of the current newsletter. This can help to gain engagement, rather than having the same header each month.

2. *Table of contents*. A compact ToC is a must, but this is often missing. For HTML e-mails, the ToC should include links to the content in the e-mail.

3. *Web-site features*. It may be useful to replicate some familiar web-site features, to 'take the website to the inbox' – for instance, Amazon uses the familiar search box from the web site on their e-newsletter to prompt an action. Menu options from the web site can be included, although this can cause confusion since they are not directly related to the e-newsletter content.

4. *Column layout*. As with print, a two- or three-column layout maximizes use of space and enhances 'readability'. Columns are good for managing the sell/inform balance – selling is often best restricted to a narrow column, with the main column providing content to inform. Cross-selling can still result.

5. *Dividers*. Section headers are used in both text and HTML e-newsletters to separate the articles. Blocks of text can also be reversed out for this effect.

Figure 5.14 An effective B2B E-newsletter template

Decision 9 – naming

There are many newsletters called Newsletter, eNews or eAlerts, so think about using a name that stands out. The name should summarize the proposition and be a clear differentiator – *What's New in Marketing*, *AvantMarketer* and *Flesh and Bones* (for medical students' textbooks) are good examples. However, if the newsletter is branded to be consistent with the organization distributing it, this is fine, since the organization name will prefix the newsletter.

Decision 10 – branding

E-newsletters traditionally mirror all aspects of an organization's branding in terms of brand name and brand image. The tone of voice and style should also be consistent.

In some cases, a brand-variant approach can be used which appeals to the reader at a different level – a different personality that is more in keeping with the informal nature of Internet e-mail. Brand imagery is still used to make the connection between brand and e-newsletter.

Decision 11 – personalization and tailoring

One of the key decisions when revising an e-newsletter is to look at the choice of e-newsletters that you offer. Whether you offer one or several, options for different e-newsletters should be revisited to assess whether the benefits of producing them are offset by the resources required to produce them.

If you only offer one e-newsletter, ask whether a 'one size fits all' e-newsletter is really delivering what the organization and its subscribers are looking for. Take the example of IBM, it offers a general IBM Weekly Update e-mail (https://isource.ibm.com/world/example_weekly.shtml) for the US market, which is tailored according to profile, and it also recognizes that other audiences require different e-newsletters.

Each company has a range of potential audiences, as listed below. IBM has taken the strategic decision to use e-mail for its business and consumer audiences as indicated:

- Customers (IBM uses iSource and customers are encouraged to update their profiles as their interests change – this consolidates from a previous situation of many separate e-newsletters to give a more consistent message and fewer communications)

- Potential customers (also use iSource)

- Different customer segments (iSource)

- Different members of buying unit (a quarterly magazine is offered for more senior managers, with separate newsletters for managers and users)

- Different products and markets (iSource)

- Resellers (IBM Partnerworld at http://www-1.ibm.com/partnerworld/pwhome.nsf/weblook/nws_ltr.html) has rationalized its communications to three targeted newsletters – a hardware edition, a software edition and a developer edition. It also offers 'a quarterly e-magazine, Business Partner Directions, which complements the e-mail newsletters by providing clear, consistent, and actionable information to help you align your strategic positioning with key marketplace opportunities'.

- Announcements (e.g. https://isource.ibm.com/world/example_announce.shtml)

- Other audiences, such as media or potential employees.

One way to assess the need for different e-newsletters is to analyse clickthroughs to different types of content according to different types of subscribers. Alternatively, you can use the profiling information to assess the balance between different audiences – for example, customers who have adopted different products or services, prospects, media and employees. A simple opt-in form can be used to acquire this information.

Of course, few organizations are likely to have the diverse customer base of IBM, coupled with its turnover and resources. Often a compromise will be to offer different newsletters in one or two of the areas listed above. For example, Tektronix (www.tektronix.com), which offers technology solutions for test, measurement and monitoring, has decided to offer newsletters for three geographies (Americas, EMEA and Asia-Pacific) and four product lines.

If you offer a range of e-newsletters and find that they are a drain on resources which isn't recompensed by the benefits, then you may want to rationalize them by reducing the alternatives and/or reducing their frequency.

Decision 12 – frequency

Think of the frequency of most e-newsletters you receive. They tend to be daily, weekly or monthly. Why is this? Perhaps we are still in the print mentality of dailies, weeklies and monthlies?

With so many e-newsletters out there, it may be of benefit to both subscribers and publisher if the frequency is less. Subscribers may be more inclined to opt-in into a communication that is bi-monthly, quarterly or even less often, since it will take less of their time and is more likely to contain important announcements. For publishers, fewer resources will be required for each e-newsletter – a significant saving, since each newsletter will take at least one person-day to produce and, if it has multiple contributors, substantially more. You also won't have to search so hard for 'newsworthy' topics each week or month; instead, major announcements and news can form the basis of the newsletter.

We don't have to limit ourselves to fixed frequencies. Where different e-mail newsletter options are offered for different audiences or different needs, then the frequencies can, of course, vary.

Decision 13 – timing

Closely related to frequency is timing, by which I mean the time of the day, week or month.

In many cases, a regular, consistent timing for e-newsletters is something to strive for, so your brand can become part of the recipients' routine. How many organizations actually achieve this regularity? More often it is Tuesday one month, Thursday the next, etc.

At the moment I receive the DM Newsletter (www.dmnews.com) and E-consultancy briefing (www.e-consultancy.com) every Tuesday, 'without fail'. Not many e-newsletters arrive on that day, so I expect these and often have time to check them out. I even look forward to them! Perhaps your taste is a satirical e-newsletter, such as Popbitch (www.popbitch.com), which arrives on a Friday when people are winding down for the weekend. Conversely, the Peppers and Rogers One to One newsletter (www.1to1.com) arrives on a Saturday, when I am, ideally, not in the office, so it rarely gets opened.

We also tend to notice e-newsletters that arrive on the first day of the month, but perhaps this approach is too common.

As for time during the day, the main factor is to deliver the e-mail when the audiences are most likely to be using their PC or PDA. This tends to increase response rates. For businesses this means during office hours, and for consumers it means during the evening or at weekends.

Decision 14 – themes

It is still common to see unthemed newsletters. These are easy to spot because they have the same subject line each and every time and, when opened, a list of news items with equal weighting. These are a lot less likely to get opened or 'clicked'.

Themed e-newsletters place an emphasis on content that delivers a greater response. The subject line can stress the theme, and this will give a higher open rate for hot topics or great offers. The themed content is then given precedence. For example, the theme for one of my newsletters was data protection, and this was flagged in the subject line and given prime position. Future themes can also be flagged up to raise expectation for future content.

Decision 15 – marketing communications integration

There is a tendency to plan our e-mail newsletters with blinkers on. If this happens, we lose opportunities to leverage the strengths of different media for different purposes. Here are some ideas on how to avoid this:

- Use the e-newsletter to preview future offers and product developments before other media. Highlight unique web offers – this will be an incentive for audiences to open the e-newsletter.

- Use the e-newsletter to reinvigorate recent or current campaigns or promotions that were first highlighted in other media.

- Use the e-newsletter to give more detail than the offline newsletter or house magazine provides – refer visitors to the online version and reduce the size and cost of the offline communication. Alternatively, put the whole magazine online, as with http://www.easyjetinflight.com.

- Rather than referring the media or other audiences to press releases or a media centre, refer them first to an e-newsletter item. This will give them a more complete picture of what the company stands for, and your current news.

Decision 16 – e-mail integration

Alongside the e-mail newsletter, there will be many other e-mail communications from an organization. This leads to decisions about what is the best way to break major news such as a product launch or upgrade.

I have seen newsletters where a major initiative such as a product launch or an event invitation becomes lost in all the other news items. Many newsletter templates could be improved by avoiding the newsletter being a list of items with similar weightings. This danger can be reduced through themed subject lines, or an e-mail newsletter design that gives precedence to certain items and is not too long. However, the danger of diluting the message still occurs. In the case of the product launch, it is best to use a separate e-mail to give this message. The opt-in form should give this option, so that the e-mail received is in keeping with the subscriber's expectations.

Decision 17 – web-site integration

One of the benefits of e-newsletters, compared with their paper-based equivalents, is the ability to deliver a large amount of valuable information at a low cost. Of course, this is a double-edged sword. Too much information will make the e-newsletter unwieldy, and your message will not get across or the recipients will not be able to locate the information relevant to them. So when you want to convey a lot of information, as is the case with many newsletters, you have to decide on the split of content between the e-mail newsletter and the web site, where more detailed content may be hosted.

Figure 5.15 shows five options for selecting the correct balance between content in the e-mail and on the web site. To simplify the example, let's say this newsletter contains just three different content areas, or three different articles. The options are:

1. *Minimal content in e-mail, full content on web site in multiple pages.* Here, the e-newsletter contains the links and a very short summary of the article, linking through to the full article on the web site. This has the benefit that the newsletter can be scanned very rapidly by the recipient for articles of interest. However, there is no indication of the quality or relevance of the content, which is possible with approaches (3) to (5). It also less easy for the other articles to be read than in the next option, (2).

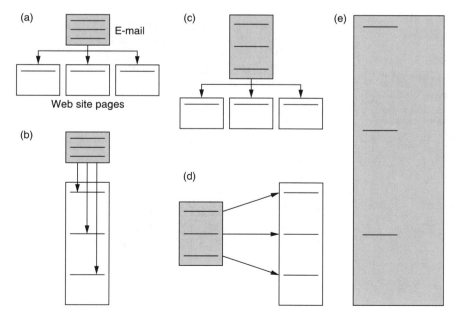

Figure 5.15 Options for split between content in e-mail (shaded) and on web site (white)

2. *Minimal content in e-mail, full content on web site in a single page.* As in the previous case, the e-mail has limited information, but on clicking through to the web site a single page newsletter is presented that contains all the articles. This has the benefit that the interested reader can rapidly find the information in all articles. This approach is used by e-Consultancy (www.e-consultancy.com), although it will not work so well for very long articles such as those in Figure 5.16.

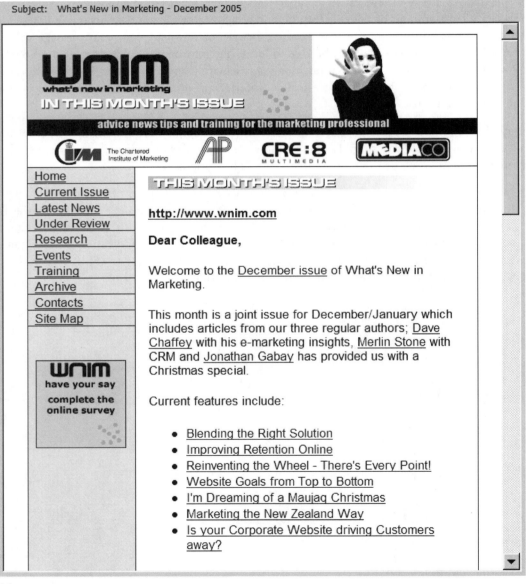

(a)

Figure 5.16   *What's New in Marketing* (www.wnim.com) (a) e-mail content

3. *Some content in e-mail, full content on web site (multiple pages).* This is similar to approach (1), but here the e-mail newsletter is longer since it contains a short extract from each article. Typically a <u>more ≫</u> option link will be available to take the user through to the web site. This makes it easier for the reader to decide whether the content is relevant to them. This is a common approach; Figure 5.14 is an example.

4. *Some content in e-mail, full content on web site (single pages).* This is similar to option (2), but again has the advantage that an idea of the relevance of the content is given in the e-mail, and also it is easier to find other content from the same newsletter on the web site.

5. *All content in e-mail.* This approach is being used by Freepint (www.freepint.com) at the time of writing. A lot of detailed content about web searching is provided in two detailed text e-mails, sent each month. Here, a clickthrough is not required to the site at all

![What's New in Marketing website screenshot showing the wnim masthead, site navigation, this month's issue content, and a subscription form]

(b)

Figure 5.16 (b) *What's New in Marketing* website

(although some longer articles may require this). It is typically used by professional or technical plain-text newsletters. This approach is arguably the best method of communicating information to the recipient. However, for the marketer, calls-to-action encouraging further participation are more difficult to achieve from the newsletter than from the web site.

This decision is difficult, since the preference on length varies according to the individual. For many, including this author, part of the power of e-mail newsletters is to be able to get a rapid briefing on developments about a particular topic. If you have to clickthrough to a web site and then understand the structure of the web site, as is the case with the *What's New in Marketing* web site (www.wnim.com), this slows down the experience.

A related question is, should we archive? For a B2B newsletter, the question is perhaps not should we archive, but how? Archiving a B2B newsletter, provided it has quality content, provides an excellent resource for your customers. They will return to the resource as they face particular issues. As mentioned above, this can also assist in generating new subscribers, since specialist articles indexed by search engines will gain new visitors who may look to tap into your expertise. For a B2C newsletter, the issue is not that clear cut. If the e-newsletter is providing news or interesting content, then similar arguments apply – it is a resource that will encourage repeat visits and can also, via search engines, act as an acquisitions tool. For B2C newsletters from an e-tail site it is inappropriate to archive the content, since product information and offers will quickly date.

When an archive is content-rich, which is typically the case with a media or news site, the utility for the user can be improved by developing 'related article' features. ClickZ (www.clickz.com) has a good related-articles feature. This lists items related to the current article according to which category they fall into, or according to similarity in key words in title or body.

Decision 18 – how do we gain subscribers?

There are two aspects to gaining subscribers: first, there are various sources where e-mail addresses can be collected; secondly, there is selling the benefits of the newsletter so that potential subscribers are happy to give up their e-mail address. You may want to refer back to Chapter 4, where approaches to gain customer e-mail addresses were covered in more detail. This explains maximizing our use of online and offline touchpoints with our audiences to explain the proposition, and offer the opportunity to opt-in without building too many barriers.

On the web site, we need to ask these three questions to maximize sign-up:

1. *Is our opt-in given enough prominence*? Is it on the home page? Is it 'above the fold'? Is there enough screen real-estate devoted to it? Is our archive and proposition indexed by search engines? Is it prominent throughout the site?

2. *Is our proposition clear*? Does the messaging say more than 'opt-in to our e-newsletter'? Does the sign-up page highlight the benefits? Are the benefits for different audiences clearly described? Is the quality of content demonstrated through an archive or example newsletter?

3. *Can we overcome barriers to subscription*? Reassure potential subscribers that you will not be overloading them with e-mail. Show how the newsletter will be relevant and targeted. Reassure them that details will not be passed on to third parties by using those six magic words: 'we will not share your information'.

For a great example from IBM of how to explain the proposition, see https://isource.ibm.com/world.

Finally, remember to try to capture the primary e-mail address. The *Doubleclick Sixth Annual Consumer E-mail Survey* (Doubleclick, 2005) showed that almost half of all consumers reported maintaining at least three e-mail accounts, an increase from 2004. Nearly 95 per cent considered one of their e-mail addresses to be a 'primary' account, while 72 per cent used a single address specifically for making purchases. This shows the importance of gaining the primary e-mail address for opt-in, particularly of an e-newsletter. To help with this, make sure you explain the proposition in detail and give examples of previous e-newsletters. If the frequency is relatively low, this may also help with obtaining the primary e-mail address.

Decision 19 – tracking and assessing satisfaction

Once we have implemented all the decisions we have reviewed above, how do we decide how well our e-newsletter is working?

If you are relaunching, you will be able to baseline against the previous incarnation of your e-newsletter.

As well as looking at opens and clicks for individual e-newsletters, as explained in Decision 2, it is also worthwhile considering what the overall levels of open rates and click rates are over a longer period – such as a quarter or a year. The e-newsletter will not be doing its job if the majority of recipients aren't interacting with it, so it may be necessary to use offline communications as a supplement for those not involved with it.

You will probably have been tracking the following in each time period, whether a month or a quarter:

- new subscribers – number of opt-ins in the period
- unsubscribes – number of opt-outs in the period
- bounces – hard bounces where the address is invalid should be removed from the list, with a process setup for contacting the subscriber if he or she is a high-value customer
- subscriber change – this is calculated by subtracting the unsubscribes and the bounces from the new subscribers in the time period
- percentage open rate – for an HTML e-mail we can tell the proportion of recipients who open the e-mail through the number of images downloaded from opened e-mails
- percentage total click rate – we can calculate the total number of clickthroughs from each newsletter through to the microsite or your website

- percentage unique click rate – it is useful to know the unique number of individuals who click through, as this gives us a better estimate of our total active audience size; each person may potentially click on several links, but the unique click through rate just records each person who has clicked

- percentage individual content click rate – tracking clickthroughs of individual content links, such as news, articles and offers, shows the most powerful content; it may also be useful to group total clicks from related content, such as news, ads and offers

- percentage outcomes – depending on the type of e-mail, conversion to particular actions such as sales or subscriptions, or clickthrough to offers, can be monitored

- percentage referrals – perhaps using 'recommend a friend' forms.

While many e-mail broadcast tools will track these variables, it is essential to view how they vary through time as a time-series graph.

What in particular should you watch out for on the time-series? I would say the trends of the key measures, such as open rate, unique click rate and outcomes.

The open rate tells you how effective the subject line is in encouraging opening. If this is low one month relative to other months, there may be a problem with how the e-newsletter is themed, or with the offer or timing.

The unique click rate gives you an overall idea of the value of the content of the newsletter – how many subscribers are actively clicking through.

Outcomes will vary for different types of e-newsletters, but you will want to achieve consistently high numbers of outcomes.

Unsubscribes should be tracked, but are not a reliable indicator of interest. The Quris (2003) survey of US e-mail subscribers showed that 92 per cent of consumers said that they 'just delete e-mails myself by hand without reading them' when they get e-mails that don't interest them. Open rate and unique click rate therefore provide a more reliable method of tracking interest in your e-newsletter.

Assessing response by audience characteristics

It is also useful to assess open and click rates by audience characteristics. That way you may find that, for example, the e-newsletter (or some type of feature) works better for communicating with, for example, the older or younger audience, or a particular type of decision-maker.

Decision 20 – listening

While the clickthrough and web-site outcome data can be used to second guess how well an e-newsletter is working, and what customers think of the company, there is no substitute for asking the question 'what do you think?', either face to face or through a structured survey, with recruitment of respondents through the e-newsletter or via a separate e-mail.

Since e-newsletters can become a large element of how your brand is perceived, it is important to know what people really think. We can see that online brands such as Tesco.com and lastminute.com poll their audiences regularly to find this out. An indication of the health of an e-newsletter can be built up using a mixture of 'watching and asking'. The Tesco.com e-newsletter seems to be in good shape, judging by the 'watching and asking' metrics provided by Kanaiya Parekh, the commercial development manager at Tesco.com, who presented the following at the 2002 Marketing Week Conference on e-mail marketing:

- 80 per cent of customers rated it as excellent
- there was a 65 per cent open rate (against the industry average of <20 per cent)
- 50 per cent of customers read the entire e-mail
- 20 per cent of customers purchased due to e-mail
- an additional 37 per cent of customers were considering purchase
- 13 per cent of customers forwarded the e-newsletter to friends/family
- there was a 5–10 per cent average clickthrough rate
- there were less than 1 per cent unsubscribes.

CAMPAIGN CHECKLIST: TOP TEN E-NEWSLETTER DOS AND DON'TS

Do:

1. Start with the business objectives
2. Remember the diverse audiences, e.g. customers and non-customers
3. Get the sell/inform balance right
4. Work hard to research powerful customer-centric content
5. Send out multi-part MIME formats, or give a choice at opt-in
6. Use template layout to distinguish content for different audiences and different marketing offers
7. Give your newsletter a distinctive brand related to the core-brand
8. Offer choice of opt-in to different content and frequencies if your resources and technology permit it
9. Use a regular time for delivery – the same time of day and same time of week or month
10. Clearly define the proposition to encourage opt-in, and clarify the offer.

Don't:

1. Underestimate the resource implications of creating e-mail newsletters
2. Personalize for the sake of it – different content areas can appeal to different audiences at a lower cost

3. Use a frequency that is too high to justify the returns – quarterly may make more sense than monthly

4. Underestimate the effect of timing – don't broadcast the e-mail at midnight on Sunday

5. Forget to theme individual e-newsletters clearly to showcase the offer

6. Forget to prepare a long-term programme of themes or incentives through time

7. Forget to plan integration between other online and offline media

8. Forget to measure success using qualitative data such as views, clickthroughs and unsubscribes

9. Forget to research qualitative feedback on e-newsletter

10. Forget to use a closed-loop approach to continuously improve e-mail marketing.

CASE STUDY 5.3: E-MARKETING EXCELLENCE – *WHAT'S NEW IN MARKETING* NEWSLETTER (WWW.WNIM.COM)

The target audience for this newsletter is marketing professionals and students. When it was first launched in autumn 2001 it was e-mailed to Chartered Institute of Marketing members (www.cim.co.uk), plus a proactive list of marketing professionals and an AP list of subscribers to the *Marketing Managers' Yearbook* (around 15 000 in total).

The execution involved a first mailing to the full list. A reminder was e-mailed a fortnight later to those who had not subscribed. Subscription occurs on the site, as shown in Figure 5.16.

The newsletter was delivered via the web site; a brief e-mail giving each month's topics directed the audience to the site. Archives were recorded on the web site, and additional traffic was driven by search engine registration.

Each newsletter recipient was encouraged to forward it to three colleagues, by being entered into a prize draw run by Proactive Productions. The prize was a DVD player and 10 DVDs. A 'chatroom' component was also added.

The initial mailing gave 3000 subscribers initially, in October 2001, and the reminder mailing increased this total to 4704. By December, there were 6600 subscribers with only 33 unsubscribes. By mid-2002, subscribers had increased to 14 000.

Some learning points:

• The web site hosting the newsletter had Flash components, so could not be read by some recipients

- Explanation in the initial mailing that subscription on the web site was necessary was not sufficiently clear
- The web site was not registered with search engines initially; this would have prevented some subscribers accessing it who had heard by word of mouth
- Additional subscription details were too limited for follow-up. In December, three new profiling fields were added to the subscription form – Job title, Industry and location.

E-MAIL MARKETING EXCELLENCE

Usability specialist Jakob Nielsen, of www.useit.com, is best known for his work on the usability of web sites, but he has also conducted usability research on e-newsletters (Nielsen, 2004). This is my summary of some of his main findings:

1. *E-newsletters build relationships.* Users tend to have a more emotional reaction and connection to e-newsletters than to web sites. Newsletters should try to leverage this connection.

2. *Spam makes e-newsletters tough, but not impossible.* Consumers can distinguish between permission-based e-mail and spam. However, it was noted that rather than unsubscribing, users often use their spam filters as a shortcut.

3. *Volume of e-newsletters.* Because we receive a lot of e-mail, we don't tend to read a lot of text (see www.marketingvox.com for e-newsletters that gets the length of text just right). The most frequent complaint in the study was that some newsletters arrived too often.

4. *Length of e-newsletters.* The most frequent common advice from participants for newsletter creators was to 'keep it brief'.

5. *Scannability.* Newsletters should use headlines, section dividers and tinted panels to aid scanning. In the first study, 23 per cent of the newsletters were read thoroughly. In the second study, two years later, only 11 per cent of the newsletters were read thoroughly.

6. *Skimmability.* This is the main mode of approaching e-mail newsletters, with 57 per cent of the newsletters being skimmed. Less common options were that they were never read (22 per cent) or were saved for possible later reading (10 per cent).

7. *'Above the fold' is key.* As would be expected, this is the area that people looked at to assess whether it was worth spending more time on the newsletter. This is the place for your main messages and calls-to-action.

8. *Headlines and table of contents.* Sometimes users will skim the headlines to get an update or overview of what's going on in the field covered by the newsletter. The study quotes one participant, who said, 'I like to keep up to date in the industry, but rarely delve deeper than the cover page.' Other times,

users deliberately pick out those few elements that are most important to them and ignore the rest. As another user said, 'I review the contents by company and only read the companies of interest to me.'

9. *Layouts must support scannability and skimmability.* Two-column layouts with clearly separate content blocks and headlines can support this.

10. *Remember the reasons that e-newsletters deliver value.* The main requirements are that the e-newsletter is up-to-date and timely. The reasons given for reading were as follows:

    - informs regarding work-related news and/or my own company's or other companies' actions (mentioned by two-thirds of users)
    - reports prices/sales
    - informs about personal interests/hobbies
    - informs about events/deadlines/important dates.

11. *E-newsletters are convenient.* If newsletters have the benefits above, i.e. they help with life or work issues, then they are likely to be successful. One user said: 'Bottom line, I'd rather have it in an e-mail newsletter than in the regular mail. I can click Delete if I don't want it; I don't have to throw anything away; and it is usually easier to unsubscribe if you don't want to get it anymore.'

12. *The here and now.* Newsletters have to justify their space in the inbox. They need to stay relevant and address the recipients' specific needs of the moment.

13. *Recipients often delete rather than unsubscribing.* Because newsletters build relationships with readers and because it's so easy to ignore individual issues, newsletters do get some leeway if they are predictably relevant at certain times. During those periods where a newsletter isn't relevant to the user's immediate needs, the user might simply ignore it for a while instead of unsubscribing.

14. *Work hard at achieving sign-up.* Users will often avoid signing up for newsletters because they feel crushed by information overload. The newsletter publisher must convince users that the newsletter will be simple, useful and easy to deal with.

15. *Standardize publication frequency.* A predictable publication frequency that is best, except for alerts. A regular publication schedule can encourage sign-up and lets users know when to look for the newsletter, thus reducing the probability that it will be deleted because it is confused with spam.

16. *Subject lines.* Writing good subject lines is especially important, both to encourage users to open the newsletter and to distinguish the newsletter from spam. The report recommends including actual content from the issue in each subject line.

17. *Opt-in.* The initial report recommends using double opt-in to ensure that users expect to receive the e-newsletter. The second report moves back from this, noting that it can be confusing. This is not standard practice in Europe and can actually confuse, because it is rare. I do not advise this (except for opt-in to lists that will be used for rental). Be specific about features and benefits – don't just talk about 'valuable offers', but provide explicit information about what types of information and offers the mailing list will contain; how frequently it is published (people are more likely to subscribe if the frequency matches their needs – consider offering different publication frequencies to serve different market segments); and how to see a sample newsletter before subscribing – people are more likely to sign up if they know what they will get.

REFERENCES

Armstrong, A. and Hagel, J. (1996). The real value of online communities. *Harvard Business Review*, **May/Jun**, 134–141.

BBC (2005). Tesco in e-mail marketing assault. Online article, Friday 11 November.

Doubleclick (2005). *Doubleclick Sixth Annual Consumer E-mail Survey*. Doubleclick.

Hagel, J. (1997). *Net Gain: Expanding Markets through Virtual Communities*. Harvard Business School Press.

Humby, C. and Hunt, T. (2003). *Scoring Points. How Tesco is Winning Customer Loyalty*. Kogan Page.

JupiterResearch (2005). The ROI of e-mail relevance. Improving campaign results through targeting. JupiterResearch Report MOA05-VO1.

Marketing Sherpa (2005). *E-mail Marketing Metrics Guide* (ed. Stefan Tornquist). Marketing Sherpa.

Nielsen, J. (2004). E-mail newsletter, Usability Executive Summary (available at http://www.nngroup.com/reports/newsletters/summary.html).

Novo, J. (2003). *Drilling Down: Turning Customer Data into Profits with a Spreadsheet* (available at www.jimnovo.com).

Parker, R. (2000). *Relationship Marketing on the Web*. Adams Streetwise.

Quris (2003). *How Companies can Enter and Remain in the Customer Email Inner Circle*. Quris.

Reicheld, F. and Sasser, W. (1990). Zero defections: quality comes to services. *Harvard Business Review*, **Sep–Oct**, 105–111.

Reicheld, F. and Schefter, P. (2000). E-loyalty, your secret weapon. *Harvard Business Review*, **Jul–Aug**, 105–113.

Revolution (2005). E-mail Marketing Report, by Justin Pugsley. *Revolution*, **Sep**, 58–60.

Seybold, P. and Marshak, R. (2001). *The Customer Revolution*. Crown Business.

Smith, P. R. and Chaffey, D. (2005). *eMarketing eXcellence – At the Heart of eBusiness*, 2nd edn. Butterworth-Heinemann.

Wodtke, C. (2002). *Information Architecture: Blueprints for the Web*. New Riders.

WEB LINKS

Database Marketing Institute (www.dbmarketing.com) gives great practical guidelines on data modelling, analysis and targeting for RFM.

DaveChaffey.com (www.davechaffey.com/Total-E-mail-Marketing) provides updates on the latest targeting techniques.

Jim Novo (www.jimnovo.com) provides guidelines on approaches to online loyalty.

Chapter **6**

Crafting e-mail creative

CHAPTER AT A GLANCE

Overview

This is a practical chapter which illustrates best practice for developing e-mail creative, including all e-mail headers and the structure, style and tone of the message copy. We also review technology constraints on message delivery.

Chapter objectives

By the end of this chapter you will be able to:

- evaluate the effectiveness of e-mail headers (from, to, subject line and date)
- assess and specify designs for e-mail structure and content
- discuss specific design issues for e-newsletters.

Chapter structure

- Introduction
- Understanding consumers' e-mail behaviour
- E-mail usage constraints
- E-mail creative structure
- E-mail headers
- Banner and headline
- E-mail creative formatting
- E-newsletter design
- Copywriting for e-mail
- Landing pages
- Testing creative
- How not to do it!
- References
- Web links

INTRODUCTION

Producing e-mail creative presents a new challenge for direct marketers – but many of the challenges are in fact not new. The limited time to achieve an action is not new. The need for a powerful opening and an appealing offer are not new. Constraints of cost and space are not new. However, there are some major differences in the delivery platform that make significant differences, and here we are talking virtual and not physical. To make creative effective, we have to understand the behaviour of processing e-mail.

We start by trying to get inside the mind of e-mail recipients. How many e-mails do they have to cope with each day? How do they process e-mails? How have they set up their system – how well can they process HTML messages? We then look at the best way to structure an e-mail, from the header (i.e. the subject line and from field) through to the body (the headline, lead paragraph, main body and close). Finally we look at the best way to write copy for e-mail marketing.

UNDERSTANDING CONSUMERS' E-MAIL BEHAVIOUR

Let's start with the types of e-mail received. Figure 6.1 shows a compilation for the US market from Doubleclick (2005). It shows that, on average, a staggering 361 e-mails per week were received, of which 70 per cent were spam. There were relatively few permission-based e-mails, but these were competing with work e-mails and friends' and colleagues' e-mails. These were only averages, so for professional business people, many more e-mails will be received weekly. It's a wonder e-mail open and clickthrough rates are as high as they are!

We also need to consider the time taken to process all these different types of e-mail. Grant Thornton (2005) showed the challenge of using e-mail to communicate with business owners. Overall, the average amount of time spent accessing and responding to e-mails in the UK is 1 hour and 12 minutes, compared to 1 hour and 30 minutes globally. However, these are averages, with 14 per cent of business owners spending 3–5 hours a day accessing and responding to e-mail, and 2 per cent using e-mail for more than 5 hours a day!

With this volume of e-mail, I think we are becoming more structured in how we approach it. Our options are essentially to:

- delete it
- read it to inform or entertain

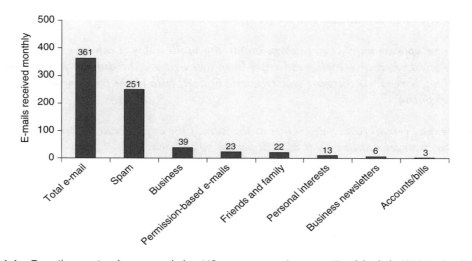

Figure 6.1 E-mails received per week by US consumers (source: Doubleclick (2005) *Sixth Annual Consumer E-mail Survey,* www.doubleclick.com)

- act on it, to find out more or buy

- archive it.

In a business context, you may prefer the '4 Ds' model of efficient e-mail processing (McGhee, 2005), which recommends that we should, in order:

1. Delete it! (or ignore it, mark it as 'read')

2. Do it! (if it takes less than two minutes)

3. Delegate it! (if you can't delete it or do it in two minutes)

4. Defer it! (if you can't delete it, do it or delegate it).

Using this approach, McGhee recommends that we spend just an hour a day processing e-mails, and in this time it should be possible to process 50–100 messages. The implication for the e-mail marketer is that with the increasing volume of e-mail, we will spend less and less time with each mail. Note that the first thing we do in either case above is delete it!

Different e-mail processing behaviour is evident from these posts to the BBC web site. Think about how your e-mail design could be changed to accommodate these, or maybe whether you could process your e-mail more efficiently. Here are some e-mail management habits, characteristic of processing e-mail at work:

> *I work on many projects at once. Each e-mail that is project-related has the project code in the header. I have a folder for each job number that I'm working on, as well as folders for general admin, personal, humour etc. When I'm very busy, e-mails just get dragged unread to the appropriate folder. Then at some point during the day I will make time to read all e-mails related to each subject.*

> *I basically scan through the sender and subject information, if I don't recognise either then I delete it without thinking. I just don't have the time to read all the spam offering me low rate mortgages or Viagra online!*

> *I receive approximately two to three hundred e-mails a day. I cannot expect to read every one I receive, so I will read what I can when I have the time to do so, the rest I will never read. Any urgent matter should be dealt with in the traditional method – the telephone!*

> *I only read e-mail twice a day. Once at the start of the day, once at the end. Anything else more urgent can be dealt with in person or by phone.*

It can be seen that there are different types of behaviour:

- 'Categorizers' will put items in folders to be dealt with later

- 'Deleters' ruthlessly delete e-mail if the subject line suggests no relevance to their work

- 'Scanners' skim most e-mails for relevance

- 'Readers' carefully read most e-mails, since they don't want to miss out on some information.

Clearly, the behaviours will vary according to the volume of e-mail received, how busy recipients are, and the type of e-mail – i.e. their interest in it.

In this chapter we will look at how to develop e-mail creative that maximizes the likelihood for action. We will focus on promotional e-mails to achieve action. Most of the observations tend to apply specifically to promotional campaigns rather than e-newsletters, which have their own structure and copy.

Recipients may well delete many messages after evaluating them for just seconds, so competition for the recipients' time is fiercer and we have limited means at our disposal to get our message across. What can we offer that will avoid our e-mail being ruthlessly deleted? Consider Figure 6.2; it shows we have less than 30 characters in the subject line to attract interest and so stop our message being deleted. Perhaps the reader will get no further than the first word of the subject line, or than the From address, which they will see first as they scan from left to right.

Of course, today, the majority of e-mail readers prefer to use a preview pane to view e-mails. Figure 6.3 shows this arrangement. Here, the recipient will make a decision according to the combination of text plus graphics if it is a HTML e-mail, so we have more scope to achieve a favourable outcome.

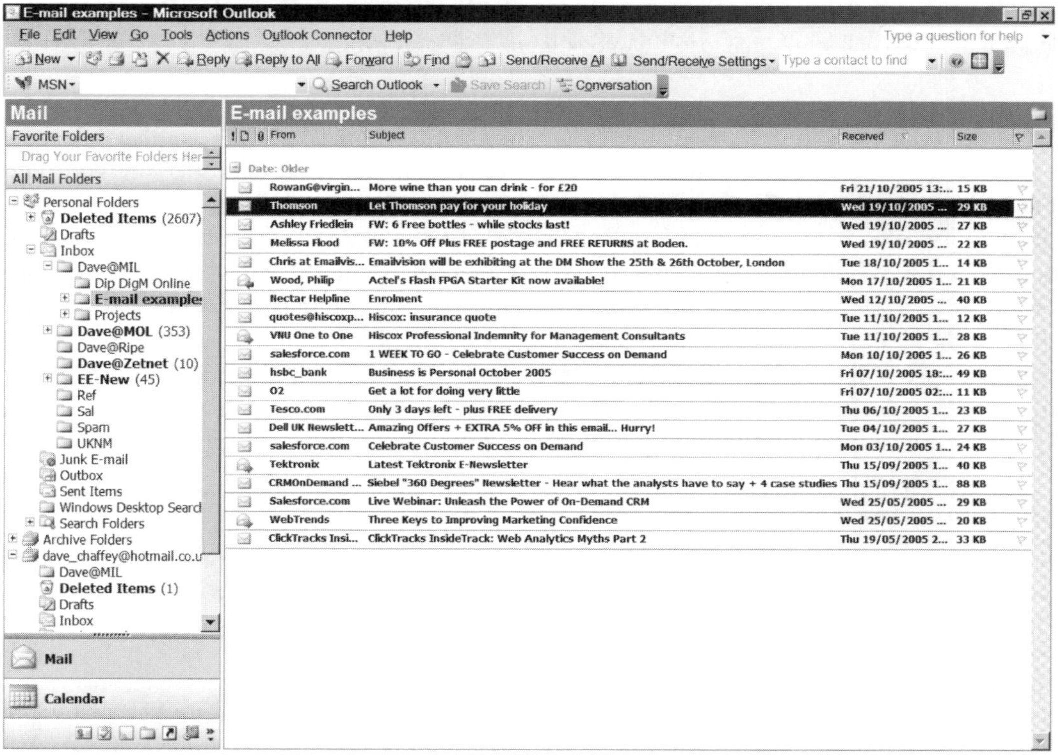

Figure 6.2 The challenge – Microsoft Outlook Inbox *without* preview pane

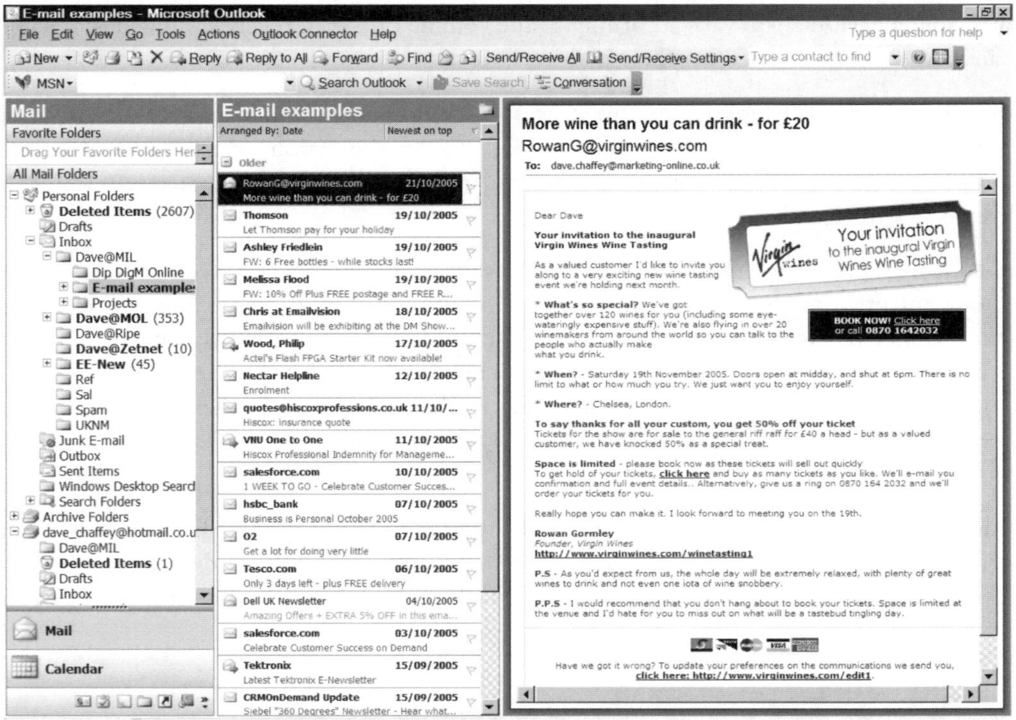

Figure 6.3 The challenge – Microsoft Outlook Inbox *with* preview pane

E-MAIL USAGE CONSTRAINTS

Before we go on to look at best practice for creative and copy, let's look at the constraints under which we operate. There are two main issues we need to bear in mind when designing e-mails. First, there are the technology constraints. To the majority these are boring technical issues, but we shouldn't unleash our creative talents if we don't know what the limits of the technology are. These are imposed by recipients using a range of e-mail readers and selecting different options for their configurations. Also, the location of access may differ – download speeds and display platforms vary depending on whether at home, at work, or even on a handheld device, phone or on digital TV. Secondly, there are the behavioural constraints. We have to consider the different ways in which e-mail users process and evaluate their e-mails.

Technology restraints

Many of the technology constraints that affect the way an e-mail is displayed are most relevant when HTML e-mails are being used. However, some also apply to text e-mails, so we will highlight this where it applies.

A general constraint on both HTML and e-mail is the resolution of the screen. This may be selected by the users, or they may be using default factory settings. It is common for designers to use high resolutions of at least 1280×1024 pixels (dots). However, the data below show that most consumers are currently using lower resolutions.

In June 2005, according to data collected from the web users monitored by the OneStat.com web analytics software, the most popular screen resolutions were:

1. 1024×768 (57.38%)
2. 800×600 (18.23%)
3. 1280×1024 (14.18%)
4. 1152×864 (4.95%)
5. 1600×1200 (1.67%)
6. 1280×800 (1.56%)
7. 1600×1024 (0.55%)

It follows that as the majority of web users are today using 1024×768 rather than 800×600 resolution, you should design and test e-mail creative for e-mail readers at this resolution. However, an e-mail that looks good at this resolution may not all fit within the message pane of the e-mail reader. It is extremely annoying to have to scroll right to read a message when it is in a preview pane such as Figure 6.3. It follows that for HTML e-mail it is still advised that a width of less than 500 pixels be used (this is often enforced through the designer using a header graphic or table of this dimension).

The HTML versus text format decision

It might be thought that deciding between whether to broadcast HTML e-mail or text formats in an e-mail campaign is straightforward. After all, as marketers, we believe that the visual design, imagery and branding associated with an HTML e-mail is likely to engage with our audience better than simple plain text. Indeed, tests performed by Doubleclick (2002) suggested that HTML e-mails give response rates that are, on average 1.4–1.7 times higher than those for text. When I wrote the first edition of this book, the merits of each approach were debated; however, today there is really no decision to be made – the default for all permission-based e-mails is HTML. We do need to offer choice, though, and remember that text is more convenient for some readers. Occasional broadcast of a text e-mail or an HTML message that is mainly text can have more impact because it looks like a service e-mail or it just looks different.

What about e-mail readers that cannot readily display HTML e-mail – for example, those on a palmtop such as a PDA or a Blackberry? Also, many business users have systems that default to text only so users do not waste time formatting or reading their messages. The technology can helps us here, since we can broadcast all e-mails as a *Multipurpose Internet Mail Extensions* (MIME) format. MIME is a standard method of formatting an e-mail with an HTML and a text component, such that when received, the e-mail client software automatically detects whether it can display the HTML version. If it can't, then the text form is displayed. Another approach used by some broadcasters to detect images, sometimes called using a 'sniffer', is to degrade the message from HTML to text if it appears that the reader can't display images. Although this sounds impressive, the variation in technology means that this approach may not be accurate.

To help distinguish between HTML and text responses, some e-mail service providers, such as Email Reaction (www.emailreaction.com), code HTML and text versions of messages with different tracking codes. This gives a true indication of how many actually receive HTML and text versions. They also calculate 'smart open rates', which take into account opens that are not recorded for messages displayed as text. These tend to be slightly higher.

E-MAIL MARKETING INSIGHT

Always ensure e-mails are broadcast as MIME formats containing both HTML and text, unless the user has specified text only. Give an option to 'View this e-mail in a browser' for those who prefer or can't see the message.

However, the MIME process doesn't work in all cases; some reader platforms think they can display HTML but perhaps they do not support the coding standards used, and the message then appears as gobbledygook. Some users prefer text, particularly for business-to-business e-newsletters, which they can digest more rapidly. Additionally, many e-mail readers now have image-blocking software that can affect the way the e-mail is rendered, and text produces a cleaner-looking result. So some e-mail broadcasters will offer this as a preference – I have seen up to 50 per cent opt for the text version, but 5–20 per cent is more typical.

E-MAIL MARKETING INSIGHT

Consider asking customers for their HTML or text format preferences when they first register.

Because of the way e-mail readers may be set up, with images blocked, the creative must be tested for the three situations shown in Figure 6.4. In this case, the message and call-to-action are clear in all three formats.

Design for different e-mail reader set-up

The main issues to consider here are the preview pane and image-blocking. Many in a corporate session using readers such as Outlook utilize a preview pane. An Email Labs (2005) survey found that 90 per cent of business users have access to a preview pane, and 69 per cent say they frequently or always use it. The preview pane can be set up differently, with 75 per cent preferring the horizontal format and 25 per cent the vertical format. The survey results also indicate that it is critical that marketers design e-mails which will maximize the preview pane's limited real estate. If insufficient information is displayed in the preview pane – due to blocked images, advertisements or poor design – nearly 19 per cent of respondents will simply delete the message.

Images are now blocked in many e-mail readers, since spammers have used the evidence of images downloaded from servers when a recipient opens an e-mail as proof that this is a live address. This feature was introduced in Microsoft Office 2003, and as more people adopt the

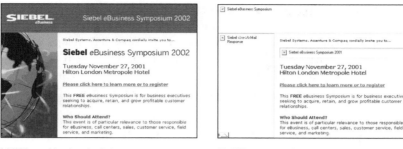

(a) With graphics downloaded

(b) Offline – no graphics

```
Siebel Systems, the world's leading provider of eBusiness applications software, presents:
Partner Relationship Management:
Maximising Revenue Through Channel Partners and Agents

http://www.siebel.com/register.htm

Thursday, March 14, 2002
2:00 p.m.—3:00 p.m. GMT
```

(c) Text – if reader can't read HTML and MIME encoded

Figure 6.4 Three different views of the same e-mail: (a) HTML with graphics downloaded; (b) HTML without graphics downloaded; and (c) Text (reproduced courtesy of Siebel, www.siebel.com)

newer version, image-blocking has increased. Since images are also used to calculate open rates, these have fallen in the last few years – although clickthrough rates haven't really experienced an equivalent decline.

The Email Labs (2005) survey found that nearly 53 per cent of respondents' e-mail clients or ISPs automatically block images in some or all e-mail messages, and 45 per cent of e-mail readers rarely or never download images within their preview pane. Furthermore, 50 per cent of subscribers rarely or never place an e-mail address on their e-mail client's safe sender list.

When designing e-mails and testing creative effectiveness, it is therefore important to assess:

- how the e-mail appears in horizontal and vertical preview panes at the most common screen resolutions
- how effective the e-mail creative is without images downloaded.

Image-blocking is more significant than the e-mail's appearance in preview panes. I see many e-mails which have no text content because text is built from blocks of images; these look great with images downloaded, but are meaningless without!

Embedded images

One approach to reducing the problem of blocked images is to use embedded images. These images are sent with the e-mail (effectively as attachments, although this is not suggested by most e-mail readers because they are referenced from within the e-mail they are associated with). This has the benefit that they are not blocked by the reader.

However, think carefully about embedding images, since this increases the size of the message – and some ISPs or firewalls may block or quarantine e-mails that have a large file size or several attachments (which is effectively the way that embedded images are implemented). However, these images do have the benefit that there is not a problem with image-blocking. Remember also that some web-mail companies, such as Hotmail, do not display embedded images, so it is necessary to send these using traditional linked images.

It is best to test these alternative approaches. Projects that have used embedded images have often outperformed linked images, but this will vary from case to case, so the message is – test!

HTML coding for different e-mail reader platforms

There is a variety of e-mail readers in which the e-mail may be displayed, so we need to check that the e-mail template designers have designed the HTML such that it is rendered as intended in as many of these as possible. We have to consider both web-based e-mail readers and e-mail reader applications.

Of the web-based e-mail readers, the ones that must be tested for are MSN/Hotmail, Yahoo!Mail, AOL and GoogleMail/Gmail. The relative popularity of these varies quite markedly, but in 2005 the Nielsen//NetRatings panel (www.netratings.com) reported that their status was as shown in Table 6.1.

Of the other e-mails readers, the most recent versions of the following should be tested for:

- Microsoft Outlook

- Microsoft Outlook Express

- Lotus Notes (common in corporate settings)

- Novell Groupwise (common in corporate settings)

- Shareware/open source readers, such as Eudora or those in Mozilla Firefox.

Table 6.1 Relative popularity of different web-based e-mail readers

Web e-mail service	Unique audience ('000)	Web pages per person	Time per person (hh:mm:ss)
All e-mail	13 463	124	1:13:28
MSN Hotmail	7 280	102	0:42:19
Yahoo! Mail	4 189	110	1:01:15
AOL e-mail	3 447	21	1:36:52
Tiscali Mail	779	139	1:02:18
Google Gmail	487	49	0:39:12

Source: Nielsen//NetRatings, NetView UK, May 2005, home and work.

Lyris EmailAdvisor (http://www.lyris.com/products/emailadvisor) includes a service for testing the appearance of e-mails in over 30 different e-mail reader versions.

At an HTML coding level, it is important to remember that HTML design for e-mail is not the same as designing for a web page. You will typically get better results if your template designer is experienced in designing e-mails for HTML. The following guidelines are based on the recommendations of Email Center, a UK-based ESP (http://www.emailcenteruk.com):

1. *Avoid scripts and dynamic HTML.* Many of the main e-mail clients cannot process scripting languages such as JavaScript. Indeed, many ISPs or corporate firewalls seek out JavaScript in an e-mail and strip it out, as they view it as a security threat. These may also give a problem: ActiveX, Audio, External Style Sheets, Frames and IFrames, Java, Meta Refresh, VBScript, Perl, etc.

2. *Code images carefully.* Images should always be referenced by providing the full absolute image location, i.e.

    <IMG SRC=http://www.yourwebsite.com/images/logo.gif alt="Company name">

    Alternative text is useful to show the context of the image for when images are blocked or not downloaded.

3. *Take care with the width of the e-mail.* Since many users have a preview or reading pane as shown in Figure 6.3, you need to make sure the majority of your e-mail appears within this pane and the user doesn't have to scroll right at the most common resolutions. I recommend a maximum width of 550 pixels to avoid this. This is usually implemented using a table or an image with this width specified.

    Another aspect of width refers to the code itself. Errors can be generated with very long lines of e-mail code or, in text e-mails, very long URLs.

4. *Review Cascading Style Sheet (CSS) capabilities of e-mail readers.* Modern e-mail readers such as Outlook are much more sophisticated at processing CSS. CSS is used by web designers to provide a consistent look and feel to web pages and e-mails – for example, a heading can be defined as a specific font and standard point size. With e-mail the <HEAD> tags in a HTML document normally contain the cascading style sheets used to define the formatting of text and links. However, at one stage Hotmail ignored the contents of these tags and the e-mail lost all of its intended formatting. The simple solution is to move your CSS code to after the <HEAD> tags and between the two<BODY> tags of your HTML. This may lead to problems in other readers, though, so sometimes different versions are created for users with different web-mail addresses.

5. *Do not expect all e-mail forms to work.* It is becoming more popular to have surveys and product searches within e-mails, and rightly so. However, these need careful testing in different e-mail readers, and the option of giving a link to reply online should be considered.

E-MAIL MARKETING INSIGHT

Use the space at the start of the message to instruct recipients to add their e-mail to the address book or to read the e-mail in the web browser.

Figure 6.5 gives a good example of a company that thinks about how e-mails appear in the user's inbox.

Figure 6.5 Firebox e-mail showing relatively narrow width and instructions to read online (www.firebox.com)

E-MAIL CREATIVE STRUCTURE

When considering the best way to structure an e-mail, it's best to think about it from the recipients' point of view. As they review it in their inbox, they will be asking the same three questions as they do for any piece of direct communication:

1. Who is it from?

2. What's in it for me?

3. What do I have to do next?

In this section we look at how we can best structure the e-mail to answer those questions effectively. We start with the message header, looking at the best way to define the From and Subject line fields, and then look at the body of the e-mail, which typically contains the following elements – many of which are shared with direct mail pieces:

- Header area message body

- Salutation or greeting to recipient

- Lead or introduction

- Main copy

- Close, including call-to-action

- Signature

- Unsubscribe

- Privacy statement or link.

Before we do anything, though, we need to decide on our overall goals for the e-mail creative, and the underlying style and tone.

Setting goals for your creative

We have discussed general campaign goals earlier in the book, particularly in Chapters 2 and 3. We now need to set specific goals for the creative. I believe that the best way to approach design of an e-mail creative is to ask yourself, what do you want your recipients:

- first, to do (response)? Your required response is for the recipient to click, read, disclose or buy, depending on the objectives of the e-mail. You should build your e-mail around these response mechanisms, not add them as an afterthought – which often seems to be the case. To achieve response, crystal clear calls-to-action to encourage clickthrough are key. You should also consider how you will persuade readers to click or read more by demonstrating relevance to the recipient personally and by offering added value. Multiple calls-to-action, some image-based, some text-based, offering different types of value work best to achieve this.

- second, to think (rational)? Your recipients will make a rational, albeit often subconscious, WIFM (What's in it for me?) evaluation when they receive the e-mail. Your message has to show clearly the benefits – the value you are offering recipients. Think through what the primary value is, then the secondary value which may get the reader to read on or click. Also ask yourself, why will they believe me (proof and resolution) and why will they trust me (reassurance)?

- third, to feel (emotional)? Your e-mail will always have some form of emotional impact on the recipient, so consider how its visual design, imagery and tone of voice will make recipients feel about you, your services and the value you are offering them. Also consider how it will make them feel about themselves. Just because this is last, it doesn't mean it's unimportant.

E-mail style and tone

We need to define the overall tone and style of the e-mail, and this will affect each creative element. Farris and Langendorf (1999) noted that since a message is likely to be interpreted literally, you should generally keep it straight – that is, adopt a professional tone. E-mail is an informal medium, lying somewhere between informal phone or face-to-face conversations and formal written communications. However, it is still a written medium, and its informality is often reserved for well-known friends and colleagues. 'Instant familiarity', which involves adopting too casual a tone with someone you don't know, will therefore be inappropriate for many recipients. You have to earn informality. For some brands, though, such as Virgin, a friendly, casual, conversational tone is right for the brand and the medium. For B2B communications, a more direct, formal tone works best.

Developing the style and tone of e-mails can be assisted by the use of design personas (see Chapter 5), where we develop a thumbnail sketch of the characteristics, needs and wants of typical e-mail recipients. We explore the tone of e-mail further in the 'Copywriting for e-mail' section.

Let's now look at how to make each part of the e-mail work to achieve a more effective whole.

E-MAIL HEADERS

We begin our detailed exploration of best practice for e-mail design by looking at the information in the e-mail headers. The message header gives the basic properties or characteristics of the e-mail contained in different header fields. These header fields are displayed in the inbox and at the top of the message when opened.

The two most important header fields are the From address and the subject line, since these will determine whether the recipient decides to open the e-mail. We consider best practice for creating these below. Other fields include CC (Carbon Copy). This should always be blank for commercial e-mail campaigns. If you disclose the e-mail addresses of other recipients, you are breaking their trust. The final header information is the date and time the message was sent. The actual time and day of week the e-mail was sent can affect the open rate, as discussed in Chapter 3.

First impressions – the 'From' fields

Many concentrate on the subject line as determining open rates, but don't neglect 'From', which is often the first thing we look at when we evaluate e-mail relevance as our fingers hover over the delete button. Figure 6.2 shows that as the recipients scan through their inbox, reading from left to right, their eyes will alight on 'From' before the subject line. In these days of spam, the From line should reassure recipients that they know this person. If they don't, they may delete the message straight away.

For house lists, it is best practice to include the company name in the From address. The only exception is where you decide to send an e-mail from the CEO or an account manager, and if the list members are familiar with their name.

For rented lists the From address is typically the name of the list owner, since it is important to indicate that the recipient's name has been provided as part of an opt-in to a known company. For house lists there is slightly more flexibility on what can be used.

For the From address, there are two separate fields that are displayed. Here is an example:

- Display name, e.g. 'Dell UK Newsletter' or 'Tesco.com'
- E-mail address: uk_gem_reply@dell.com or online@tesco.co.uk

While using an appropriate display name is most important, there is also another aspect of From addresses to take into account. Many e-mail readers display the e-mail address itself in the inbox or at the top of the e-mail when displayed, so it helps to use a friendly e-mail address – judge for yourself which of those above is best. Of course you also need to monitor this account, since customers who hit 'Reply' and send a message to you will return e-mails to this address. Any e-mail address can be specified when setting up your campaign.

Changing the From address could be worthwhile for special campaigns to show that the e-mail isn't just 'more of the same'. Being creative can help your e-mail 'cut-through' in the inbox – i.e. stand out from all the others.

A final point on the From address is that this is the address that handles bounces and returns. It must be a valid e-mail address that can be accessed to view any queries, complaints or unsubscribe requests. There may be many replies from a large broadcast, so make sure that if you have used the CEOs e-mail, it is not their main account! However, make it look as though there could be a human at the other end of the line – directresponse@company.com does not do this.

Gaining attention – the subject line

The importance of the subject line is self-evident. Think about what you are trying to achieve. For many years those that have developed adverts and direct mail have used the AIDA framework as they try to achieve Attention, Interest, Desire and Action. Where do you think the e-mail subject line fits in here? Certainly you are trying to achieve Attention, since the e-mail is competing for attention with many other e-mails. Furthermore, you have to achieve Interest and Desire in order for the recipient to open the e-mail. The initial action is opening the e-mail, but through the subject line we are conditioning the recipient to take the ultimate Action of clicking on a link.

Although everyone knows the subject line is important, remember that *the first two or three words* of the subject line are the most significant as users scan through their inbox. Remember also that you have a limited number of characters to get your message across, particularly where the preview pane is used (see Figure 6.3). The subject line should be designed for 30 characters, or you should at least be aware that beyond this, characters can be deleted.

Table 6.2 shows some examples of subject lines, from Chittenden and Rettie (2003), of 30 rented list campaigns using Claritas data for rented e-mail lists. The top three achieved more than a 10 per cent clickthrough rate and the bottom three less than 1 per cent responders. You can see how the combination of offer and language works much better for the top three examples.

Table 6.2 Some examples of From addresses and subject lines

Product	Incentive	Subject line
Whisky	Holiday prize draw	Exclusive all-expenses paid weekend in Speyside
Market research	Amazon voucher	Free Amazon e-voucher for giving us your opinions
Fashion	Milan weekend prize draw	Win a £6000 holiday in Melbourne
Dental care	25% off offer	25% off at Boots Dentalcare
Utilities	Acquisition	In 10 minutes you could start saving £150 off your bills
Online shares	30 days' free commission	Are you interested in making more money?

Approaches to devising the subject line

The subject line can use a number of techniques to gain attention. Common techniques include:

1. *The teaser*. This is intended to intrigue – it says 'read me'. It is often combined with a question.

2. *The question*. The question will usually allude to the benefits. It will work on a need or problem the customer may be facing, such as financial or time-based.

3. *The event tie-in*. This relates to different type of events, which can be annual holidays or company-type events. The JD Edwards campaign in Chapter 3 is related to Valentine's Day, and although the service has no direct relationship to Valentine's Day, an indirect link has been found. 3M Health Care developed an acquisition campaign based on a product centenary.

4. *The direct approach*. Clearly state the offer or benefits, without trying to be intriguing or humorous.

5. *Personalization*. The name of the recipient can be incorporated into the start of the subject line, which is good for increasing attention since this approach it is not commonly used. This may be with good reason, since it can lead to false sincerity – 'Special offers for Dave Chaffey', for example. The subject line can also be personalized according to particular product interest if a customer has previously purchased a similar product.

In many cases a combination of techniques is used within any one subject line. Look at the examples selected from my inbox (Figure 6.3). In many cases a combination of techniques is used within any one subject line. Which technique(s) does each subject line use?

Don't forget the importance of subject lines – don't leave constructing them until just before the e-mail is broadcast. Think about them at the planning stage, early in the campaign, and refine them from there. One approach to refining e-mails is to think through synonyms for each word and evolve them as follows by brainstorming different alternatives:

1. Free break in Scotland

2. Free weekend in the Highlands

3. Exclusive weekend in the Highlands

4. Your exclusive weekend on Speyside

5. Exclusive all-expenses paid weekend in Speyside.

You can then pick the best combination. Here option (4) is arguably the best, since it is reasonably specific and intriguing without being as long as option (5).

What to avoid in the subject line

Finally, this is a checklist of what to avoid in the subject line:

- Make sure the subject line is not too long. If you leave the best to last, the offer may be truncated.

- SHOUTING!!! Shouting is using capitals. It looks unprofessional. Worse still, it is often associated with spam – and spam filters stop e-mails with too many capitals in the subject line. Exclamation marks are not a good idea for similar reasons!!! Some capitalization can work – for example, just on the first word or on the first letter of each word.

- All spam characteristics. These are many and various, but some are deeply worrying; some spam filters remove any message with 'FREE' in the subject line. Messages starting with 'RE:', suggesting a response to the e-mail, are used by spammers, but are not likely to be filtered since they could be valid e-mails. Other filters (described in more detail in Chapter 8) are perhaps less obvious. One bank that was offering preferential discounts to under-18s was filtered by spam filters looking for X-rated content.

BANNER AND HEADLINE

The start of the creative or e-mail body content is very important, particularly with the widespread use of preview panes. An Email Labs (2005) survey indicated that 49 per cent of e-mail readers only look at the first few lines in the preview pane to decide whether they want to continue reading the message.

The banner and headline can be combined, but are often best separated. The banner should not look too much like a banner, since when we are online we suffer from 'banner blindness'. Instead, it should be a bit like the masthead on a newspaper. I think this is a useful analogy, since the mastheads of newspapers have evolved from simply being a name and price to also featuring the top content – effective use is made of this area, and the same is required in an e-mail.

The masthead area should reinforce who the message is from, so include your brand ident prominently to help generate trust. The banner area for an e-newsletter can also incorporate

Figure 6.6 BBC Shop e-mail showing use of headline area (www.bbcshop.com)

site menu options, such as product categories or a search box, and an injunction to shop now, to capture those impulsive clicks.

At the same time, many e-mail marketers make the masthead area too wide and push down the initial call-to-action into the body of the e-mail. Figure 6.6 shows an example where good use is made of the headline area, although there isn't a specific headline adding to the subject line.

Avoiding technology problems

The top of the e-mail message is also often used, particularly by consumer brands, to counter problems with the technology. A short message in small-font text is placed above the banner (not part of the main creative), and this directs those who want it to a browser version of the e-mail personalized to the individual. Some prefer this, or they may be unable to see the original message. It also gives instructions about how to add the 'Safe Senders List' (see Chapter 8). Examples include:

> *If this e-mail is not displayed correctly, please click on the link below: http://view.ed4.net/v/IYMN ...*

> *To ensure that your Tesco e-mails get to your inbox, please add mailto:online@tesco.co.uk to your e-mail Address Book or Safe List. For instructions, click here.*

The headline

The headline or title is equivalent to the headline on a print ad or direct mail piece. Headlines are often used less often for e-mail – perhaps designers believe the subject line has this role. I believe a powerful headline is very important, adding to subject line and encouraging the recipient to click or read more.

The headline should not repeat the subject line, but build on it, explaining more about the offer or setting the scene or the mood of what is to follow. For example, a Vodafone e-mail used a heading to detail the offer:

> **_Get your e-mails on your phone anytime, anyplace anywhere._**

Heal's, the furnishing retailer, set the tone of a wine-based offer as:

> **_fine and mellow._**

Headlines often work best in a larger font or a different font-type to the body – testing has shown that large fonts perform best for most categories. However, a headline can be as simple as bold text, which will only take up the limited space. Sometimes the headline is built into a graphic, but care should be taken here because many recipients will simply scan for text – they filter out text contained in images, since they are conditioned to ignoring standard banners. Don't make the banner look too like a banner. Also, the banner image may be blocked by the e-mail reader, so I advise that an HTML text-based image be used.

It may be better to put the headline just before or just after the salutation, as shown in Figure 6.7. Note how this e-mail uses repetition of the subject line, but adds to it by using 'foolproof'.

We will look at alternative headlines in the section 'Copywriting for e-mail'.

Salutation

The initial greeting to the recipient is not the most important part of the e-mail in determining response rates, but it is one of the first things that will form an impression for the reader. It can set the tone of the e-mail as being formal or fun. Tests show that, generally, including the name improves response. An appropriate salutation will vary according to the individual's preference, but we can generalize that an older audience will prefer the more formal approach of Dear Mrs Smith (or Mr Smith). A younger audience may prefer Dear John (or Joan), but this can suggest false intimacy, which may annoy some. The preferred salutation can be prompted for when a prospect first registers for opt-in, but that is probably one question too many.

Lead/opening/first paragraph

As with any direct mail piece, the first paragraph of an e-mail must:

1. *Engage.* When reading this, perhaps in the auto-preview window, recipients are deciding whether to delete or read further. Therefore, as for any creative, the opening needs to be powerful.

Figure 6.7 Virgin Wines e-mail showing repetition of core message

2. *Add detail to the subject line or the headline.* Repetition is less important in e-mail than in direct mail, since it is processed so quickly. The recipient will remember the gist of the subject line, and it is always there at the head of the e-mail, so reinforcement is the main objective of the message here.

3. *Summarize the whole.* The opening of an e-mail is often compared to the opening of a press release, which typically uses an 'inverse pyramid' structure to summarize the main points of the message in decreasing order of importance, as briefly as possible.

4. *Include a call-to-action.* If the reader likes the offer or wants to know more, don't make them scroll down to find an elusive hyperlink; it should be there in the first paragraph. This is a mistake often made by e-mail 'newbies' – leaving the best until last.

After the header and salutation, you will likely not have much space left 'above the fold' (the space for opening copy before readers need to scroll down, if they bother) – so use one to two snappy sentences, maximum, for the lead. In this space we need to develop the initial interest to encourage the user to scroll down to find more and click that call-to-action. Better still, if you can manage it, put the call-to-action 'above the fold', in or immediately below the lead. This way, if prospects have decided to act, don't delay them. The lead should flow smoothly from the subject line – there should not be a disconnect. You should not, however, repeat the subject line; think about how it can be modified to express the offer in a different way that helps to convince the recipient to click.

E-MAIL MARKETING INSIGHT

Make sure there is not a disconnect between the subject line, and that your lead reinforces rather than repeats the subject line.

What should the copy of these one or two snappy sentences contain? Typically, you will be expanding on the initial offer made in the subject line. Since your subject line is very short you will need to repeat the basic offer, but provide additional description of the features or benefits involved in the offer. You also need to reinforce the credibility of your company to deliver. Why is this offer better coming from you? A statement summarizing the positioning of the company can help here. Try to incorporate hyperlinks into the copy of these sentences.

Body copy

The main copy is for those readers who want to know more – those who haven't lost interest, and those that haven't clicked the initial call-to-action already. The person who gets this far likely wants detail and reassurance. Since we have a fair amount of detail here, this is often the place to use bullets with bold headings so that it can be taken in by readers who are scanning (Figure 6.7 uses this approach). The main copy should therefore include:

- a detailed description of the offer features. If the offer is for a holiday, what is on offer? If the offer is for a seminar, what are the topics and what is the track-record of the speakers?

- a detailed description of the offer benefits. In the case of the seminar, what benefits will those attending the seminar receive? You can combine features and benefits by adding 'which means that . . .' after each feature.

- clear instructions about what to do next to receive the offer

- a description of how the process for fulfilling the offer works.

As in a direct mail piece, the main body of the e-mail typically details the features and benefits of the offer in order to encourage a response. With e-mail, you shouldn't use too much detail – the best place for detail is arguably the web site, and you can encourage clickthrough to find out more. A common approach is to use a bulleted list in the main body to describe features and benefits. Some e-mails seem to take this too far, though, with the e-mail becoming little more than a series of such lists. Although most would agree that 'brief is best' when it comes to e-mail, we do need to make the body copy long enough to create engagement, set the tone and explain the offer – and bullets alone are often not the best way to do this.

The body should also Explain and Instruct. It should explain because you may have developed a great offer and method of redemption, but it may be too complex for the embattled e-mail recipient as they wade through hundreds of e-mails. Explain clearly how the offer works. Instruct is related to Explain – most of us seem conditioned to follow instructions, as they make our lives easier – so the main body copy can instruct the recipient what to do next to receive the offer.

The close

The main aim of the final part of the text should be to achieve action, so the close should always include a link to execute the action. The section on achieving the call-to-action (see below) explains the best form for this. The reader will often have had to scroll down to get to this point, and it may be worth briefly repeating what has been said so far – in particular, the offer.

Sign-off

The sign-off can be personal or impersonal. Personal – from a named person – is best if the recipient knows an individual in your organization, such as an account manager or a customer service representative. Alternatively, if the company has a well-known figurehead the e-mail could be from this person, but many may think that this is false familiarity unless the copy is written to avoid this. An impersonal sign-off is often more appropriate for rented lists.

The postscript

The postscript is a device, often used in direct mail, which is known to capture attention and will encourage action. The PS is not seen that often in e-mails, perhaps because e-mail is seen as more of a conversational communication and the PS adds an element of formality, or perhaps because it is too overt a sign of selling. My view is that it can be used to good effect, since our eyes are drawn to the PS – so it is a good mechanism for getting a key message across to the reader.

Mandatory inclusions

These are what must be included to be legally compliant. Currently, this implies an unsubscribe mechanism, a privacy statement and a contact point (name and company address) that the recipient can contact if required. It is also good practice to include a 'statement of origination' – a short piece of text explaining why the recipient has received the e-mail – because some recipients may have forgotten signing up to your e-communications and will consider your e-mail to be spam unless you include this.

The unsubscribe is simply an instruction. It should be reasonably prominent and straightforward if you believe in permission marketing. The instruction will usually take the form of typing Unsubscribe into the subject line of the reply, or clicking on a link. You don't have to be formal here; Kangol uses this 'cool' approach for the unsubscribe to their newsletter:

> *PS think your life is so complete you don't need to hear from us again? Click here and kiss the cool times goodbye.*

A privacy statement or link must be included, but since it is not desirable to have a full privacy statement in the e-mail body, this is usually a link back to the privacy statement on the web site. The required contents for privacy statements have been covered in Chapter 2. Related to the privacy statement is the 'statement of origination', which explains who has sent the e-mail and why. The importance of this is also described in Chapter 2.

To wrap up this section on structure, let's look at an example that puts it all together. Figure 6.8 is an e-newsletter that targets engineers and their managers. It is kept succinct, and has a clear

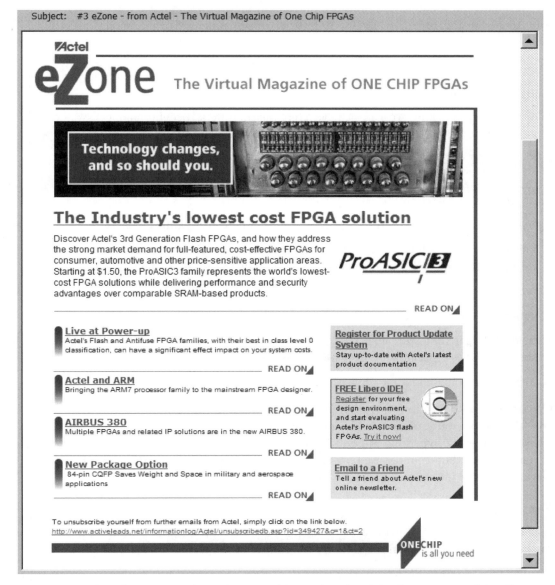

Figure 6.8 Technical B2B e-newsletter from Actel (reproduced with kind permission of Actel)

headline and header image plus a clear call-to-action at the beginning. It then uses bullets and panels to indicate other stories. The only thing it is really missing is a close, which would help make it more personal.

E-MAIL CREATIVE FORMATTING

The aim of creative formatting is to produce a pleasing visual design that enables us to connect emotionally with our recipients, while at the same time achieving the *emphasis* to attain our goals of Do, Think, Feel! Getting the right balance between visuals and text is important for this. For consumer brands, images will be equal to or exceed the text to help to create warmth about the brand, while for a B2B or informational e-newsletters the balance will be different, with text predominating although Figure 6.8 shows how images can also be important here.

Achieving emphasis

We need to think how we can achieve emphasis of offers, benefits and calls-to-action for those scanning. Think about how you can use:

- CAPITALIZATION, particularly in text e-mails – but don't overuse it
- the space before and after words and between lines – this can be powerful in highlighting offers or calls-to-action
- bullets – asterisks work best in text e-mails to highlight the features or benefits of your offer
- panels – reverse-colour panels or using a different HTML background colour works well to draw attention to particular parts of your e-mail and to aid scannability
- section dividers or sub-headings – these need to be in a sufficiently large font to be effective
- chunking – using short paragraphs of one or two sentences
- bold or larger font sizes in HTML e-mails, including in the headings – the scanners' and skimmers' eyes especially are drawn towards these
- hyperlinks – blue underlined hyperlinks attract the eye online.

Of course many of these forms of emphasis are familiar from direct mail, but there are some you should be wary of online. Using underlining should be avoided, since readers may think this shows a hyperlink and will be annoyed if they can't click on it. Italics are difficult to read online, but can be used in short paragraphs for testimonials. Use of exclamation marks should be limited to humour or outstanding items.

Fonts

For text e-mails, the e-mail will be displayed using the default, non-proportional font (such as courier); you have no control.

For HTML e-mails, you have a choice of serifed fonts (such as Times) or sans-serifed fonts (such as Arial). Reading sans-serifed fonts is easier online and looks better to most people.

This is the reverse of the offline world, where most print publications use serifed fonts. Look in your own inbox – almost all the commercial HTML e-mails will be sans-serif. You will quite often find that HTML spam has serifed fonts, so avoid this. However, you might use a serifed font in an e-mail if you wanted to be distinctive and appeal to an older audience.

Calls-to-action

I have called this sub-section 'calls-to-action' because you should always consider multiple calls-to-action in your e-mail. There should be at least two calls-to-action because of the limited screen area the e-mail is being read in. Also, different recipients may want to click at different times. Some people who like the offer will click on it impulsively at the top of the e-mail, but others may want to scroll down for the details and will then click if the offer suits. What we want to achieve ideally is, therefore, a call-to-action which is viewable and clickable when the e-mail is first opened, and then each time the recipient scrolls down using the 'Page down' key. There should be a call-to-action at the end of piece, but also near the middle or top, even if they are the same link.

E-MAIL MARKETING INSIGHT

Use multiple calls-to-action

You will also need to decide how focused to keep your calls-to-action. For specific campaigns, it is best to have a single landing page with multiple calls-to-action leading through to this. What you don't want is a hyperlink leading to a home page giving general detail about the company. However, for an e-newsletter multiple links to different areas of the web site are more acceptable, provided they are not too prominent and do not distract from the main offers.

Clicking on the hyperlinks within an e-mail will take the recipient to the landing page. The form of the hyperlinks will vary according to the format of the e-mail. In text e-mails, the call-to-action must be the physical address of the landing page, such as http://www.company.com/landing_page.htm?id=testing_tags. Try to keep this address as short and simple as possible, although this may be difficult if you are coding the response with testing tags. We showed in Chapter 3 that different calls-to-action can be tagged so that, when looking at the web-site statistics, it is possible to see which has been the most effective call-to-action. Of course you won't want to use the text 'testing tags' in your e-mail. If you find the banner at the head of an HTML e-mail or the first link 'above the fold' works best, then this is where you should concentrate your creative efforts in future. For example, if you have two links in your e-mail to the same landing page, you might test them as follows:

http://www.company.com/landing_page.htm?id="top"

and

http://www.company.com/landing_page.htm?id="bottom"

To highlight the call-to-action, the link should be separated on a different line and a clear instruction made to click on it. CAPS work in both text and HTML e-mails.

More examples of copywriting for calls-to-action are given in the checklist later in this chapter.

An example that combines much of the best practice for emphasis in e-mail marketing is shown in Figure 6.9. This uses bold formatting in the opening to gain attention, and bullets in the main body. It also has alternate text and image hyperlink calls-to-action at the top and bottom of the e-mail, with an injunction to act now.

E-NEWSLETTER DESIGN

Many of the principles of effective design we have covered above apply equally to all types of e-mail campaigns, whether e-promotions or regular e-newsletters. However, there are some

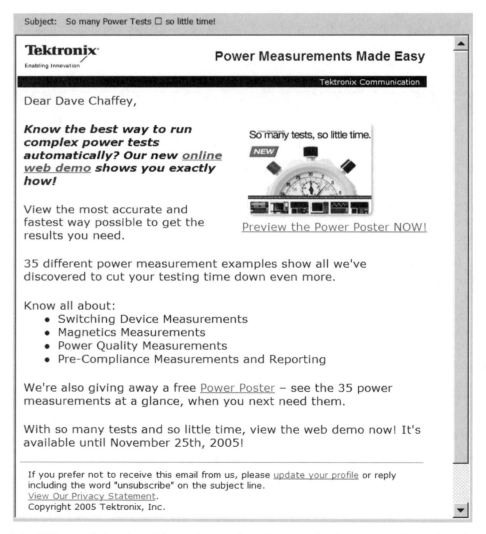

Figure 6.9 B2B e-mail showing different forms of emphasis and calls-to-action (reproduced courtesy of Tektronix, Inc.)

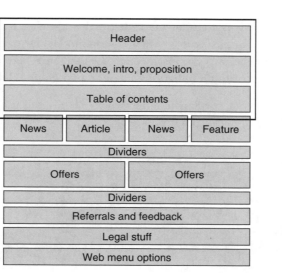

Figure 6.10   Generic e-mail newsletter layout showing different components

specific issues for e-newsletters as a result of their format. In Chapter 5 we looked at different issues concerned with e-newsletters, such as audience, proposition, frequency and length. Here, we will briefly look at some of the issues of newsletter layout and design.

I am often asked whether companies should use a fixed e-newsletter structure. Looking at most print publications answers this. Newspapers and magazines only modify their page layouts and overall structure when they need rejuvenation, not every issue. Agreeing on a standard format or template will also help crank out the e-newsletters each month. Figure 6.10 illustrates a generic newsletter layout which gives a checklist of the type of content you may want to use. It is important that an e-newsletter has the right standard features. The clicks on these may not be high, but they can be important. Consider these options for standard template features which should appear above the fold:

1.   Links to main site sections and possibly search/shop options for e-retailers

2.   Table of contents linking to different sections in the e-newsletter

3.   Subscribe (for use where the e-mail has been forwarded)

4.   Forward to a friend/colleague

5.   Print

6.   Communications preferences/My Profile (best at bottom of e-mail).

The header is an area that is used to brand the e-mail and can also be used as a navigation element. Menu options may link to headings further down the piece (an underused feature), and sometimes these menu headings will link back to the web site. If they are to the site, highlighting this may prevent confusion. If the newsletter is long, with a number of news items or articles, it is conventional to have a table of contents, although since this can fill a lot of the space above the fold it is not always used. Below this, articles, features and promotions can be included in standard positions. A two- or three-column layout maximizes use of space, as for print, with the number of columns varying through the newsletter, but not too much. For shorter e-newsletters, such as those with more focus, a single or two-column layout can be most effective.

Figure 6.11 shows the layout for a newsletter which blends the use of images and text well, and also makes good use of background tints.

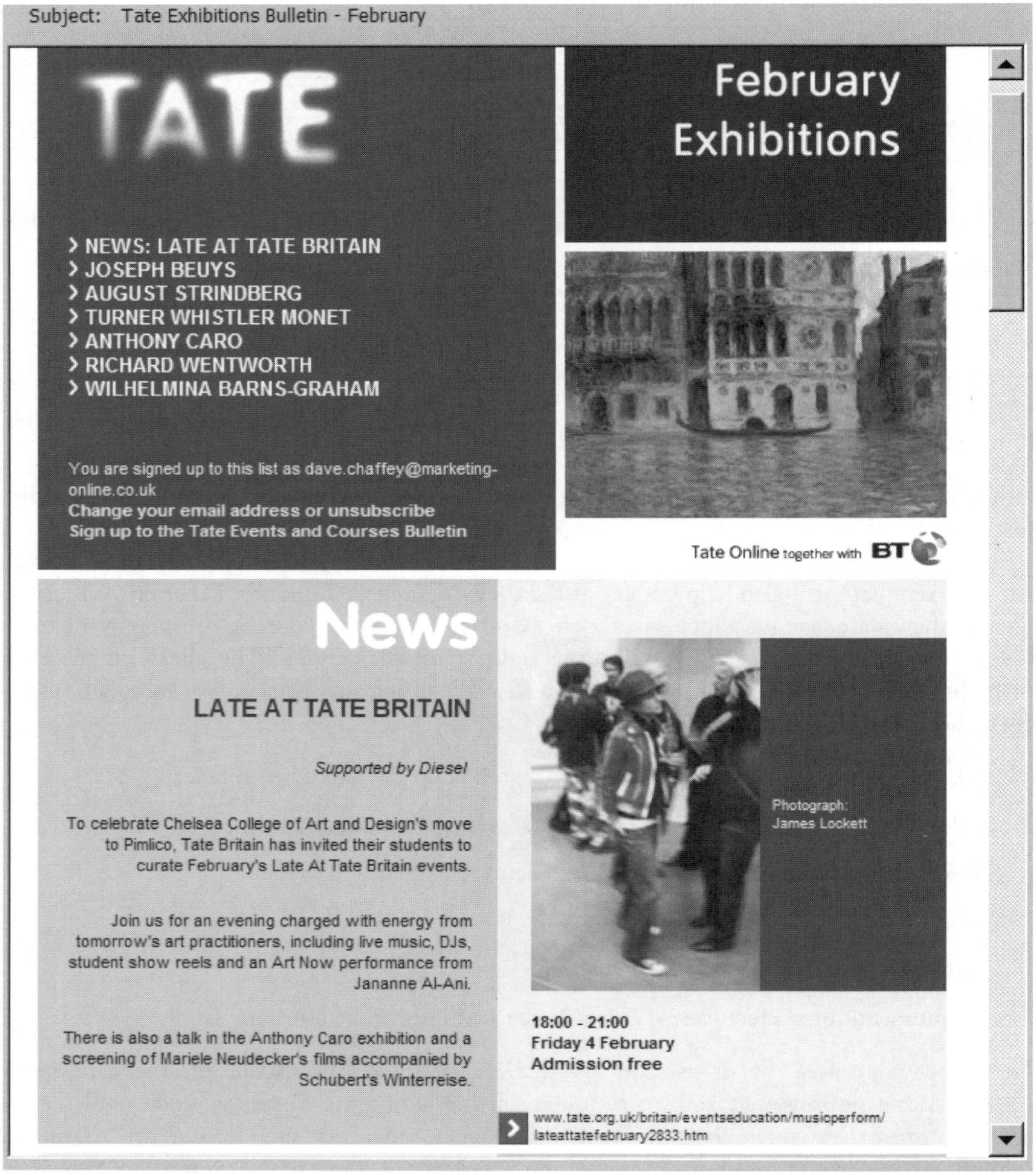

Figure 6.11 Tate e-newsletter

To write successful e-mail copy, we need to adopt a mindset based on how readers interact with e-mail. If you are familiar with writing copy for print, consider these three important differences, which are discussed below:

1. Readers scan, don't read, e-mail

2. E-mail is conversational

3. E-mail readers are cynical.

Readers scan, don't read, e-mail

The scanning behaviour of online readers is well known. For example, Nielsen (2000) reports on research that shows that, in a test, 79 per cent of test web users scanned while just 16 per cent read word-by-word. Since we tend to read 25 per cent more slowly from a computer screen, this behaviour is likely to be exhibited in all on-screen copy, whether web or e-mail.

One implication of this is that we should write less copy when writing for the web or e-mail – Nielsen suggests 50 per cent of the original for web copy. We can suggest that for e-mail, which tends to be read in a smaller window and in a different context, this should be even shorter.

To achieve brevity, Steve Krug, author of *Don't Make Me Think!* (Krug, 2000), suggests we should abide by the following:

1. *Omit needless words!* He says we should remove half our original words and then strive to remove half again.

2. *Marketing happy talk must die!* Avoid that introductory text intended to make the customer feel comfortable or extol the virtues of a company.

3. *Instructions must die!* This refers to online forms rather than e-mails, where it is achieved through making the options clear without extensive text. For e-mail we can argue that instructions are often useful to explain to readers what they need to do to redeem the offer and to convert them to action. However, we can certainly keep instructions succinct.

Brevity is therefore key, but what not to include? Jennings (2002) suggests that you should focus copy on what the 'readers want to know, need to know or both'. She suggests you put yourself in the readers' shoes and focus on answering their questions, rather than expounding on details of the company and its achievements that you are proud of. So ask whether the reader will be influenced by copy; if not, leave it out.

Krug's comments originally focused on web pages, but some e-mail marketers seem to have taken him literally, with e-mails simply becoming a list of bullet points. As with any rule, there are exceptions. If every e-mail becomes a list of bullets, it becomes difficult to differentiate and explain your offer, or to engage and then have a dialogue with the reader.

Of course, the other implication of scanning behaviour is that we should make our e-mails scannable! Nielsen suggests using these approaches:

- highlighted keywords (we will look at different forms of highlighting for text and HTML e-mails later in this chapter)

- meaningful, not 'clever', sub-headings

- bulleted lists

- one idea per paragraph

- the inverted pyramid style, starting with the conclusion

- half the word count (or less) than conventional writing.

E-mail is conversational

Although we receive many unsolicited communications, many e-mails are from work and friends.

Cyberatlas (2003) reported research from JupiterResearch which showed that in 2003, for 4000 US adults, the main types of e-mails from different sources were:

- Spam (44%, up from 35% the year before)

- Friends and family (31%)

- Opt-in – business (16%)

- Work or school (5%)

- Other (4%).

We are therefore used to using e-mail in a conversational, informal way with friends, family or work colleagues. It follows that copywriters can be more conversational with e-mail than with other media, and this can help us to get closer to our prospects and customers.

Some have said we should 'write like you talk' – a good test is to ask whether you would say it to someone face-to-face. If not, it is probably the 'marketing happy talk' we referred to above.

Other ways to make e-mail conversational are to use simple words and colloquial expressions. Pronouns such as 'I', 'we', 'you' and 'they' are also effective. Some talk about the 'we–we test' – reviewing the e-mail to see whether the emphasis is on the sender 'we' or the recipient 'you'. The example below shows an e-mail that passes this test:

> *You already know how easy it is to get instant online insurance cover from Norwich Union. But did you know that Norwich Union can also offer you online access to low-cost life-cover? For example, £X would cost you as little as £Y per day.*

E-mail readers are cynical

The figures above show that, in some cases, approaching half our e-mail is now spam. With offers for holy water, losing weight while sitting at your computer, receiving millions from the deceased relative of a government member, every e-mail reader is going to be super-cynical about what you are offering. Professional e-mail marketers therefore have to work extra hard to establish credibility and prove their benefits, so, as you write, put yourself in the position of a cynical customer who is fed up with insincere and bogus offers – how are you going to prove that you are a credible supplier?

These are some approaches to overcome cynicism and build credibility through e-mail:

● Try to achieve 'connection' with the readers to show that you understand them, by using customer language and buzzwords

● Spell out the benefit the feature gives – for example, a bulleted list might use different fonts or formats to emphasize benefits

● Back up with facts and numbers

● Build testimonial elements into your e-mails, such as customer quotations, number of customers, client names, and independent reviews and awards.

Customer-centric copy

It is often said that to write good direct mail copy, you need to write for your reader – in other words, to imagine the person who is reading your carefully crafted words. To do this, though, we need to remember the different types of position that our readers are in. Write down how their backgrounds vary. These are some of the different aspects you should consider:

● *How well do the recipients know your company?* Are they prospects, customers or first-time customers?

● *How well do the recipients know your products?* Have they bought single products or a range of products?

● *What style of communications will appeal?* What will they expect from previous interactions with your brand? Do they like a direct approach, or do they prefer a more involved dialogue? What is their age? They may prefer more or less formal communications accordingly.

● *How technologically literate are they?* Some may have been using e-mail and web sites for five years, others for only five weeks. Make it obvious for the newbies, but avoid patronizing the old hands.

● *Do they scan or do they read?* Depending on time available, and their character, some recipients will just scan the e-mail body, while others prefer to read more carefully. You need to provide copy and design that works for both.

Through using customer personas and asking these types of questions, you will build a picture of the range of people you are writing for. If it is not practical to write for such a wide range, consider separating your mailing into, for example, recently acquired customers and established customers.

Figure 6.11 shows a good example of customer-centric copy. It is written in an informal way, but still manages to communicate the serious business benefits of attending this event. Figure 6.9 is another great example of copywriting for the B2B audience.

Does your e-mail have CRABS?

Smith and Chaffey (2005) use the acronym CRABS to summarize effective web-page copy. This is even more appropriate to e-mail copy, since we typically have even less space to communicate. CRABS stands for:

- *Chunking*. Chunking means that paragraphs must be shorter than in paper copy – think one or two sentences, three or four maximum. This helps scannability.

- *Relevance*. With limited space, we have no room for fillers. Stick with what matters – the details of the offer and how to receive it.

- *Accuracy*. Don't get carried away with your copy; don't set expectations so high that you overpromise and can't deliver something you offer.

- *Brevity*. Brevity goes with chunking and scannability. Write your copy, reduce the word count and then reduce it again. Give yourself targets and beat them, without sacrificing good English and understanding.

- *Scannability*. This is reading without reading every word, just picking up the sense of each paragraph from the keywords. The eye will pick out words at the start of paragraphs and those emphasized in bold.

The title of Steve Krug's (2000) book on web usability gives a useful guideline for copywriting for e-mail – *Don't make me think*. He also suggests that you should consider the amount of copy you have, halve it and halve it again.

If you have produced copy that follows the CRABS guidelines, you are only a small part of the way there, as there are many issues of style that must be considered in order to make successful copy. Check the following eight copy questions against your e-mail copy.

CAMPAIGN CHECKLIST: EIGHT KEY COPY QUESTIONS

Question 1: Does your copy excite?

You have a great offer, but have you supported the offer by writing enthusiastically to appeal to the reader's emotions?

For the consumers, you are offering riches, dreams and experiences – does the copy effectively communicate how your offer will improve their life?

For business people you are offering time, knowledge and control – does the copy effectively communicate how your offer can help them 'work smarter'?

The copy also needs to excite from the outset – see Question 7 for tips on headlines.

Question 2: Does your copy convince?

You may believe that your service or offer sells itself on its features because you believe in it, but the recipients are less likely to be believers – they don't have the interest or knowledge you have. Have you backed up your promise with enough detail to convince them that the offer is worthwhile? Is the unique selling point clear?

The style of writing also needs to enthuse about these benefits. This may be difficult if you cannot personally relate to the customer's needs – which is sometimes difficult for technology markets. The only way to succeed is to develop empathy with your reader by researching and maybe even living the role, as actors do.

Question 3: Is your copy natural?

We have said that e-mail is a social, conversational medium – it is mainly used to chat to friends or communicate with colleagues – so we want to avoid our e-mail reading as if it was written by a machine.

If you can, make copy conversational; write at the same level as your audience and make it flow naturally, then you will get closer to readers and predispose them to what you are offering. However, don't overdo the informality – some e-mails appear as though they are written by someone you have known from 'back at school'!

Question 4: Is the copy length right?

Let's look at the extremes. Which is best – short copy or long copy?

There can be no right answer, because it depends on the purpose. Most people answer that short is best, since readers don't want to read your carefully crafted words, just to assess WIFM – 'What's in it for me?'

My view is that you can combine short and long copy in one e-mail. For those who are more likely to respond to short copy, use the introduction and the start of the main copy which is above the fold. For 'the scanners', who scan through the whole e-mail, you may impress with detail, provided that detail stands out. For 'the readers', who read every word and want the details, you need long copy.

I would argue that the e-mail cannot be too long, provided that it is relevant and entertaining, and another call-to-action and summary of the total copy are included at the start.

These 'E-marketing insight articles' are long in comparison with many web articles, but that is not necessarily bad – many readers want additional insights that they can then print out and read offline. Getting a reader to print an e-mail is often a good outcome for the marketer.

Some argue that the detail can always be covered in a link to a more detailed web page, but I think that this can cause loss of focus – once readers click through to their web browser, you have lost control.

Question 5: Have you repeated yourself?

This is a difficult one. Direct mail wisdom says repeat to reinforce, whereas e-mail wisdom says the reader doesn't have the time to see information repeated. However,

I think some repetition is desirable. Reinforcement of messages is effective in any media.

We need to repeat and build on what is available in the subject line in the headline. Then, because the reader has scrolled, repeating the offer in the final call-to-action makes sense.

Question 6: Which copy stands out?

You have satisfied yourself that you can answer the other questions, but now, looking at the big picture, what will the 'scanner' notice – what techniques have you used to emphasize the key points in your e-mail?

In text e-mails, you have these options to make copy stand out:

- CAPITALIZATION, particularly in text e-mails – but don't overuse it

- the space before and after words and between lines can be powerful in highlighting offers or calls-to-action

- bulleted lists using asterisks or dots.

You can see that the options in text e-mails are limited. However, in HTML e-mails there is much more scope for emphasis – which is perhaps one of the reasons why, in many markets, HTML e-mails receive higher response rates. With HTML we can use the options for text e-mails listed above, but also:

- text formatting – bold and italics. Take care with this, as italics may be difficult to read in small point sizes. Never use an underline that looks like a hyperlink – readers will try to click on it.

- font sizes – using a large font size for the headings or separate messages works well for scanners.

- font colour – use a different colour from body copy, using vibrant colours such as red and orange.

- graphical animations of copy – but make sure your animation doesn't prevent the message being viewed by scanners

- hyperlinks – blue underlined hyperlinks attract the eye online.

Question 7: Do we have a powerful headline?

Copycat suggests in WNIM 17 (http://www.wnim.com/issue17/pages/copycat.htm) that, online as offline, many more people will read or remember a headline than the body of an ad. While this is not proven online, many e-mails do not have a title at all – online copywriters seem to think they aren't necessary because that's what the subject line is for. Not so! Headlines do help engagement if they build on the subject line to engage the reader.

In his excellent book *The Online Copywriter's Handbook* (Bly, 2002), Robert Bly recommends the following approaches that can be used for e-mail titles:

- Get a terrific benefit upfront
- Appeal to personal self-interest
- Get the right sort of attention
- Add news
- Offer to teach
- Ask a provocative question
- Use 'quotes'.

Question 8: Will our copy achieve action?

The last of our eight questions is the most important – will our e-mail achieve action? Arguably this should be the first question, since then the whole copy can be structured around the outcomes we want to achieve!

Approaches that can help achieve action include:

- a text-based call to action in the first screen (for the impulsive) and the last screen (for those with the time to read)
- a time-limited offer that uses copy to encourage the reader to Click NOW!
- instructions such as 'forward to a friend' or 'print this e-mail as a reminder' can give other useful outcomes
- using hyperlinks to highlight the offer at the right position in the paragraph.

As an example of highlighting the offer through a hyperlink, think of marketing to an IT manager to download a best practice guide. Which of these approaches do you think would be best?

A   Click below to receive your complimentary guide to reducing Total Cost of Ownership:
　 FREE guide to reducing TCO.
　 Sign off
B   Click here to receive your complimentary guide to reducing Total Cost of Ownership
C   To receive your complimentary guide to reducing Total Cost of Ownership, click here.
D   To help you lower the costs of running your IT infrastructure we have prepared a complimentary guide to reducing Total Cost of Ownership.

In A, separating out the hyperlink on to a separate line does increase its prominence, but spoils the flow of the copy.

I prefer B to C, since it is more direct and the eye will be more naturally drawn towards the underlined hyperlink at the start of the sentence within the copy as a whole. However, approach C can encourage the scanner to read the copy before the end of the sentence.

Design practice for web pages would favour approach D, which makes the call-to-action part of the copy. While this may work best for web pages, where we are perhaps not seeking the hard sell, for simplicity and encouraging action approach B is best.

Think carefully about the colour of the hyperlink. On the majority of web pages – Yahoo! and Amazon, for example – users are used to seeing a blue hyperlink on a white background. You will get a higher response with this combination because of familiarity. If other colours are used, high contrast is essential.

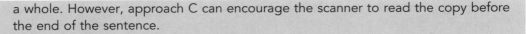

E-MAIL MARKETING EXCELLENCE – BEST PRACTICE FOR E-MAIL COPY

David Mill, of specialist e-marketing agency MediaCo (www.media.co.uk), gives these best-practice guidelines for e-mail copy: You can read more detailed advice by David on copywriting and all aspects of online marketing in his book *Content is King*, which is also part of the *E-marketing Essentials* series (Mill, 2005).

Body Content

You have some 10 seconds to grab the attention of recipients after they have opened the message. Therefore, the content should:

- *be relevant and focused*. The more it appeals to your audience, the better the results.

- *Make the objective obvious*. For example, 'Enter our competition to win' or 'Here is the latest news on . . .'. In addition, it is often good practice to take an early opportunity to tell recipients why they are receiving the e-mail – for example, 'You have received this newsletter because . . .'.

With regard to the message itself, it should:

- be clear and concise.

- be written in plain language.

- avoid jargon – no buzzwords, jargon, funky phrases or punctuation unless expected by the target market.

- be kept short – short copy delivers results but, if it must be long, a synopsis or content list should be provided at the outset. HTML versions that can be viewed in one screen are also most effective. If they are longer, key elements should be viewable above the fold.

- be immediately of interest – have the key points and main clickthrough links in the immediately viewable area.

- be creative, so it stands out from the crowd.

Generally speaking, the content should:

- use compelling active voice and action verbs

- talk about THEM not you

- place readers in the action

- stress benefits, not features

- build real and perceived value

- have personality, so you and the recipient connect.

A newsletter is most effective when it does one of two things:

1. Reflects the typical reader's personality, appealing to the reader at another level – i.e. a personality the reader can both recognize and accept within the context of the newsletter.

2. Has a personality that adds to the human element of the newsletter and boosts the one-to-one characteristic of e-mail marketing, bearing in mind it is not an audience that's being addressed – it's an individual sitting alone in front of a screen.

LANDING PAGES

There should be a specific landing page for every major campaign unless you are a retailer simply directing consumers to product pages. The landing page should:

- support the tone of the campaign

- include a summary of the offer, but not too much detail unless this was not possible in the original e-mail

- provide more detailed information

- not ask for too much information or too many fields

- not give too many links to elsewhere in the site (i.e. don't include complete template to all other parts of the site)

- be tested for attrition unless you have run similar campaigns before

- include privacy statements.

Table 6.3 Combinations of creative elements for Crayola.com e-mail test from MercerMC (2001), with changes in response rates compared to worst case shown

Creative element	Worst combination	Best e-mail script
Subject line	Help us to help you (0%)	Crayola.com survey (7.5%)
Salutation	Greetings (0%)	User name (3.4%)
Call-to-action	As Crayola.com grows (0%)	Because you are … (3.5%)
Offer	No offer (0%)	$25 Amazon gift certificate drawing (5.2%)
Close	Crayola.com (0%)	Editor:Crayola.com (1.2%)
Overall response	9.7%	33.7%

TESTING CREATIVE

In the last part of Chapter 4, we described approaches to testing the different components of a campaign. However, a common problem with testing the creative is that there is a wide variety of options. To avoid the need to test all options, Mercer Management Consulting recommends using an experimental design or multivariable testing. MercerMC (2001) gives the example of campaign testing for Crayola using Mercer Management's Nexperiment methodology. To evaluate a combination of 3 different salutations, 5 offers and 6 price points would have required 360 test e-mails. However, Nexperiment used a subset of the combinations. This helped to identify a combination of creative that was more than three times as effective in generating a response. An indication of the approaches is shown in Table 6.3.

Multivariate testing of different elements of e-mail creative and landing pages is possible using automated tools such as Offermatica (www.offermatica.com) and Optimost (www.optimost.com).

HOW NOT TO DO IT!

We end this chapter by looking at how *not* to do it. eMarketer (2002) reported on a survey of 1250 US e-mail users, and asked them about the most annoying features of permission e-mail marketing. These, mentioned from highest to lowest (including multiple responses), were:

- Suspect that the company is sharing your address (74%)
- Tried unsubscribing in vain (69%)
- Messages too frequent (66%)
- Nothing of value being sent (59%)
- Too much e-mail in general (53%)
- Messages not targeted to interests (53%)
- Product I seldom buy (46%)
- Not good price (43%)
- E-mails do not affect purchase decisions (37%)

- Messages too 'hard sell' (36%)
- No longer interested in topic (27%)
- E-mails use 'rich media' (15%)
- E-mails use HTML (7%).

Clearly it is not the design and style of the creative that bugs people; it is when the targeting, timing, relevance and offer are wrong. All these factors therefore have to be right before we even start on the creative.

E-MAIL MARKETING CHECKLIST: TOP TEN E-MAIL CREATIVE DOS AND DON'TS

Do:

1. Set SMART business objectives before you start!
2. Brand the start of the e-mail to connect with the customer and reassure
3. Encourage clickthrough near the top of the e-mail to encourage impulsive clickthroughs
4. Develop different creative treatments for key audience to boost response
5. Limit the number of offers, but use secondary offers to encourage clickthrough
6. Use the opening paragraph to summarize the whole
7. Use the body to explain fully how the offer works through features and benefits
8. Use a sign-off from a named individual – this is more personal and may be a legal requirement
9. Think about using a postscript
10. Test to improve the template and other creative features.

Don't:

1. Forget the headline – you need this as well as the subject line
2. Make the e-mail too short (to explain the offer) or too long (to reduce engagement)
3. Use images unless they add to brand, create a personality or help convert to clickthrough
4. Get the tone of voice wrong – it must be right for the brand and the customer, and must connect
5. Forget to put copy in small chunks
6. Forget to make copy relevant

7. Forget to make copy accurate

8. Forget to make copy brief

9. Forget to make copy scannable

10. Forget a final call-to-action at the close of the message.

REFERENCES

Bly, R. (2002). *The Online Copywriter's Handbook: Everything you need to know to write electronic copy that sells.* McGraw Hill.

Chittenden, L. and Rettie, R. (2003). An evaluation of e-mail marketing and factors affecting response. *Journal of Targeting, Measurement and Analysis for Marketing,* **11(3)**, 203–217.

Cyberatlas (2003). The deadly duo: spam and viruses (by Robyn Greenspan). *Cyberatlas,* **July**.

Doubleclick (2002). *Q2 E-mail Trend Report* (available at www.doubleclick.net – note that current trend reports do not report text e-mail results).

Doubleclick (2005). *Doubleclick Sixth Annual Consumer E-mail Survey.* Doubleclick.

Email Labs (2005). Email Labs Survey Implications: Use of Preview Pane and Image Blocking will drive B2B Marketers to rethink their Email Newsletter Design Strategy. *E-mail Labs Press Release,* 19 November.

eMarketer (2002). Consumers want more from e-mail marketing. eStatNews from eMarketer, 20 May.

Farris, J. and Langendorf, L. (1999). Engaging customers in e-business: how to build sales, relationships and results with e-mail. White paper, available at www.e2software.com.

Grant Thornton (2005). *Grant Thornton's 2005 International Business Owners Survey* (IBOS), 28 February.

Jennings, J. (2002). Evaluating your e-mail campaign, Part 2 (available at Clickz, www.clickz. com), 28 February.

Krug, S. (2000). *Don't Make Me Think.* New Riders.

McGhee, S. (2005). 4 Ways to Take Control of Your E-mail Inbox. Recommendations published at http://www.microsoft.com/atwork/manageinfo/email.mspx.

Mercer MC (2001). Making CRM Make Money. A Mercer Management Consulting Commentary (available at www.mercermc.com).

Mill, D. (2005). *Content is King. Writing and Editing Online.* Butterworth-Heinemann.

Nielsen, J. (2000). Mailing list usability. *UseIT Alertbox,* **August** (available at www.useit.com).

Smith, P. R. and Chaffey, D. (2005). *eMarketing eXcellence – At the Heart of eBusiness,* 2nd edn. Butterworth-Heinemann.

WEB LINKS

Writing and Editing online (http://www.writingediting.co.uk) is David Mill's site for *Content is King*, including extracts from the book.

Chapter

7

E-mail marketing management

CHAPTER AT A GLANCE

Overview

This chapter is about making it happen. We will look at the best way to set up, run and manage your e-mail campaigns using e-mail management services and software. We will also briefly review managing inbound e-mail enquiries.

Chapter objectives

By the end of this chapter you will be able to:

- assess the best approach for resourcing your e-mail marketing
- develop a strategy for managing inbound e-mail.

Chapter structure

- Introduction
- Selecting solution providers
- Managing a campaign
- Choosing e-mail management software and services
- Managing the house list
- Managing inbound e-mail
- References
- Web links

INTRODUCTION

An important part of your e-mail marketing strategy is the development of a resourcing strategy. This involves identifying the best partners for helping to develop and broadcast campaigns, and manage your lists. This can be a complex decision, since different suppliers will often be selected for different aspects of e-mail marketing. You may decide that one agency manages your e-mail promotion campaigns and another your e-newsletter. You may also have different suppliers managing your web site and customer data. Additionally, who you use will change through time. You may start by outsourcing your e-newsletter development, since you don't have experience in this and want to learn through your supplier. If you are unhappy with the supplier, you may change, before perhaps bringing the e-newsletter in house – by which time you have the necessary experience and skills to manage this at a lower cost.

Then there are the options for resourcing different aspects of each campaign. A typical range and sequence of activities is strategy, creative design, media buying, e-mail creative execution, web-site design and hosting, data management and e-mail broadcasting. In-house skills may be available for some of these activities, but not for others. Perhaps the skills are available, but time is not. Where there is a resource shortage in terms of skills or time, or if it is thought that outsourcing may be cheaper, then the outsourcing option will be explored.

SELECTING SOLUTION PROVIDERS

There are two main outsourcing options. These are a specialist full-service e-mail marketing agency, or a traditional marketing/direct marketing agency. Since e-mail marketing is still relatively new there is a strong argument for using the specialist e-mail marketing agency, since it will likely have experience of more campaigns – so it will have experimented and tested, and will know what works and what doesn't. It will also be able to participate in all aspects of the campaign. Unless a more traditional agency has recruited expertise, its staff members could be learning as they complete your job.

Figure 7.1 summarizes the main options for resourcing e-mail campaigns. The client can complete all the work, or can work with a variety of partners. The client may decide on a single 'one-stop shop' or 'full-service' partner to manage all aspects of the campaign; often this will be a specialist e-mail or web marketing agency or, increasingly, it could be e-mail and e-marketing specialists within a traditional marketing agency. This agency will manage the strategy and design of the campaign, and this work will usually be done internally, although other specialists with HTML or graphic design skills may be brought in. If an acquisition campaign is being run, the client (or the client's agency) has the choice of approaching a list owner (such as a magazine publisher) direct, or may go through a specialist list broker. Acquisition centres offer a further option for acquiring consumer e-mail addresses, as described in Chapter 4. Finally, the agency or client may broadcast the list, or this can be managed through an e-mail service provider.

MANAGING A CAMPAIGN

In Chapter 3 we looked at key issues in developing a campaign, such as the targeting, offer, creative and timing. In detail, there are many more activities that need to be managed within the campaign. Figure 7.2 summarizes all the tasks under the three main headings of (A) Design, (B) Obtain list and (C) Deploy. All the tasks under Stages A and B can happen at a similar time

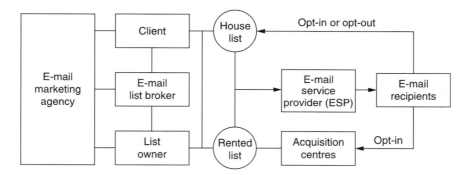

Figure 7.1 Structure of the e-mail marketing industry

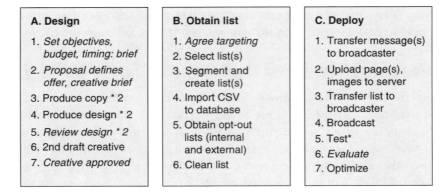

Figure 7.2 A three-stage campaign plan

once objectives are agreed, but Stage C is dependent on the other two stages. All these tasks are either handled internally or shared between the client and the agency. Figure 7.2 also shows in italics the tasks where client input is required. Note that if the client is busy with other projects, then these can potentially be bottlenecks since all hand-offs between one group of people and another will create delay. If the whole project is in-house, then it could take place in less than 24 hours, with dedicated staff and simple creative; however, more often it will take days or even weeks. Putting a time against each of the tasks in A and B and plotting them on a Gantt chart can certainly help to keep the tasks under control.

The process in Figure 7.2 will be swifter if the first two stages are efficient. The clearer the brief produced by the client and the proposal received from the selected consultant, the quicker the overall process will be. What, then, should go in the brief? Some general guidelines based on what we have discussed in previous chapters are given in the Campaign checklist below.

CAMPAIGN CHECKLIST: WHAT GOES IN A CAMPAIGN BRIEF?

1. Describe how the required campaign fits into the overall marketing strategy and communications strategy, including targeting marketing and differentiation strategy.

2. State clearly the success criteria or objectives for the campaign.

3. Ensure that the brief should not be too prescriptive about the form of the execution; briefs often describe the exact media and offer to use and, by being too prescriptive, creativity is stifled. However this may be more practical if time is tight.

4. Detail the characteristics of the target audience(s). This may include database selects based on demographic profiles, or previous purchase or response patterns, and should include psychographics as well as demographics. Agencies

will often not know the psychographics of the recipients. Thumbnail profiles or personas that show how the audience lives and what appeals to them can help here.

5. Outline competitors and how they differentiate their services.

6. Specify the testing required before the campaign and how the campaign will be modified (if needed) mid-campaign.

7. Provide brand guidelines, including tone, style and personality, for consistency with other campaigns.

8. Give the constraints – time and money.

CHOOSING E-MAIL MANAGEMENT SOFTWARE AND SERVICES

We now turn to look in more detail at software and services that can be used to manage the creation, broadcast and tracking of an e-mail marketing campaign that covers Stages A, B and C in Figure 7.2.

Selecting the right combination of services is challenging, since there are many suppliers and different formats with a range of costs. Choosing the right supplier will help you use the best-practice advice on targeting and tracking, given in this book. We will start by looking at the different aspects of campaign management that a supplier can assist with, and criteria for selecting tools, then we will look at some of the alternative approaches. Finally, we will look at some examples at different price points.

E-mail campaign management capabilities

At a simple level, there are four main requirements or tasks involved with managing e-mail campaigns and e-newsletters:

1. Creating the content

2. Managing the list

3. Broadcasting the message

4. Tracking and reporting the results.

You should assess potential e-mail management systems against detailed criteria in these four areas, which are summarized in diagrammatic form in Figure 7.3.

1. Creating the content

Producing creative requires software to construct the HTML and text versions of the e-mail. To do this, many companies will employ HTML editing tools that are used for web content. Dreamweaver is probably the best-known HTML authoring tool used by web-design professionals. Some prefer the simplicity of the Microsoft tool Frontpage, while

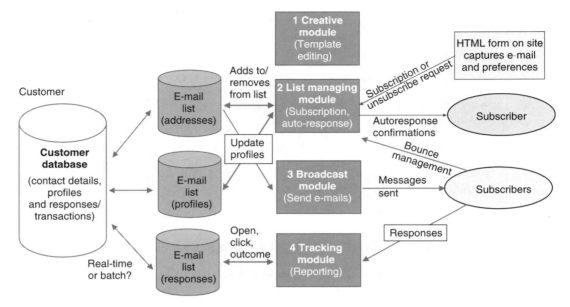

Figure 7.3 Components of an e-mail management system

for simple e-mails Microsoft Word can be used to save a basic e-mail format in HTML format. Care needs to be taken with using some versions of the Microsoft tools, since they can add unnecessary XML/HTML formatting; this will add to the overall size of the e-mail and may not be rendered well in different e-mail readers. Refer to the section in Chapter 6 which recommends testing for different e-mail reader types, and some of the HTML coding approaches to avoid.

An alternative approach is to use specialist e-mail template authoring software. This is designed to shield marketers who are creating e-mails from some of the complexity of a web-authoring package such as Dreamweaver. These provide a WYSIWYG ('What you see is what you get') editing approach, which shows the final version of the e-mail (or, alternatively, a preview mode) as it will appear to the user. They also allow the creator of the e-mail to work within one of a series of templates created for e-mail marketing, so using an existing layout and amending the copy and images for the new version. It is often most effective, in terms of response, to have different types of e-mail templates for different types of communication, such as new product launch, promotion, event or e-newsletter. Many of the e-mail service providers we will review later in this chapter have this capability.

You should test the capability to personalize messages according to fields in the database using merge fields and, as a minimum, incorporate the name. More sophisticated tools will enable branching, for example:

IF product category purchased = TV THEN

Insert Text Block

ELSEIF product category purchased = HIFI THEN

Insert Text Block

ELSE

No insertion

ENDIF

Other issues to remember regarding content creation include:

- form or microsite creation. It is often convenient for marketing to create separate pages for subscription and updating communications preference. Not all packages have this capability.

- version control. Can previous versions of e-mails or forms be accessed?

- permissions. It is helpful in a large organization to have different permissions for which activities are permissible, such as administrator (can do anything), template creation, copy-editing (just copy, not images or text) or reporting (with or without password control).

- content pods (different sections of e-mail). As suggested in previous chapters, these are defined areas of the screen that are used to deliver different messages to different types of people on the list. If you envisage doing this type of targeting, then check how easy it is to add the rules to display the messages in each content box.

- embedded forms for surveys. It is increasingly common to complete online surveys within e-mails. Some tools may not support this capability. Also, remember that this approach may not work well for some web-mail platforms, such as MSN and AOL. It is essential to have a link to a web-based form.

- web versions of e-mail. If the e-mail cannot be displayed, will the e-mail broadcast package readily display the e-mail in a browser, and will it be personalized – i.e. will the page be dynamically generated?

2. Managing the list

A basic part of managing lists involves facilitating subscriptions entry of customer profile details and also unsubscribes. This facility will typically be set up to occur automatically via the web site. It should also enable adding e-mail and other profile details collected offline, such as by phone and events. You should assess the package to see whether it enables you to import these details readily from other packages such as Excel. This is a basic capability, and most packages will enable you to tailor profile fields you add into the database.

You will need to decide whether to collect e-mail addresses and profile data via your web-site content management system or customer database management system, or through a data collection module which is part of your e-mail package. Some e-mail subscription management simply uses a white page, which does not give a great customer or brand experience because it is clearly not integrated with the main site. If using your e-mail package, this sometimes require a separate web address; however, it is best if it can be set up as a virtual sub-domain of your own site, with your own branding, which makes it appear more integrated. HSBC,

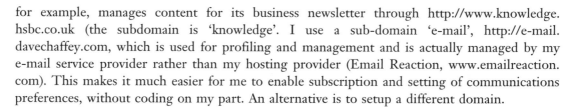

for example, manages content for its business newsletter through http://www.knowledge.hsbc.co.uk (the subdomain is 'knowledge'. I use a sub-domain 'e-mail', http://e-mail.davechaffey.com, which is used for profiling and management and is actually managed by my e-mail service provider rather than my hosting provider (Email Reaction, www.emailreaction.com). This makes it much easier for me to enable subscription and setting of communications preferences, without coding on my part. An alternative is to setup a different domain.

A more complex aspect of list management is integration of data related to the e-mail campaign with the customer database. In most organizations this is a major issue, since the data integration between the two (or more) systems can dramatically affect the capability to target, personalize and analyse campaign effectiveness. It is important to realize that your e-mail management system effectively has its own separate customer database additional to your existing customer database(s). As within any separate databases, this raises issues of data integration between the two – when data (such as an e-mail address or personal details) are updated in one database, the two need to be synchronized to the most recent one. Data from the customer database will be needed within the e-mail broadcast system to personalize any messages (using merge fields). It will often also be useful to import measures collected by the e-mail system into the customer database – for example, for each individual, which e-mails they opened and clicked on, and which items they clicked on. It may also be required to return data to the customer database about communications preferences, including e-mail subscribes and unsubscribes. The options to achieve data integration are:

1. An *ad-hoc* import/export process, i.e. customer profile information for personalization is exported from the customer database before a campaign as required, and changes to communications preferences are updated after each campaign

2. A regular batch synchronization process, where the system can be set up to exchange data at a regular time – daily, weekly or monthly

3. A real-time synchronization process, where direct communications are set up to occur between the e-mail database and customer database using application programming interfaces (APIs).

The best option will depend on the frequency of the e-mails you send, the size of your list and the degree of personalization. As size or complexity increases, you are likely to need to move from (1) to (3). Real-time synchronization is also preferable if you are undertaking a lot of event-triggered e-mails (where e-mails are sent according to response to other media or at particular points in the customer lifecycle).

A further aspect of list management is *bounce management*. While all e-mail broadcast tools will have some capability to deal with replies, they will differ in the wide variation of replies or bounces from different receiving mail servers in different languages. Bounces or returned e-mails are particularly important for large lists, since a large volume of replies can be generated from out-of-office autoreplies, particularly in holiday periods. Hidden amongst these will be genuine replies that may include feedback or requests for further information, so a method is needed to sift the wheat from the chaff and forward these replies to someone who can respond appropriately.

Since there are many different message codes and bounce replies, it makes sense to have a tool that can readily identify messages that are of value. One of the best-known options, and particularly useful if you are broadcasting from an internal package, is b*Bounce (www.bbounce.com). This identifies over 3000 different types of bounces (including international types), which it groups into the following types:

- *Hard* – the mail server could not send the e-mail; the most common example of a hard bounce is if the user doesn't exist on that domain, which usually indicates a mis-typed e-mail address

- *Soft* – the mail server is temporarily unable to accept your e-mail; this usually happens when the user's mailbox is full, or if the mail server cannot be reached

- *Blocked* – recipients' mail server is blocking you from sending e-mail to them

- *Temporary* – the mail server is temporarily unable to transfer your e-mail

- *Auto reply* – an e-mail auto-generated from the recipient, usually indicating that the recipient is out of town or out of the office for the time being

- *Subscribe* – indicates that somebody is wanting to subscribe to your list

- *Unsubscribe* – indicates that somebody is wanting to unsubscribe from your list

- *Challenge response* – the recipient subscribes to an e-mail service whose aim is to eliminate all unauthorized e-mails; the challenge response system works by requiring human intervention in order for e-mails to reach the intended recipient

- *MDN* – the message is a Message Disposition Notification, commonly known as a 'read receipt'

- *Generic* – the system is unable to detect what type of bounce the message was.

To simplify the range of responses required, most e-mail broadcasting systems use a system based on rules such as this:

- *Ensure failed message/hard bounce is a true problem*. If mail server sends a hard bounce reply, either re-send after an interval of, say, one day, or re-broadcast to the address when a campaign is next run. Since there is a wider variety of mail servers and different problems can befall them, it is not safe to assume that a hard bounce means the person has left the company or suspended the mail account.

- *Ensure messages that fail due to transient errors get through*. If the mail server receives a temporary failure message, then the message can be retried over the next few days until it gets through.

- *Ensure replies get through to a customer service/sales person*. Review all messages that have not failed against out-of-office style messages to identify the ones that are genuine replies.

3. Broadcasting the message

For most campaigns, in terms of the interface, this is straightforward. After completing the two previous stages, you simply hit the 'send' button. It may be necessary to setup the subject line and From at this point, although these are often associated with message creative (see Step 1,

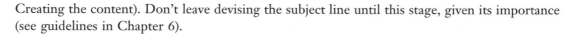

Creating the content). Don't leave devising the subject line until this stage, given its importance (see guidelines in Chapter 6).

The broadcast module is used to prepare the e-mail to send. First, the members of the list you want to target have to be selected – for example, if you only want to send the e-mail to female subscribers from the last two months, you can select these. This creates a separate campaign contacts list, which is then broadcast by the outbound module. After the 'send' button is pressed, this module simply processes the list of recipients and sends the appropriate message to each (Text, HTML or MIME) via the organization's or ISP's SMTP mail server. If the message is not received (a bounce), it will usually record this and the SMTP server will continue trying to send it for a specified period. If there is a hard bounce, the recipient can be removed from the list.

Another big issue here is the time of broadcast. As discussed in earlier chapters, it is important not to broadcast at the dead of night when the server load is low, since this will have a lower impact in the inbox than if the e-mail is received during the day. If e-mails are broadcast at a high rate, this can lead to classification of the message as spam.

The other broadcast capability that should be assessed is *event-triggered e-mails*. For example, can e-mails be broadcast to notify about a birthday or renewal, or perhaps different stages during pregnancy?

4. Tracking and reporting the results

To evaluate and improve e-mail marketing requires good reporting capabilities, and for me this is a key differentiator between e-mail management services. Almost all packages should report these basic campaign metrics (reviewed in the Measurement section of Chapter 3):

- number of e-mails broadcast
- deliverability rate
- open rate (unique and total)
- clickthrough rate (unique and total)
- unsubscribe rate for campaign.

Note that some of the desktop mailers we mention below will not provide all of this information, but application service providers will.

You should check to see whether more advanced tracking reports are within the capabilities of a system, including the following:

1. Reporting on *response behaviour of individual list members*. It is essential to use advanced e-mail techniques such as sending a follow-up e-mail to list members who have clicked but have not responded. It relies on having a different link coded for each list member.

2. *Activity scoring*. Each customer is scored according to his or her response, whether the number of opens, clicks, leads or purchases. Different communications can then be sent

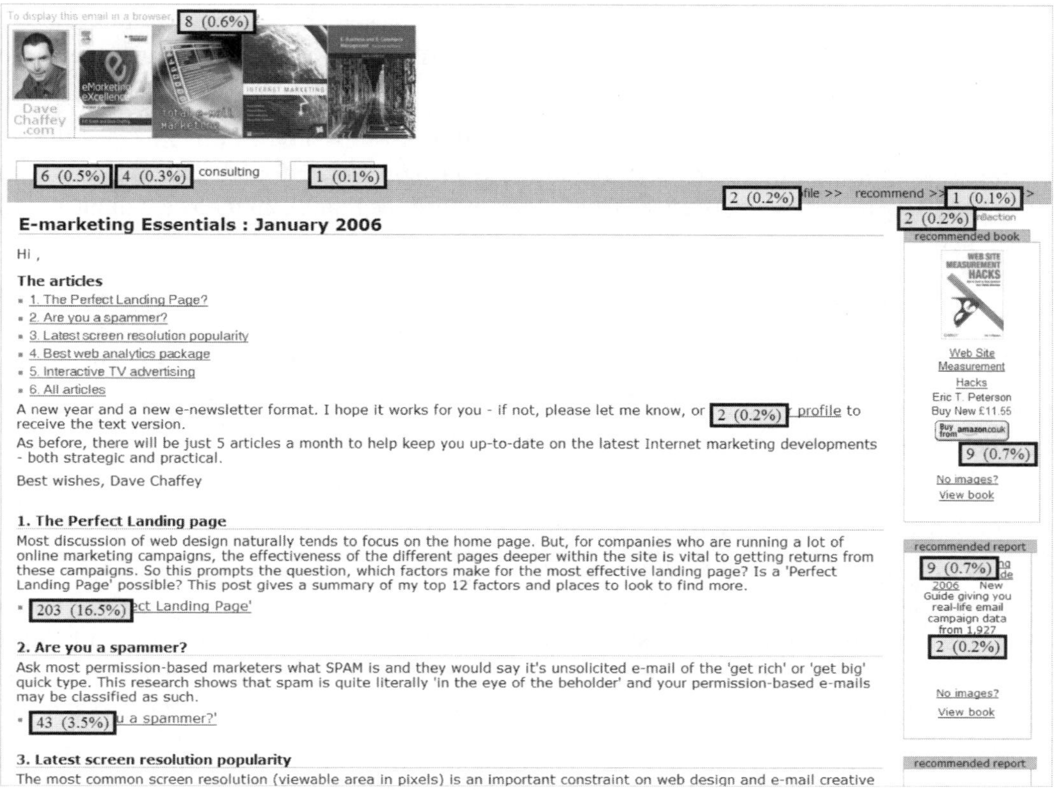

Figure 7.4 Reporting of clickthroughs on an individual e-mail broadcast (reproduced courtesy of Email Reaction Ltd, www.emailreaction.com)

to list members depending on their historical level of activity. Customers who don't seem to be responsive to online messages can be targeted through other approaches, such as direct mail or phone.

3. Reporting on *clickthroughs on each link*. Most modern systems allow these to be overlaid on top of e-mail creative, as shown in Figure 7.4.

4. Estimates of *overall open rates* based on assumptions that the same proportion of text-subscribers to a list open the e-mail (this will increase reported open rates).

5. Data on *forwards to colleagues and friends*, which is also essential for assessing viral marketing campaigns. This approach typically uses cookies to assess where e-mails are forwarded, and is subject to privacy laws in some countries.

6. Reporting '*after the click*' on the web site. For follow-up 'sense and respond' communications, it is useful to know which content on the web site was visited after the landing page. Was it related to the original offer or to different content? More generally, bounce rates can be reported on the web site (bounces are where the site visitors exit from the page they entered on). This type of reporting can be delivered by some ESPs, or it may require integration with a web analytics system. For example, Email Reaction

(www.emailreaction.com) can be set up to determine when an outcome (such as a lead or sale) is achieved on the microsite, and a value attributed to it to help calculate return on investment (ROI).

7. *Reporting of segment response.* It is useful to break down response as open or clickthrough rate by segment. For example, a vendor of a fashion brand found that the e-mail was more effective at generating clicks from older age groups than from its core, younger target audience.

8. *Reporting of long-term response across campaigns.* You may know that you get an average 30 per cent open rate, but it is helpful to know whether the same 30 per cent are regularly opening the e-mail across the whole year or, alternatively, whether there is wider engagement and 70 per cent of your audience is interacting with the e-mail.

9. Reporting of *recency, frequency and monetary value* (see Chapter 5).

10. Reporting on *list quality* using the measures indicated earlier in the book – for example, total subscribers, unsubscribers for campaign, activity of list and cost/value of list.

11. *Reporting of deliverability by ISP.* This is essential for large-scale consumer campaigns to assess whether there is a problem with deliverability of one domain – e.g. AOL, Hotmail or Yahoo!Mail. Ensure you check for deliverability problems by reporting hard bounces, and also opens and clicks, broken down by the main ISPs, since there may be a problem only for some. Techniques to improve deliverability are covered in more detail in Chapter 8.

12. *A/B testing capability.* Finally, another facility that will be essential for advanced e-mail marketers is a tool for A/B or split-testing. Some systems make it easier to execute this than others.

Price

Finally, when the service fulfils all the other criteria satisfactorily, look at price. The more capable systems may seem like a major investment, but over a period of years they can repay through higher response. Use lifetime value modelling, such as that highlighted in Tables 5.2 and 5.3, to calculate the returns over a longer period. We have looked at many criteria. The E-mail marketing checklist given here lists my top ten 'must-have' features for advanced e-mail marketing, although not all the providers have them.

E-MAIL MARKETING CHECKLIST

My top ten questions to ask about marketing capabilities of an e-mail system are, does it:

1. Track response at an individual level to outcome?

2. Track response across time/multiple campaigns?

3. Track response by demographic profile?

4. Integrate response with customer database?

5. Manage profiling and subscription/unsubscribe?

6. Provide details of bounces and replies – e.g. out-of-office auto-replies?

7. Deliver WYSIWYG for marketing staff, with rules-based fields for personalization?

8. Monitor viral pass-alongs?

9. Archive e-newsletters on web site?

10. Broadcast smartly – i.e. throttle back to avoid spam assessment?

Selecting an e-mail management solution

There are four main types of e-mail solutions that companies use, described here in order of increasing sophistication:

1. Standard office software

2. Desktop mailer software

3. List-server software

4. Application service providers (ASPs).

As companies' needs grow and they send out a larger volume of e-mail, they typically then use the more sophisticated methods for broadcast.

Standard office software

It is possible to use standard office groupware such as Microsoft Outlook to manage mailing lists. To send e-mails, a group is set up with each recipient added to the Blind Carbon Copy field (BCC) or through a list compiled using the address list, perhaps through a mail-merge facility, so that recipients only see their own e-mail address. This solution is only really practical for relatively small lists, since each contact has to be added and removed manually. No tracking is available with this approach, and all bounced e-mails have to be processed manually.

To automate this process (this is really essential for any list numbering thousands of subscribers) there is a range of software solutions available. These can include software that you install on your own PC for list management, or a server-based product that can be located elsewhere in the organization or delivered by an external application service provider (ASP) which is usually accessed via a web browser.

Desktop mailer software

With this approach, e-mail lists are managed and e-mails broadcast using a software application running on the user's PC. Most of the software tends to be from US suppliers; such software is sometimes referred to as 'bulk mailers'. Some of the well-known suppliers are:

- *Infacta GroupMail* (www.infacta.com), which has a separate tracking package, GroupMetrics

- *Gammadyne Mailer* (www.gammadyne.com/mmail.htm)
- *Broadcast* (www.mailworkz.com), which has a separate tracking module, ezTrackZ.

These packages have the advantage of low cost, since they only require an initial licence and there is no fee for each message sent. They offer some personalization, and now have additional tracking packages. The main disadvantages are that volumes are limited by what is permissible by the ISP. They are mainly suitable for small businesses.

Related to desktop mailers is low-cost sales and contact management software which can also be used for e-mail management and tracking contact history. These typically have their own desktop mailer engine, or can integrate with Outlook. They include:

- *Act*, from Sage (http://www.act.com)
- *Goldmine*, from Frontrange (http://www.frontrange.com)
- *Centerbase* (http://www.centerbase.com).

Desktop mailers are probably the best option for small businesses, but make sure the tracking of individual action and reporting is adequate for your needs.

List-server software

For businesses requiring higher volumes of e-mail broadcast from a server, there are different list-server options. List servers are software tools, hosted on a server computer, which are used for managing e-mail communications. They are well-established tools; the first version of Listserv was introduced in 1981. Many list servers are applications service providers that are used by many companies worldwide.

List servers are used for broadcasting e-mails, but also manage the addition and removal of subscribers to an e-mail list. Addition and removal of subscribers was traditionally carried out by e-mail subscribe and unsubscribe messages, but these may be confusing for novice users; therefore, when selecting a list server, the option to be able to use a web form to add or remove a subscriber from the list is essential for commercial organizations. They were formerly used for managing e-mail newsletters and alerts, but can also be used for promotional e-mail campaigns. The mailing lists can be one-way (which is the case with a standard newsletter) or two way (where they are used for a discussion mailing list, which is usually a moderated forum about a particular topic). Discussion mailing lists, such as UK NetMarketing (www.chinwag.com), may involve tens of messages or 'posts' each day, so list servers offer two different methods of e-mail delivery: the first is where single messages are delivered as soon as they have been posted; the second is 'digest delivery', which contains all the messages for a day or week in a single message. A further option to consider for such mailing-list software is whether web-based list management is possible. This allows subscribers or non-subscribers to view current or archived messages.

Examples of list servers include:

- *Lyris List Manager* (www.lyris.com), which is a list manager that is widely used for marketing purposes by companies who want to manage broadcast internally. A web-based interface is used by subscribers and list managers. By default it has a double opt-in mechanism, where subscribers have to reply to a confirmation e-mail after the initial opt-in. Like L-Soft, Lyris also offers an ASP or outsourcing service.

- SparkList (www.sparklist.com), which is based on the Lyris List Manager and is also a popular list server.

- *Listserv* (www.lsoft.com), which is based on development of the original list server. This package is available for Microsoft Windows-based servers as well as UNIX. There is an advanced web-based interface for subscribers and list managers. L-Soft, the supplier of Listserv, provides an outsourcing service which involves hosting the list. The list is then managed remotely in the company using web-based tools. The cost of hosting the list varies according to the number of lists and subscribers.

- *ListProc* (www.listproc.net), which is most commonly used by educational organizations, since the fee is waived for these users.

- *Majordomo* (www.greatcircle.com/majordomo), which, according to ServerWatch, is the most popular list server since it is free. It is a modular package which includes some graphical subscription and viewing interfaces; this may make installation lengthy and complex.

Some of the ASP providers mentioned in the next section, such as Email Reaction (http://www.e-mailreaction.com) and EmailCenter (http://www.e-mailcenteruk.com), also provide the capability for their ASP solutions to be installed in-house.

Application service providers

An application service provider (ASP) provides a web-based service that can be used by clients to manage their e-mail activities. Rather than buying software that you host and manage on your server, the software is effectively used on a subscription basis and runs on another company's server. In other words, it provides the technical infrastructure that is needed to run the campaign – this could comprise all of the four key capabilities mentioned earlier in the chapter, including hosting of the microsite or landing pages, the broadcast tools for dispatching the e-mails and the database containing the prospect or customer profiles. For example, you could use an ASP which hosts your newsletter archive, manages the subscriber list, and broadcasts and tracks the newsletter each month. For the e-newsletter, you will likely create the content each month and upload it to the ASP service for dispatch.

From a user-experience point of view, the user logs in to a web-based 'booth' such as that shown in Figure 7.5 and from this one point is able to create the e-mail, select the targeting, and broadcast and track the results in real time.

The Aberdeen Group (2000) identifies these differences from purchasing licensed software. According to them, with licensed software the customer must:

- develop and support the IT infrastructure of the application

- make a large capital investment in acquiring and installing the software (for this reason, licensed software is relatively difficult to trial)

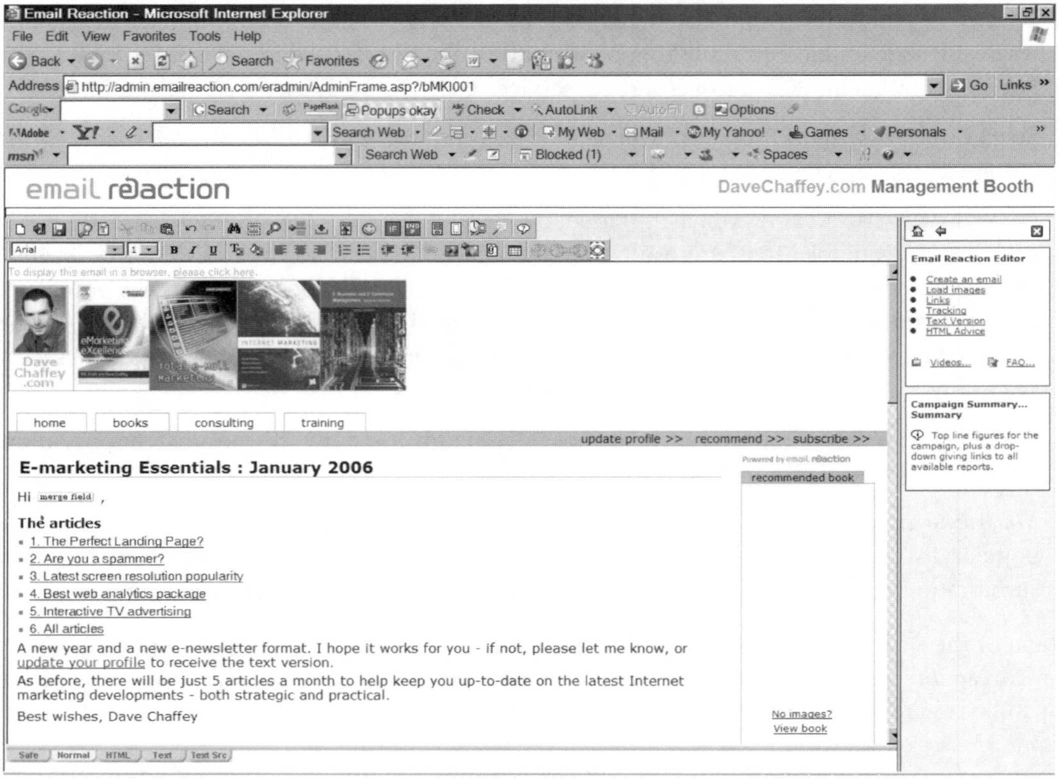

Figure 7.5 Email Reaction ASP e-mail service provider (reproduced courtesy of Email Reaction Ltd, www.emailreaction.com)

- develop considerable internal expertise in the use of the software to fully realize its potential

- cope with regular software upgrades, bug fixes and version releases.

The ASP model removes many of these problems. It offers:

- reduction or elimination of the many of the up-front capital expenses associated with implementing new software systems and databases

- access to skilled IT professionals – the ASP has to pay good rates, perhaps more than you can afford, to deliver a world-class service

- a guarantee of a specific and agreed-on service level

- reduced deployment time

- the potential to reduce systems integration expenses.

The Aberdeen Group (2000) distinguishes between two different types of ASP. Today, these are both referred to E-mail Service Providers (ESPs). The first is the ASP, which just provides a software service to dispatch and monitor e-mails. Secondly, there is a service that can also deliver strategy, creative design and testing – a service bureau.

Not included in the original report are these typical benefits of e-mail ASP services:

1. *Experience in managing deliverability*. The ASP should know the different factors that trigger a spam alert, such as high broadcast rates (typically $> 10\,000–15\,000$ messages per hour), and should be able to monitor deliverability both by checking blacklists and by reporting on deliverability. If there is a problem with e-mail delivery, then the e-mail service provider should have the contacts with the ISPs and web-mail companies to resolve blacklisting issues. They also tend to be very careful that they are not classified as spammers and put on blacklists, and that their servers are not hijacked by spammers – although it is a good idea to ask how often this has happened in the past, as it is possible. For large-volume senders it may be helpful to have your own IP address, since with some ESPs it is shared across several companies which may flag a spam alert on the receiving ISP.

2. *Improved tracking and bounce management*. E-mail broadcast ASP services tend to have more sophisticated tracking and management of bounces than do internal systems, particularly if you are using a standard e-mail package such as Microsoft Outlook to broadcast your messages.

The following services use an applications service provider model. I maintain an up-to-date list of the providers, from low to high cost, at: http://www.davechaffey.com/Total-E-mail-Marketing.

Some of the most widely used high-end systems employed in large organizations in the UK at the time of writing were:

- *Email Reaction* (www.emailreaction.com)
- *E-dialog* (www.e-dialog.com)
- *Email Vision* (www.emailvision.com)
- *EmailCenter* (www.emailcenteruk.com)
- *e-rm* (www.e-rm.co.uk)
- *Exact Target* (www.exacttarget.com)
- *messageREACH* (www.messagereach.com)
- *Responsys* (www.responsys.com).

The e-mail broadcast/management (e-mail service provider, ESP) solutions that are most cost-effective (below $50 per month for low volumes), as recommended to me by delegates on my courses, are:

- NewZapp (www.newzapp.com), which is a relatively low-cost, capable UK-based solution
- Newsweaver (www.newsweaver.co.uk), which is a European-based solution, but more expensive
- Jangomail (www.jangomail.com), which is one of the best for database integration

- Ezinedirector (www.ezinedirector.com)
- Constant Contact (www.constantcontact.com).

MANAGING THE HOUSE LIST

As was noted in Chapters 4 and 5, there will be a high turnover of your e-mail addresses or 'gone-aways' (in traditional direct mail speak). Research by MercerMC (2001) showed that, on average, 20 per cent of customers in a typical database will change their contact information over the course of a year. Changes vary from 16 per cent for the address and 17 per cent for the job to 25 per cent for the e-mail address and 33 per cent for a cell-phone number. Furthermore, they estimate that the cost of updating or reconsenting these databases can run into tens of millions of dollars for a large database – not to mention the opportunity costs from lost customers. These figures highlight the importance of creating measures to capture these changes. Worse still, the permission provided for contact may change through time, since you will have asked different questions about how personal data will be used to market to the customer. Options for managing this change include:

- periodic checks by call centre staff and at other touchpoints
- a 'change personal details' option on the web site (this is required by data protection laws in some countries)
- e-mail or telesales campaigns aimed at updating data (Case study 4.1 shows how this process works).

Software designed specifically for cleaning a list is Winpure (www.winpure.com), although many ESPs also contain this capability.

Note though, that changing e-mail address seems to have stabilized more recently. The *Doubleclick Sixth Annual Consumer E-mail Survey* (Doubleclick, 2005) showed that, when asked how long they had maintained their e-mail addresses, most consumers had kept the same address for four to six years. Nearly two-thirds of consumers had never changed their e-mail address.

The survey (Doubleclick, 2005) also showed that almost half of all consumers reported maintaining at least three e-mail accounts – an increase from 2004. Nearly 95 per cent considered one of their e-mail addresses to be a 'primary' account; 72 per cent used a single address specifically for making purchases. This shows the importance of gaining the primary e-mail address for opt-in, particularly for an e-newsletter. To help with this, make sure you explain the proposition in detail and give examples of previous e-newsletters. If the frequency is relatively low, this may also help with gaining the primary e-mail address.

MANAGING INBOUND E-MAIL

Inbound e-mail is all incoming e-mail to the organization. This includes bounces, which we have covered earlier in the chapter, but also managing e-mail enquiries from customers. There are two conflicting concerns in managing inbound enquiry or support e-mails that will determine the inbound customer contact strategies; the first is customer service quality and the second is cost. Customer contact strategies are a compromise between delivering quality customer service with the emphasis on customer choice, and minimizing the cost of customer contacts. Typical operational objectives that should drive the strategies and measure their effectiveness are:

- to minimize average response time per e-mail and range of response time from slowest to fastest; this should form the basis of an advertised service quality level

- to minimize clear-up (resolution) time – for example, number of contacts and elapsed time to resolution

- to maximize customer satisfaction ratings with response

- to minimize average staff time and cost per e-mail response.

Of course, the challenge is to balance the level of service with the cost of delivering this service. Technology can help here – a common approach is to use a web self-service approach of 'Frequently Asked Questions', which should reduce the number of form-generated e-mail enquiries.

Now let's look at cost. Farris and Langendorf's (1999) survey found that the cost of manually managing each inbound e-mail averaged $2.75. By using automation to manage the inbound e-mails, they suggest the cost could be reduced to less than 25 cents. How many e-mails does your organization receive that are processed manually? Multiply that number by £2. Is this a cost you would like to reduce? If so, this section explains some of the techniques, used by companies that receive hundreds of thousands of e-mails, to reduce cost.

Customer contact strategies for integrating web and e-mail support into existing contact centre operations usually incorporate elements of both of the following options:

1. *Customer-preferred channel.* Here, the company uses a customer-led approach, where customers use their preferred channel for enquiry – whether it is phone callback, e-mail or live chat. There is little attempt made to influence the customer as to which is the preferable channel. Note that while this approach may give good customer satisfaction ratings, it is not usually the most cost-effective approach, since the cost of phone support will be higher than either customer self-service on the web or an e-mail enquiry.

2. *Company-preferred channel.* Here, the company will seek to influence the customer on the medium used for contact. For example, easyJet encourages customers to use online channels rather than voice contact to the call centre for both ordering and customer service. Customer choice is still available, but the company uses the web site to influence the choice of channel. Visit the easyJet web site (www.easyjet.com) and see Case study 7.1 to see how this is achieved.

Other management options for contact management strategy that concern resourcing include:

- *Call-centre staff multi-skilling, or separate web contact centre.* Many companies start with a separate web contact centre, and then move to multi-skilling. Multi-skilling is the best way of effectively answering queries from customers whose support query may refer to a combination of online or offline activities. Multi-skilling also reduces hand-offs, and can increase variety for contact-centre staff.

- *Balance between automation and manual processes.* Automated responses, intelligent routing and autosuggestion are all techniques, described in the next section, which can be used to reduce the number of queries handled by human operators. If the automated approach fails, however, then inappropriate responses may be received by customers.

- *Insourcing or outsourcing.* Software, hardware and staff can be deployed internally or outsourced to an application service provider, who will work according to a service-level agreement to achieve quality standards.

Developing a plan for managing inbound e-mail

To develop a plan for managing inbound e-mail, the best approach is to consider the typical stages in which an e-mail is received and responded to (Figure 7.6).

The five stages are as follows.

Stage 1: Customer defines support query

The first stage starts before the customer has even sent the e-mail since, if we are concerned with reducing cost, we want to minimize the number of e-mails that need to be responded to. Provided the customer doesn't have to spend too much time seeking out an answer, then this can also give rise to better customer service. As Case study 7.1 shows, easyJet encourages users to view the Frequently Asked Questions first, before giving them the option to e-mail or phone.

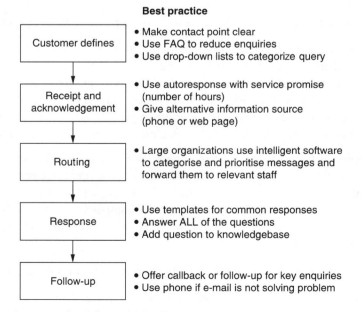

Best practice

Customer defines
- Make contact point clear
- Use FAQ to reduce enquiries
- Use drop-down lists to categorize query

Receipt and acknowledgement
- Use autoresponse with service promise (number of hours)
- Give alternative information source (phone or web page)

Routing
- Large organizations use intelligent software to categorise and prioritise messages and forward them to relevant staff

Response
- Use templates for common responses
- Answer ALL of the questions
- Add question to knowledgebase

Follow-up
- Offer callback or follow-up for key enquiries
- Use phone if e-mail is not solving problem

Figure 7.6 Stages in managing inbound e-mail

To reduce costs, we therefore need self-service tools on the web site that help the customers to find answers to their query. Many sites have Frequently Asked Questions (FAQ) that have usually been compiled without too much thought as to what customers are actually asking. Start with moving from a brief list of FAQ to a more extensively researched and structured list of FAQ. This can be compiled based on questions already fielded from customers. If you supply complex products, such as hardware or software, then FAQ will probably not be enough. A knowledgebase can be used here. The most used knowledgebase is probably the Microsoft knowledgebase, which contains articles written by engineers in response to customers' questions. To be effective, the knowledgebase requires suitable query tools which offer both keyword-based search and restricted searches in particular categories, such as the product type and problem type. Some knowledgebases contain specific responses to individual customers, but the Microsoft approach of writing a more detailed article gives a better quality of response and avoids duplication.

Another approach that can be used for some products is an automated diagnostic tool that steps users through their problem by asking a series of questions and then offering appropriate solutions. Epson (www.epson.co.uk) provides an online tool to diagnose problems with printers and suggest solutions.

CASE STUDY 7.1: E-MAIL MARKETING EXCELLENCE – EASYJET MANAGES E-MAIL VOLUME (WWW.EASYJET.COM)

If easyJet customers select the 'Contact Us' option, rather than listing phone numbers and e-mail addresses, they are led through the three steps shown below, which are intended to reduce the need for them to call the contact centre.

Step 1: Links or Frequently Asked Questions (FAQ). The FAQs are based on careful analysis of phone calls and e-mails received by the contact centre. Examples include questions concerning use of the site and booking online, fares, availability and pricing, airports, check-in, and travel information.

Step 2: E-mail enquiry through web form completion. Examples include technical queries relating to the site, customer service and route feedback, and general feedback – for comments and suggestions (these e-mails are categorized to help prioritization and routing to the right person).

Step 3: Telephone numbers. Phone contact is only encouraged at the final stage. As easyJet explains: 'We've tried to make the FAQ and e-mail service as simple and efficient as possible in order to keep the cost down and provide you with a good service, but if you're really stuck then, of course, you can call us.'

Companies should also consider how easily the customer can find contact points and compose a support request on site. Best practice is clear e-mail support options. Often, finding contact and support information on a web site is surprisingly difficult. Standardized terminology on a web site is 'Contact Us' or 'Support'. Options should be available for the customer to specify the type of query on a web form, or alternative e-mail addresses such as products@company.com or returns@company.com should be provided on site, or in offline communications such as a catalogue. Utilities provider Servista (www.servista.com) provides a good example of such a form.

When the site visitor finally comes to complete the support form, then it is vital to have a field on the form that identifies the type of query – for example, 'Product fault', 'Delivery enquiry', 'Product information required' or 'other'. This is best achieved through the aid of a drop-down product list box from which the customer chooses an option. This can help in assigning the e-mail to someone who is able to answer the problem, since there is a restricted range of options.

Finally, the web site should determine expectations about the level of service quality – for example, inform the customer that 'Your enquiry will be responded to within 24 hours'.

Stage 2: Receipt of e-mail and acknowledgement

Best practice is that automatic message acknowledgement occurs. This is usually provided by autoresponder software. While many autoresponders only provide a simple acknowledgement, more sophisticated responses can reassure the customer about when the response will occur and highlight other sources of information. Blackstar (www.blackstar.co.uk) provides a good example of best practice here:

> *Thanks for e-mailing blackstar.co.uk. There are currently 51 e-mails in the queue in front of yours, so our expected response time is approximately 1 hour, 10 minutes.*
>
> *Don't forget that you can track your order status on line at: http://www. blackstar.co.uk/circle/order_status (where you can also cancel your order if you've made a mistake, or have just changed your mind).*
>
> *Many other common questions are also answered in our help section: click on the big question mark in the header bar or go direct to http://www.blackstar.co.uk/help/*

Stage 3: Routing of e-mail

Best practice involves automated routing or workflow. Routing the e-mail to the right person is made easier if the type of query has been categorized at Stage 1. It is also possible to use pattern recognition to identify the type of enquiry. For example, Nationwide (www.nationwide.co.uk) uses Brightware's 'skill-based message routing' so that messages are sent to a specialist advisor where specific enquiries are made. Such software can also be used at Stage 1 to give an auto-response appropriate for the enquiry. Using this approach, Mark Cromack, operations manager at Nationwide, says '40 per cent of messages no longer reach our advisors' (see Case study 7.2).

Stage 4: Compose response

Best practice is to use a library of pre-prepared templates for different types of query. These can then be tailored and personalized by the contact centre employee as appropriate. The right type of template can again be selected automatically using the software referred to in Stage 2.

Through using such autosuggestion, the Nationwide has seen e-mail handling times reduced by 25 per cent for messages requiring advisor intervention. Sony Europe identifies all new support issues and adds them, with the appropriate response, to a central knowledge base.

Stage 5: Follow-up

Best practice is that if the employee does not successfully answer the first response, then the e-mail should suggest a phone callback from an employee or a live chat. Indeed, to avoid the problem of 'e-mail ping-pong', where several e-mails may be exchanged, the company may want proactively to ring the customer to increase the speed of problem resolution. Finally, the e-mail follow-up may provide the opportunity for outbound contact and marketing, perhaps enquiring whether there are any further queries while advising about complementary products or offers.

CASE STUDY 7.2: E-MAIL MARKETING EXCELLENCE – CUSTOMER SERVICE AT THE NATIONWIDE

The Nationwide is a financial services organization which has been active in using the Internet as a customer service tool. Bicknell (2002) reported that the volume of customer service was as follows: 900 000 registrants on site, with 2.4 million visits to the site in August 2001. Of the 1.2 million who entered the online bank, 900 000 made transactions, resulting in 60 000 online contacts that required customer service.

These figures highlight the number of transactions that will have reduced customer contacts in real-world branches and by phone, but this still leaves 60 000 online contacts. The Nationwide believes that customers should expect service to be fast and accurate. Mark Cromack, operations manager, said:

> There was a huge demand for more and more information and an explosion in the level of information that people wanted. That had implications for staff morale. What we needed was an autoresponse facility which provided quality, compliant and consistent answers.

To reduce the volume of calls, Frequently Answered Questions (FAQ) was not sufficient. The Nationwide purchased two products from Firepond to improve service: *Concierge* is provided on the home page to provide a facility with natural language searching to help customers find the answers to their queries more rapidly, while *Answer* is an automated message routing tool that provides automated answers to simple questions that can be reviewed by contact centre staff before dispatch, and yet is able to spot the phrasing of more complex queries for completion by call centre operators.

Using these solutions, the quality of answers improved to give a first-time resolution rate of 94 per cent. With the reduced staff time involved, the cost per contact was reduced from £4 to £2.

REFERENCES

Aberdeen Group (2000). e-Marketing: to outsource or not to outsource – that is the question. An executive white paper. The Aberdeen Group.

Bicknell, D. (2002). Banking on customer service. *e.Businessreview*, **Jan**, 21–22.

Doubleclick (2005). *Doubleclick Sixth Annual Consumer E-mail Survey*. Doubleclick.

Farris, J. and Langendorf, L. (1999). *Engaging Customers in e-Business*. e2 white paper (available at www.e2software.com).

Mercer MC (2001). Making CRM make Money. A Mercer Management Consulting Commentary (available at www.mercermc.com).

WEB LINKS

The web links on e-mail broadcast tools are contained within the chapter.

Chapter

8

E-mail marketing
challenges and innovation

CHAPTER AT A GLANCE

Overview

This chapter looks at issues that will affect the future of e-mail marketing, many of which are significant already. They include challenges such as achieving deliverability, given the rise of spam, and attaining the right balance between frequency and return on investment. There are also technological innovations, including wireless access devices such as PDAs and mobiles, and the new opportunities for rich media, such as video streaming provided by increased bandwith. The impact of Really Simple Syndication (RSS) on e-mail marketing is also covered.

Chapter objectives

By the end of this chapter you will be able to:

- assess different approaches being developed to control spam.

- evaluate the relevance of rich media e-mails.

- identify the options for e-mail using wireless access devices.

- assess the role of RSS in the future.

Chapter structure

- Improving deliverability

- Touch frequency

- Rich media e-mails

- Messaging through mobile or wireless access devices

- Really Simple Syndication

- References

- Web links

IMPROVING DELIVERABILITY

Newmediazero (2002) reported that, according to a new Forrester report, the 'spam flood will drown E-mail marketing'. Forrester predicted that all attempts by ISPs to filter spam and efforts by governments to legislate against spam would be ineffectual. Four years later, we can see that the gloom of this prediction has not transpired. Response data showing e-mail responsiveness measured by clickthrough of e-mails delivered have remained similar despite the volume of spam increasing to over 90 per cent of all messages, according to Messagelabs. This is because consumers seem to be good at identifying permission-based e-mail in their inbox – the permission marketing concept works!

What has transpired, though, is that e-mail marketers have had to work much harder to get their e-mails delivered, given the increase in efforts by ISPs and web-email companies to reduce the amount of spam arriving in their end-users inboxes. This results in *'false positives'*, where permission-based e-mails may be bounced or placed into junk-mail boxes, or simply deleted if the receiving system assesses that they are spam. Although deliverability rates remain high, it may be that some e-mails which appear to be delivered do not get through to their recipients.

Know your enemy – what can lead to you being identified as a false positive?

Spammers work hard to understand why their messages are not read and find methods to avoid being blocked. Here, legitimate e-mail marketers are much like the spammer, since they and their suppliers also need to understand what is stopping their messages getting through and identify solutions to this. There are four general points where spam or legitimate permission-based e-mail is identified, and which can stop e-mail being read by the recipient:

1. *Inbox identification by the user.* The simplest way that spam is identified is by the recipient; if it looks like spam from the header, it will be quickly removed using the delete button. Alternatively, recipients can report spam to their anti-spam software and, if enough people do this, there is the danger that may be added to a blacklist.

2. *Software filtering.* E-mail can be identified as having the characteristics of spam by anti-spam software, which may run at a variety of locations – at the ISP, a third-party mail-scanning service, a company firewall or mail server, at a web-based e-mail service server or on the end-user's computer.

3. *Domain blocking.* Here, the domain from which the e-mails are broadcast is blocked since its IP address is deemed to be a known source of spam.

4. *Sender authentication systems.* Here, the recipient's system or administrator identifies that the e-mail has not been sent from a recognized broadcaster.

Let's now look at these in a little more detail.

Inbox identification

An e-mail will look like spam if recipients don't recognize the sender – i.e. it is not a company or product known to them as indicated by the From, subject line or preview pane. If it is not clear from the subject line, a preview of the text in the e-mail will usually show whether or not it is relevant. For an in-house e-mail list you must therefore use the company or brand name in the From address, or in some cases (like an e-newsletter where the name of the e-newsletter is in the From address) use the name of the company or brand in the subject line.

For campaigns using rented lists or co-branded with a partner, it is more tricky. Many companies concatenate both list owner and the brand being promoted in the From as in 'Freeserve-Accucard', but since this may get truncated it is perhaps better to put the brand in the subject line.

Another vital step to avoid being identified as spam by the recipient is to use copy within the message that explains that the message is *not* spam. This is commonly headed as a 'statement of origination' or, more informally, 'Why am I receiving this e-mail?' This should explain either that the recipient has opted in, ideally with the place and time of opt-in, or that the e-mail has been sent because the recipient is an existing customer. You should also explain that the message is within the law of the country.

For e-mail campaigns using rented or shared lists, it is essential that the statement of origination is clear, typically at or near the top of the message. For house-list campaigns it is still useful to have a statement of origin, but is probably best at the foot of the message.

It is also best practice to invite the recipient to add the e-mail to the *'safe senders list'*. Some e-mail providers have set up pages to explain how the end-user can do this for different web mail and desktop mail packages. For example, Tesco has this message at the top of its e-mail, in a discreet colour:

> *To ensure that your Tesco e-mails get to your inbox, please add mailto:online@ tesco.co.uk to your e-mail Address Book or Safe List. For instructions, click here.*

Software filtering

There are now many techniques that are used by different types of anti-spam software to identify spam. We will now review some of the most common ones, which are often combined in a single anti-spam tool, and describe the type of steps that marketers can take to avoid being wrongly identified as spam.

Keyword and key phrase filters

First-generation anti-spam software uses a simple 'look-up' table of words that are commonly used by spammers, such as 'viagra', 'sex', 'over 18' or 'free'. If these words are contained in either the message header or the body, then it is deleted or assigned to a junk-mail folder.

Such words do not present a problem to most companies, but what if your company is in Sussex, or you are a bank that by law has to say that your product is only available to those who are over 18? Or maybe you are offering a free trial. In these cases, one alternative may be to use these 'naughty words' as part of graphics embedded within the e-mail, which will not be recognized by most filters. Of course, the spammers use variants of words, such as 'v'iagra' or 'vlagra'.

Do not be overly concerned by using words such as 'free' in the subject line – I have seen tests where such e-mails pull a higher response than more subtle approaches. The reason is that many spam filters now use a more sophisticated approach ...

Message rating filters

Second-generation anti-spam software uses a scoring system where different keywords and different phrases score different points – for example, 'free' might score 2 points and 'sex' 10 points. If the e-mail is rated over 15 points, it will be classified as spam. Some programs now have Bayesian filters, which use a mathematical model to learn the characteristics of spam and watch for patterns typical of spam. You may have noticed gobbledy-gook phrases at the bottom of some spam messages; these are used to overcome such an approach. An example of a spam rating available from the ESP Email Reaction (www.emailreaction.com), based on the Spam Assassin rating, is shown below. Such facilities are available to help you assess your e-mail for 'spamminess' before you send it. You can see that, in this case, some factors are set to 0, but for some firewalls these could be given higher values.

Words likely to trigger content filters

These words may trigger some content filters: viagra.

HTML and technical issues

Content analysis details: (4.4 points, 5.0 required)

pts	rule name	description
0.0	SUB_FREE_OFFER	Subject starts with 'Free'
1.8	SUBJECT_DRUG_GAP_VIA	Subject contains a gappy version of 'viagra'
0.5	TO_ADDRESS_EQ_REAL	To: repeats address as real name
0.2	HTML_IMAGE_RATIO_04	BODY: HTML has a low ratio of text to image area
1.5	HTML_IMAGE_ONLY_12	BODY: HTML: images with 800–1200 bytes of words
0.0	HTML_WEB_BUGS	BODY: Image tag intended to identify you
0.2	HTML_FONT_BIG	BODY: HTML tag for a big font size
0.0	HTML_TITLE_EMPTY	BODY: HTML title contains no text
0.0	DRUGS_ERECTILE	Refers to an erectile drug
0.1	MIME_BOUND_NEXTPART	Spam tool pattern in MIME boundary

These are some tips from David Hughes of Email Vision (www.emailvision.com) on how to reduce problems of content filtering:

- Avoid or minimize spam phrases, particularly in subject lines

- Minimize use of capitalization

- Keep HTML simple

- Carefully word your unsubscribe method so it doesn't look like that commonly used by spammers; don't mention spam compliance as such

- Don't overuse large fonts and garish colours

- Newsletters are less likely to be blocked, so show clearly that you are a newsletter

- Avoid the message being too small – spammers and phishers today often find that a single embedded image with their message in it gets through the filters, particularly if it has a paragraph of legitimate newsletter-like text at the bottom of the e-mail.

Messages are also blocked if the original From address has been masked, so it is important for legitimate marketers not to do this. If your e-mail management system doesn't contain these spam rating features, then you can try using this service (which is currently free): Lyris Content checker (http://www.lyris.com/contentchecker).

Blacklists

Blacklists are lists of known spammers, such as those reported to Spamhaus Project (www.spamhaus.com) or SpamCop (www.spamcop.net). If a recipient is on the blacklist, it is deleted or put in the junk-mail folder. Blacklists are often used in conjunction with filters to block e-mails. One of the most widely used systems is that developed by Brightmail (www.brightmail.com), which uses a global network of e-mail addresses set up to trap and identify spam. Brightmail is increasingly used by ISPs such as BT to block spam.

Blacklists are also used by many types of anti-spam software, such as the two most popular – McAfee SpamKiller and Norton AntiSpam.

It is unlikely that legitimate marketers will be placed on these, but it may be worth checking. However, there is an argument for companies who send out a lot of consumer e-mail to test whether messages pass through the main filters. Filtering used by major ISPs such as BT, AOL and Freeserve, and also web-based e-mail services such as Hotmail and Yahoo!Mail, should also be tested.

Using seed addresses at some of these accounts can help, but you may be missing some. Email Monitor (www.emailmonitor.co.uk) estimates that 99 per cent of e-mails in the UK are ultimately delivered through 20 ISPs. It offers a tool, known as MailBox Monitor, which is configured with addresses at these 20 ISPs in order to test for blocking due to blacklists or the different filters described above. It also has a tool known as Message Check which tests an e-mail address, before sending, against the main filters.

Lyris EmailAdvisor (http://www.lyris.com/products/emailadvisor) also includes a blacklist monitor and deliverability service. Blacklist monitor (http://www.blacklistmonitor.com) is a low-cost service, with a free trial that enables you to see whether the IP address of your e-mail marketing broadcaster is blacklisted.

Whitelists

An organization whitelist is a list of *bona fide* e-mail addresses that are likely to want to contact people within an organization. It will include all employees, partners, customers and suppliers who have obtained opt-in from employees to receive e-mail. A personal whitelist is one created by the user of e-mail software, listing message senders he or she is happy to receive e-mail from.

The organization whitelist approach has not been adopted widely because it is difficult to set up, but it probably offers the best opportunity for the future. The personal whitelist feature is becoming more common in anti-spam software, and is now built into Outlook or the popular Qurb (www.qurb.com) service, which guarantees to 'block 100% of Spam'!

However, there is little action marketers can use other than recommending that their company be put on the recipient's whitelist. Some e-mail recipients may use such tools rather than opting out.

Challenge/response authentication

In this approach, if an e-mail is sent from someone who is not on your whitelist (or is possibly on your blacklist), a message is automatically sent asking the sender to provide manual confirmation or authentication of identity by following a link from a challenge e-mail that requires a response. This approach is available as part of anti-spam solutions from companies such as Spam Interceptor (http://si20.com) and SpamBully for Outlook (www.spambully.com). The theory is that spammers are not going to be able to respond; the problem is that permission marketers will not be able to either. Fortunately, it seems that this approach is not widespread . . . yet.

'Peer-to-peer' blocking services

These take advantage of the fact that humans are good at identifying spam; when they do so they then notify a central server, which keeps an index of all spam. SPAMNet from CloudMark (www.cloudmark.com) requires users to identify spam by pressing a 'Block' button in Microsoft Outlook, which then updates a central server so that when others download the same message at a later time it is automatically identified as spam. I have used this service and it works effectively, but I have noticed a problem in that legitimate e-mails I have opted in to can be classified as spam by other users. They can be marked as legitimate, however, by the recipient.

Domain blocking

ISPs or firewalls can block individual domains or web IP addresses that are known sources of spam, or where the pattern of broadcast suggests spamming. This approach is intended to trap known spammers who hijack servers and send out a large number of e-mails. However, it can lead to legitimate e-mail marketers being blocked, particularly if their e-mail platform is co-hosted by a machine that has been hijacked. This may also be a problem if you send out a large number of e-mails in a short period, such as when your e-mail broadcaster or in-house system sends more than 10 000–15 000 e-mails per hour. Web-based e-mail vendors such as Hotmail, Yahoo!Mail or AOL may blacklist companies who broadcast too many.

One solution is to send out the e-mails over a longer period or 'throttle back' the rate at which e-mails are sent. However, it is difficult to know which ISPs are blocking your domain.

Also check whether your broadcaster has a deliverability monitoring tool. One of the first tools developed was IP Block Alert, also from IPT Limited's Email Monitor (www.emailmonitor.co.uk). Most of the major e-mail broadcasters now offer this facility.

Sender authentication systems

These approaches seek to prove the sender of the e-mail is legitimate – that senders are who they say they are. The SMTP standard used for e-mail allows any computer user to send e-mail claiming to be from anyone, so its easy for spammers to send e-mails from forged addresses. Authentication uses different methods, which require senders to establish who they are. There are several approaches.

Reverse DNS look up

DNS stands for Domain Name System – it's how computers find each other on the Internet, a bit like the Yellow Pages. The DNS is a mapping of the IP address (e.g. 64.233.179.104) that uniquely identifies each computer attached to the Internet with its physical addresses. For example, the IP address given above maps to the domain google.com.

Many ISPs now perform what is known as reverse DNS to check that the e-mail sender has a valid domain with a published DNS record. This is only possible for servers with a static IP address, such as legitimate ESPs. Spammers may be using software installed on infected end-user machines known as 'zombies', which typically have dynamic IP addresses (they change every time the user logs on).

Sender Policy Framework (SPF)/sender ID

In 2004, there was an announcement of intent for international cooperation by governments to encourage ISPs to create an effective infrastructure to limit spam. Initially this was to focus on reducing the ease with which spammers can spoof or mask their real address in e-mail headers by replacing it with another domain name. This would prevent spammers using common domain names, such as Yahoo.com or Hotmail.com. However, some believe it will not prevent spoofing of less well-known names. Providers such as Sendmail (www.sendmail.com) are now developing 'sender authentication technology', which allows organizations to verify the source of a message before accepting it by automatically checking if an e-mail comes from where it claims it does.

Microsoft announced its Sender ID technology in 2004, but the standard with which it is linked (Sender Policy Framework (SPF, http://www.openspf.org) is better known and supported by more open-source server providers. It is due to be ratified by the Internet standards body (IETF). Both techniques are based on the broadcasting domain publishing a DNS that shows it is a genuine sender. This verification is automatically performed by the ISP or recipient's mail server before the e-mail message is delivered to the user.

When the e-mail is received, the receiving mail server checks the domain indicated in the e-mail header against that published in the public DNS (i.e. against a registered list of servers that the domain owner has authorized to send e-mail). As Figure 8.1 shows, if the two do not match, the e-mail is not transmitted. See http://en.wikipedia.org/wiki/Sender_Policy_Framework for more details.

Domain Keys

Yahoo! Domain Keys also aims to combat domain spoofing and to assist in tracing spammers. It will generally be deployed alongside SPF. The approach used is different. When the e-mail is sent from a domain, it is encrypted using a private key that can only be used on the domain (effectively a digital signature). The receiving SMTP server then checks this digital signature against the public key for that domain, and if it is an authenticated, genuine sender they will be same. This approach has so far been implemented on Yahoo! Spam Guard, BT Openworld and Gmail.

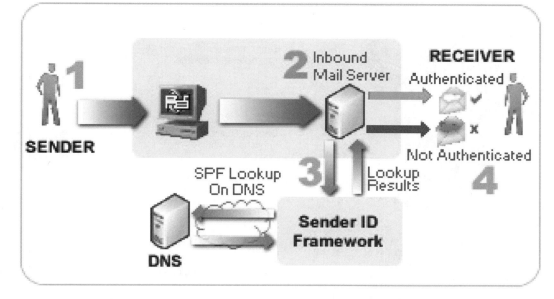

Figure 8.1 Microsoft Sender ID

Sender-warranted e-mail

Sender-warranted e-mail use some type of watermark to identify legitimate e-mail. Habeas (www.habeas.com) is one company that has promoted this approach. This is a great example of lateral thinking. The e-mail message contains a defined signature which is based on a small *haiku* poem – for example, the footer might contain 'X-HABEAS-SWE1-Winter Into Spring'. E-mail marketers who use the Habeas service have the right to include these identifiers in the foot of their message. Since Habeas has an agreement with the major ISPs, such as AOL, and anti-spam services, such as Message Labs, such messages are never classified as spam because they are from a trusted sender.

Of course, some spammers have started using the Habeas codes within their e-mails, but two prosecutions have been brought against them.

A similar approach is the concept of a 'bonded sender', developed by Ironport (www. bondedsender.com). Senders of opt-in e-mail post a financial bond to prove they are a reputable company. Senders of spam would not be able to afford to pay the bond. Recipients who feel they have received an unsolicited email from a Bonded Sender can complain to their ISP, IT manager or IronPort, and a financial charge is debited from the bond.

Pay per e-mail

An additional component of future approaches could be to charge a tiny amount for each e-mail sent, particularly where multiple messages are sent. This would eliminate the economic incentive for spammers, particularly if they could not hide the source address. What is of

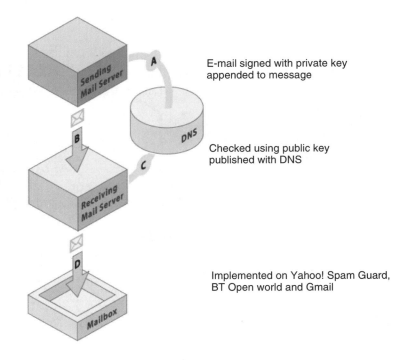

E-mail signed with private key
appended to message

Checked using public key
published with DNS

Implemented on Yahoo! Spam Guard,
BT Open world and Gmail

Figure 8.2 Yahoo Domain Keys

more concern is proposals to charge large-volume e-mail broadcasters. Although companies using third-party broadcasting services are already paying between 0.5 p and 10 p per message, companies broadcasting their own e-mails would also see an increase in costs. However, any small increase in price per message may be able to be borne by companies if current response rates prevail. Indeed, one argument is that with less spam, response rates will increase.

E-MAIL MARKETING INSIGHT

Review the authentication used in the broadcast of e-mail messages from your internal servers or those of your ESP. Best practice is to use Sender Policy Framework and Domain Keys as a minimum.

Given that there are so many methods used by different web-mail providers and ISPs for countering spam which may also block legitimate e-mails, it is important, particularly for large-volume senders, to test to see whether particular providers are blocking your areas. A recent post on E-consultancy (www.e-consultancy.com) highlighted how a B2C company was sending hundreds of thousands of e-mails to MSN/Hotmail but none were getting through. Worst still, there was no notification of this – it is not practical or desirable for the receiving mail server to send back hundreds of bounces; they are simply discarded. How, then, can you find out if this is happening? Well, it's simple if you look. You can simply report on open rates and click rates by provider – you would see in this case that there were no opens or clicks from people on your list with Hotmail addresses.

E-MAIL MARKETING INSIGHT

Ensure you check for deliverability problems by reporting hard bounces and also opens and clicks by the main ISPs.

TOUCH FREQUENCY

A further challenge suggested by the Forrester research, and referred to at the start of the chapter, is achieving the delicate balance between frequency of campaigns and response. As suggested in Chapter 4, finding the right touch strategy is important to maximize the value from an e-mail list while at the same time not annoying customers or losing response owing to too high a volume of e-mail.

Consider the example where a retailer is broadcasting a fortnightly e-mail and finds that, through running a test, increasing the frequency to weekly also increases sales. It then rolls out at this frequency to the entire list, but over time the negative impact is felt with decreased sales, increased unsubscribes and a negative perception from list members. What approaches can be used to resolve this dilemma? Here are some suggestions:

1. Offer more customer choice by offering communications preferences – enable customers to tailor the type and frequency of communications received. Amazon provides this facility, although not at opt-in (users are opted into all communications by default); it is available to customers if they feel they are receiving too many messages. Contrast this with other e-retailers, where the only option is all or nothing.

2. Customers who are responsive to e-mail must be monitored at a more granular level than the whole list. Customer responsiveness can be assessed relative to typical values, and customers who are less responsive (for example, if they are not regularly clicking through on the e-mail) should be e-mailed less frequently. More periodic e-mails with stronger offers may have a stronger response.

3. Increase the relevance of messages by matching them with customer intent – i.e. a sense and respond approach where e-mails are sent in response to customers at different stages of the lifecycle, or when they are visiting the web site unprompted by an e-mail.

4. As you use more advanced targeting, it becomes increasingly difficult to monitor the number of e-mails received by customers; will vary according to different selects against the database. Producing a touch frequency plot such as that shown in Figure 8.3 can help to assess whether some customers are being e-mailed too often or not often enough.

5. Put limits on e-mail frequency, such as minimum or maximum e-mails in a period, as described in Chapter 4.

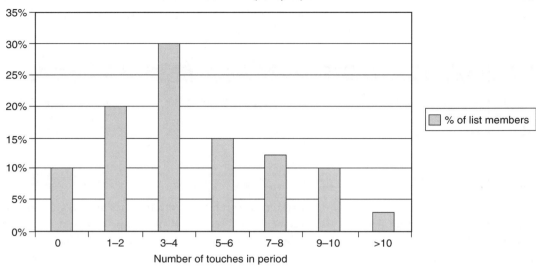

Figure 8.3 E-mail touch frequency plot

RICH MEDIA E-MAILS

Rich media e-mails go one step beyond the use of static or animated graphics in HTML e-mails, and give a richer experience through more complex animation, video and/or sound. Some refer to HTML as rich media, but more commonly the term is used to refer to e-mails with more dynamic or interactive content. A video can be streamed when the user opens the e-mail, or the message displayed in the preview pane and the video downloaded and displayed in real time – for example, Trailermail (www.trailermail.co.uk) is used to provide video trailers for movie companies. Alternatively, Flash animations can be integrated into the e-mail.

Many brands have experimented with rich media e-mail, but they don't seem to be increasing in popularity. There are several potential reasons why they have not been used more widely:

- E-mail, as with other digital media, tends to support impulsive behaviour – we don't want to wait for downloads unless the download is compelling
- Many corporate firewalls can block streaming media and, because of the high at work usage of e-mail, companies cannot risk reducing the visibility of their message
- Again in the corporate setting, e-mail recipients often won't want to be seen listening to or viewing a video clip by their boss, unless they control the media and turn on audio
- There is not a clear relationship between the incremental cost of rich media and the returns generated either through response or uplifts in brand awareness and favourability.

Owing to the technical issues of delivering rich media within the e-mail, increasingly companies are using an approach where the message directs the viewer to a web site to download or stream a clip. Of course, this means that the e-mail has less impact itself. If rich media is used in e-mail, it is more likely to be relatively simple – perhaps a flash animation – and is used to complement a text or static image-based message which will be effective even if the rich media element doesn't download.

E-MAIL MARKETING EXCELLENCE

One example of a successful rich-media e-mail innovator inbox (www.inbox.co.uk) is given by BUPA, where a rich media message was used to target personnel managers in organizations with more than 500 employees. The message was offering health cover to employees through a company scheme. The creative consisted of a personalized video showing the time savings that companies could potentially make. The results were:

Open rate	52%
Click rate of open	21%
Request call of open	8%
Conversion to appointment	18%

During the campaign, the company monitored which recipients opened the e-mail and these were then followed up by phone.

MESSAGING THROUGH MOBILE OR WIRELESS ACCESS DEVICES

Mobile technologies are not new; it has been possible for many years to access the Internet for e-mail using a laptop connected via a modem. With the ongoing convergence of devices, we are now seeing a range of hybrid devices combining PDA features such as calendar, address list, task list and office tools with phone features.

The importance of mobile access devices for messaging in the future is evident from Figure 8.4. This shows that, in the UK, the usage of mobile phones far exceeds that of the fixed Internet. This pattern is repeated throughout the world. What does this mean for e-mail marketing? First and foremost, messaging to mobile devices offers greater reach than Internet-based e-mail marketing. However, messaging to mobile devices brings a host of new technical and ethical issues. The main form of messaging to mobile phones is now SMS text messaging, but with the advent of RIM Blackberry devices, phones are being used more and more for viewing and responding to e-mails.

Since the mobile phone is arguably a more personal device than the fixed PC, companies can be even more unpopular if they are perceived to have delivered spam. There is also the constraint of the limited space for communicating by SMS (restricted to 164 characters). How do you explain your offer and proposition in this space without recourse to a landing page for the direct response? Although these current limitations are significant, they will be

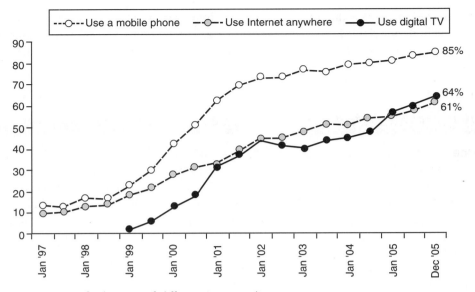

Figure 8.4 UK rate of adoption of different new media

swept away in the future by the advent of new-generation phones which use the wireless Internet to access e-mails using conventional inboxes such as Outlook Express. Many users already access their e-mails on their mobile through Yahoo!, but the limited, largely text-based user interface offers limited potential for marketing. The new technologies, such as WAP, GPRS and 3G, have been much criticized for their disappointing speed and the cost of the licences, but the technology will be widely adopted, worldwide. It is only a matter of when.

So, what are the options for mobile messaging and what are the latest developments? We start with mobile or wireless marketing and concentrate on the marketing applications rather than the technology. If you want to check out the technology, there's a good summary on Wikipedia (http://en.wikipedia.org/wiki/Mobile_phone) of the standards from 0G to 4G.

Mobile (m-commerce) or wireless commerce

We seem to like mobiles in the UK, Europe and Asia. The UK figures speak for themselves:

- 83 per cent of adults use mobiles
- there is 101 per cent mobile penetration amongst UK adults (some have more than one handset)
- more than 15 million handsets are replaced per annum, which is about a third of all handsets; the average upgrade time is 18 months
- 84 million text messages were sent person to person every day in the UK in April 2005
- 133 million text messages were sent on New Year's Day 2005 versus 111 million the year before.

If those numbers aren't mind-boggling enough, since recording started in 1999 we have sent over 100 billion text messages in the UK. (source: IDM, 2005, and Mobile Data Association; see www.text.it for the latest figures and case studies.)

In fact, in the whole of Europe there are 460 million mobiles, according to Admap (2005), which is much higher than in the US, where only 55 per cent of adults have mobiles.

Characteristics of mobile marketing

When thinking through the opportunities for mobile marketing, we should remember the inherent characteristics of the medium in order to best exploit its strengths and weakness. Chaffey (2004) describes the characteristics this way:

- Fixed-location web access is not necessary; this is more convenient for the user, who is freed from the need to access content via the desktop. This makes access possible when commuting, for example.

- Location-based services are possible. Mobiles can be used to give geographically-based services – for example, an offer in a particular shopping centre. Future mobiles will have global positioning services integrated.

- There is instant access/convenience. The latest GPRS and 3G services are always on, avoiding the need for lengthy connection.

- Privacy. Mobiles are more private than desktop access, making them more suitable for social use or for certain activities such as an alert service for looking for a new job.

- Personalization. As with computer-based access, personal information and services can be requested by the user, although these sometimes need to be setup via PC access.

- Security. In the future, mobiles may become a form of wallet; however, thefts of mobiles make this a source of concern.

A further issue related to privacy is the legal constraints involved, and it is vital that mobile marketers understand and comply with the Privacy and Electronic Communications Regulation 2003, which mandates that consumers opt in to receive text messages and can readily opt out. Several mobile providers have fallen foul of this or related data protection laws; see www.informationcommissioner.gov.uk for further details.

Some consumers will see their mobile as a personal device where they don't wish to receive promotional messages, and in this case it may be best to get them to opt in to receive e-mails. Using mobile messaging for permission-based customer communications is still at an experimental stage – maybe where e-mail was three to five years ago. We can expect a lot more brands to start giving the choice of text message contact, although it can be argued that e-mail is far more powerful since you are not limited to 60 characters and there is better response mechanism, which is a link through to a web site. Picture messaging, the growth in WAP sites and 3G phones will reduce these limitations.

Some areas of mobile marketing have worked particularly well – hair and beauty salons find mobile messaging great for updating customers on offers and boosting capacity when the salons are less full. Using SMS messaging to remind business people about events has also proved cost effective. As we become more familiar with such services, and if the value is there, it is likely that the opposition to these services will decline.

We have to respect consumer privacy and security fears with our mobile marketing, but remember that there are many opportunities to use the mobile to communicate with customers when they are away from their fixed web devices.

We will see that mobile phones have a great variety of response mechanisms which can be integrated with other media. These are often based around short codes – easy to remember five-digit numbers combined with text that can be used by advertisers or broadcasters for a personalized response from the customer.

Applications of mobile marketing

From the statistics above, you may think that the only application of mobiles is texting. Far from it; here are 20 marketing applications of mobile marketing, starting with the text-based ones. These are a summary of the main mobile marketing applications produced by Helen Keegan of Beep Marketing (author of the IDM (2005) module on digital marketing). The applications use Helen's categories, with my examples added.

1. *Text and win.* This is a convenient way to manage a competition or prize draw and is surprisingly popular with consumers. Think of the recent on-pack promotions by Walkers to win a million iPods – there was a draw every five minutes. Admap (2005) reports that a Cadbury on-pack 'Txt'n'Win' campaign offering £1 million in prizes received more than five million messages – a response rate of 8 per cent – thanks partly to the novelty of this approach and the ongoing popularity of prize draws.

2. *Voting and participation TV.* Text voting for reality TV programmes such as *Big Brother* and *The X-Factor* are incredibly popular (see Table 8.1).

3. *Quizzes.* Quizzes work well on mobile phones, using either text messaging or a java application for a deeper level of interactivity than text alone (graphics and sound can be incorporated). The typical way to start a quiz is to text in a keyword to a shortcode and a question is sent to you by return. Mobile quizzes are a good way for brands to engage

Table 8.1 Examples of popularity of different text messaging votes (source: Mobile Data Association)

Rank	Programme	Total number of votes by text message
1	*Big Brother 5*	> 10 million
2	*I'm A Celebrity Get Me Out of Here 2004*	> 10 million
3	*The X-Factor*	5.4 million
4	*Big Brother 3*	5.3 million
5	*Big Brother 4*	3.1 million
6	*Fame Academy 2*	1.6 million
7	*Eurosong 2002*	700 000

consumers. In 2005, Birds Eye asked consumers for their preferences for a new food style and combined this with the chance to win in a prize draw.

4. Mobile content (pictures, ringtones, video). Thanks to the popularity of ringtones, the mobile content industry is already huge and has increased rapidly.

According to Cellular News (2005), a recent Mintel report put the UK content market at $1 billion, with ringtones accounting for the largest share of downloads (33 per cent of volume sales), followed by games (26 per cent of the market). The remainder is made up of wallpapers/screensaves (13 per cent), gambling (9 per cent), music (8 per cent) and others (11 per cent), which includes news updates from football clubs, the Stock Exchange and other special groups. The volume of sales is expected to increase from 30 million downloads in 2002 to an estimated 760 million in 2005 – a massive 25-fold increase.

According to IDM (2005), brands are now capitalizing on the popularity of mobile content and are using it as part of their marketing effort. A picture or ringtone can be a second- or third-tier prize in a free prize draw or other competition which doesn't involve physically sending out many prizes.

Any service such as a ringtone delivered by WAP can be invoked from a text message. For example, *Parker's Car Guide* now prints ad text 'go parkers' to 89080 (a short code) for quick access to the Parker's WAP site, which provides car prices 'on-the-go' at £1 for 10 minutes.

And I managed to review mobile content without talking about the Crazy Frog!

The popularity of online content is partly down to the ease of payment. No credit card is required, and no complex authentication. Users of services are simply billed through their network provider for these services. This payment service has been used in novel ways – for example, during the 2004 tsunami over £1 million was raised through SMS donations.

5. *Games*. Mobile games are very popular, and are even spawning new converged hardware. You may have seen addicts playing on the Nokia N-Gage or a Gizmondo. Again, these games make good low-cost competition prizes or incentives to sign-up for permission-based text or e-mail marketing. Coca-Cola has signed a deal to produce Coca-Cola branded games which customers will buy rather than download for free.

6. *Applications*. These are various types of productivity software that run on higher-end mobile phones which run the Symbian operating system or Windows CE. They can be used in a business-to-business environment for inventory and order tracking, as well as time management.

7. *Customer Relationship Management (CRM)*. Through combining some of the techniques above, such as offering mobile content for incentives and text messaging for communications, mobiles can be a useful element in a wider CRM initiative. It can help build relationships with consumers who don't have ready access to e-mail, or who simply find mobiles more convenient. The cost per message makes mobile CRM quite effective too, varying from 3p to 10p per message, according to volume.

8. *Interactive Voice Response (IVR).* IVR is best (or rather worst) known as the system for connecting your call to the right department in large organizations, but it can also be used to pay for mobile content and for premium rate services in response to TV ad campaigns.

9. *Multi-media messaging (MMS) in/out.* This technique is increasing in potential as it becomes more readily available on handsets. However, it is limited by the cost and technical limitations of handsets. MMS can be pushed to the phone at higher costs than simple text messages (several times higher), or there is the cheaper option of 'virtual MMS' or WAP push. Here, the message is downloaded to the phone. Most marketers stick with text because it is cheaper and doesn't suffer these compatibility problems.

10. *Direct ad-response/Red Button Mobile.* Red Button Mobile describes direct-response campaigns using the mobile phone as opposed to using the red button on interactive television (or, potentially, outdoor or print advertising, unlike true red-button advertising). The mobile 'red button' is based on a shortcode available optionally coupled with different relevant keywords, dependent on the response mechanics. Options include:

   - text to screen – with TV, comments texted in can be automatically populated on screen as used by reality TV programmes (text to screen)

   - text to e-mail – where you text in your e-mail address to a short code and an automatic HTML e-mail is generated to the respondent

   - text to post – this works in a similar way, where you text your address or postcode and street number

   - text to WAP – here, respondents are directed to an advertiser's WAP site through a link where they can access content or opt in

   - text to mobile content – content such as a ringtone or a coupon is received through texting a shortcode.

   As an example of the potential effectiveness of these campaigns, Axa PPP ran a direct-response campaign involving press advertising for their personal health insurance provider. Customers were asked to respond to the advertisement either by freephone (0800 number) or via text message; 50 per cent of all the replies came via text message and all texts routed direct to the call centre to manage outbound calls.

11. *Barcodes.* Barcodes can be sent to a mobile phone and then redeemed in-store using the usual Epos systems. For example, Ann Summers uses this technique if you text in response to a print or other advertisement (so I am told!). There are practical issues with this owing to the large number of different handset displays on which the bar code has to be displayed. A new take on bar codes is 'camera codes', where a consumer takes a picture of the barcode from a TV screen, poster, newspaper, magazine or website, or anywhere really. This then initiates the response mechanism or can be used for couponing.

12. *Location-based services (LBS).* This technique has been prominent recently, with companies offering services that allow children's whereabouts to be tracked via their phones. With ChildLocate, parents pay a monthly fee of £9.99 to have access to the service. The monthly fee includes 10 free location requests and 10 free text messages. Additional

location requests are charged at 30p and text messages at 10p. Trials have also been run in shopping centres, where shoppers can opt in to receive promotions, but this is generally seen as an idea implemented before its time. 'Find me' services are available, which are useful for evenings out, and the mobile version of Google can also help with this.

13. *WAP portal*. WAP sites are the mobile versions of media sites, such as the BBC or Channel 4 or the network owner. WAP e-mail is also popular on some smartphone or PDA devices – check your e-mail renders clearly on these devices in text mode.

14. *Java portal*. This is a different form of portal, where you do not have to visit the portal but instead content is downloaded in line with your preferences. Avant Go! uses this technique to download content while a smartphone is being synchronized with a PC.

15. *Mobile search*. All the main search providers have mobile (WAP)-specific versions of their search engines. These are now becoming more sophisticated. Google Mobile search (www.google.co.uk/mobile) offers Local search to find a local business, and will then display a map (Google Maps is integrated) or phone number with the option of click-to-call on the appropriate handset. Google Local uses listings from Yell.com.

16. *Mobile music*. Beyond ringtones, many handsets are now designed to play and store MP3 music files and potentially rival the iPod – although we now have an iPod mobile version. As access speeds increase, tunes may be offered in promotions.

17. *Podcasting*. Podcasting involves streamed delivery of a radio programme, tune, speech or video. Podcasts can be accessed on any device with the appropriate MP3-playing capabilities (see http://www.voxmedia.org/wiki/How_to_Podcast).

18. *Blogging and RSS*. Blogs are proving incredibly popular with those in the know. Technorati (www.technorati.com) lists around 20 million blogs (it is estimated that around 3 per cent of American are bloggers, while more than 60 per cent read blogs). RSS feeds of blogs (see http://www.wnim.com/archive/issue2203/new_media_innovation.htm) can also be accessed by mobile. While this format works best on conventional fixed web access, mobile blogging is used by those on the move. RSS and blogging are described in more detail at the end of this chapter.

19. *Moblogging*. Moblogging (or blogging from your mobile phone) is possible and, although it can be text-based, makes best use of the potential of the device when images or video clips are submitted by MMS or WAP. We now have citizen journalists who report breaking news before the main networks. Sony Ericsson has used the technique of posting images to a blog to promote its K300i phone, by encouraging users to upload their images to http://www.shameacademy.com.

20. *Bluetooth/infra red*. These techniques enable a message to be sent from one electronic device to another. From a marketing application viewpoint, we are only just starting to see this technique used (many phones don't have Bluetooth). While individuals can exchange a business card or use their phone as a modem which links by Bluetooth to their mobile, a much more exciting application is Bluecasting. This technique was used with the launch of the latest Coldplay album, where a London-based campaign involved 13 000 fans downloading free pre-release video clips, never before seen interviews,

audio samples and exclusive images onto their mobiles via Bluetooth from Transvision screens at mainline train stations.

In this campaign, 87 000 unique handsets were 'discovered' and 13 000 people opted-in to receive the material – a response rate of 15 per cent. The busiest day was Saturday 4 June – two days before the official album launch date – when over 8000 handsets were discovered and over 1100 users opted in to receive a video file. The Bluecast systems can deliver time-sensitive content – so, for example, in the morning the users would get an audio clip of the tracks *Fix You* and be prompted to tune in to Radio One, and in the afternoon the clip would be the same but users would be prompted to watch Jonathan Ross on BBC1.

And yes, in case you're wondering, the first cases of Bluejacking other phones, Bluetooth viruses and Bluespamming have already been reported.

REALLY SIMPLE SYNDICATION

The last technology we will review is arguably the most exciting. I believe that in the long term it will both complement and rival e-mail as a strategic marketing communications medium.

From a technology view point, Really Simple Syndication (RSS), also sometimes known as Rich Site Summary, is an Internet standard for publishing and exchanging content using XML. From a practical viewpoint, it enables two things. The first is that content can be syndicated or published on one site that originates on another site. Secondly, and of much greater interest to the e-mail marketer, it is a relatively new method of distributing messages to subscribers.

At the time of writing, most consumers and few business people have heard of RSS – it is mainly used by journalists and analysts as a convenient way of keeping up to date with press releases. Initially the RSS messages were received by specialist software that could be downloaded for free, such as RSS Reader (www.rssreader.com), or sites that receive feeds, such as Bloglines (www.bloglines.com). These RSS readers, or aggregators, poll for RSS at a defined interval, often once an hour.

RSS will not become widespread until it is incorporated into standard software, but this will happen. In 2006 you can receive RSS feeds within your web browser, and once they are included as a different type of inbox within e-mail packages, I believe they will be much more widely used. Currently, though, the proposition of RSS against e-mail isn't strong enough for most audiences, although it is superior for some audiences such as journalists and technology followers. I also think improvements to the RSS readers to incorporate features similar to e-mail packages, such as rules and keyword-based filters, will help to manage the volume of RSS.

RSS has been embraced by major publishers such as the BBC, and if you visit the BBC web site, you can see its potential. It enables you to subscribe to very specific content that interests you, and then provides you with an alert when a new story is published. For example, I subscribe to the e-commerce news channel and that for Arsenal, my football team. In this arrangement subscription does not require opt-in, it just requires a request of the feed.

RSS is therefore potentially a threat to the permission marketing model, since there is no data exchange and it is easy for subscribers to switch on and off.

RSS will become much more widely adopted when it extends beyond specialist readers to the still ubiquitous Internet Explorer and Outlook products. Going forward, e-mail marketers need to manage the risk of reduced use of permission-based e-mail as customers realize the benefits of RSS, including:

- more granular control of communications (e.g. customers can choose content updates from any channel on the BBC site, such as the e-commerce section (see the BBC web site for an explanation of the RSS consumer proposition)

- that it can be switched on and off without registration, which reduces the control of marketers – someone could subscribe to holiday offers within a two-week period from a travel web site, for instance

- little or no spam, since messages are pulled to the reader from the server (this is currently the case, although ads may be placed within a feed).

There are certainly disadvantages to RSS from the consumer viewpoint. It requires a separate inbox or reader to set up and monitor, and this has deterred many. It also only suits certain types of information, published as single alerts, so it is mainly used for short stories and press releases. It has not traditionally been used in a newsletter-type format with an edited collection of stories, but this is possible within the specification.

RSS is a threat to e-mail marketers because typically users profile and qualify themselves before opting in to e-mail. With RSS this permission marketing isn't necessary, since it is a pull service where the user retrieves information from the web site hosting the RSS feed. The user just subscribes to the feed without the need to share any information with the organization. This has been the typical model to date, but Silverpop has recently launched RSS Direct, which uses a more familiar e-mail permission marketing model where the user provides information before signing up to feeds. I'm sure many e-mail marketing service providers will move to offer this service, and indeed the data-capture technology looks straightforward – involving simply placing a data-capture form with which to configure the feeds – so could also be implemented in-house.

It will be interesting how this plays out over the next couple of years. Will marketers provide free access to RSS to maximize volume of subscribers, but be limited by their capability to profile and target customers? Alternatively, they may use the permission-based opt-in RSS model, which will have lower volume but improved profiling and targeting.

RSS certainly presents opportunities for new types of communications. As the BBC web site shows, subscribers can access much more specific, timely information, and from the content-providers' point of view, all they have to do is publish it on the site and subscribers will be notified. Marketers will have to think how the page layout of the template can be used to achieve wider objectives, such as generating awareness, interaction and response (for example, sign-up to e-mail subscription). In some sectors RSS has potential – updating about new holiday offers (perhaps you will just switch it on for a two-week period, for example, to just show holiday deals in Cuba), books from a favourite author, or new gadgets from a favourite supplier.

In reality, I think more complex e-mail/RSS communications preferences will be offered to consumers. Perhaps certain types of high-value information will only be offered through e-mail. Time for some more testing ...

REFERENCES

Admap (2005). How marketers can exploit new mobile services (by Dan Steinbeck). *Admap*, **Jul/Aug**, 41–43.

Cellular News (2005). UK Mobile Content Market Worth Over US$1 Billion. Article dated 22 September (available at http://www.cellular-news.com/story/14147.php).

Chaffey, D. (2004). *E-business and E-commerce Management*. FT-Prentice Hall.

IDM (2005). Course material on IDM Certificate in Digital Marketing – modules on mobile messaging and interactive TV and Radio. IDM.

Newmediazero (2002). E-mail marketing warning. *NewMediaAge*, **April**.

WEB LINKS

Mobile Marketing Association (www.text.it)
SPAMcop (www.spamcop.net)
SPAMAssassin (www.spamassassin.org)

Index

Pansong
1436 Havard St .